World without End

World without End

Christian Eschatology
from a Process Perspective

Edited by

Joseph A. Bracken, S.J.

William B. Eerdmans Publishing Company
Grand Rapids, Michigan / Cambridge, U.K.

Wm. B. Eerdmans Publishing Co.
255 Jefferson Ave. S.E., Grand Rapids, Michigan 49503 /
P.O. Box 163, Cambridge CB3 9PU U.K.

Printed in the United States of America

09 08 07 06 05   7 6 5 4 3 2 1

Library of Congress Cataloging-in-Publication Data

World without end: Christian eschatology from a process perspective /
   edited by Joseph A. Bracken.
        p.   cm.
   Includes bibliographical references.
   ISBN 0-8028-2811-6 (cloth: alk. paper)
       1. Good and evil.   2. Eschatology.   3. Suchocki, Marjorie.
   I. Bracken, Joseph A.

   BJ1406.W68   2005
   236 — dc22
                                                2004056405

www.eerdmans.com

Contents

Editor's Preface   vii

The End of Evil   1
    Joseph A. Bracken, S.J.

"Deliver Us from Evil" or Doing Away with Humankind?   12
    Jürgen Moltmann

Eschatological Visions   28
    Robert Cummings Neville

The Mystery of the Insoluble Evil:
Violence and Evil in Marjorie Suchocki   46
    Catherine Keller

Subjective Immortality in a Neo-Whiteheadian Context   72
    Joseph A. Bracken, S.J.

God's Advent/ure: The End of Evil
and the Origin of Time   91
    Roland Faber

CONTENTS

An Alternative Theory of Subjective Immortality   113

    Lewis S. Ford

Eschatology as Metaphysics under the Guise of Hope   128

    Philip Clayton

Behind the Veil: Evolutionary Naturalism
and the Question of Immortality   150

    John F. Haught

Endings and Ends   177

    Anna Case-Winters

"Afterwords"   197

    Marjorie Hewitt Suchocki

Contributors   219

Index   221

Editor's Preface

In the twentieth century Eschatology moved from being little more than a minor theme (the doctrine of the last things) within various treatises on systematic theology to an overriding concern in both New Testament studies and systematic theology. As Hans Schwarz notes, interest in eschatology was initially sparked a century ago by the work of Johannes Weiss and Albert Schweitzer who in different ways claimed that the mission and ministry of Jesus as set forth in the Gospel narratives could only be understood in strictly eschatological terms.[1] The same orientation to the future resurfaced in mid-twentieth century with systematic theologians like Wolfhart Pannenberg, Jürgen Moltmann and Gustavo Gutiérrez. In their hands eschatology was seen as the basis for hope in a better future within this world as well as for hope in the Second Coming of Jesus and the definitive establishment of the Kingdom of God.[2] Finally, in the closing decades of the twentieth century eschatology became a controversial topic of conversation between natural scientists, philosophers and theologians whose views of the far-distant future were notably different. Two recently published sets of papers on this topic have been *The End of the World and the Ends of God* and *The Far-Future Universe*.[3]

---

1. Hans Schwarz, *Eschatology* (Grand Rapids, MI: Eerdmans, 2000), 107-15.

2. *Ibid.*, 142-62.

3. *The End of the World and the Ends of God: Science and Theology on Eschatology*, ed. John Polkinghorne and Michael Welker (Harrisburg, PA: Trinity International, 2000);

The present volume is different from the above-cited texts in that it does not include among its contributors some well-known natural scientists interested in the religion and science dialogue. Rather it brings together philosophers and theologians with a common interest in the process-relational metaphysics of Alfred North Whitehead insofar as it can be used as a theoretical underpinning for contemporary Christian Eschatology. The focus for their reflections is a book entitled *The End of Evil* published some years ago by Marjorie Hewitt Suchocki as both a historically and systematically oriented Christian Eschatology. Likewise included in the book is Suchocki's response to her colleagues and critics, especially insofar as they seek to move beyond both Whitehead and herself in terms of their own process-oriented understanding of Christian Eschatology. The value of such a collaborative venture is that it quite clearly presents a challenge to natural scientists, classically trained Christian theologians, and process theologians to rethink their basic presuppositions about the end of the world and/or the final destiny of the human race.

As John Haught makes clear in his essay, for example, perhaps it is time for natural scientists to admit the limitations of their own disciplines to address the deeper questions of meaning and value in human life. For, if natural science can predict with certainty only the eventual demise of the present universe,[4] what is the enduring worth even of scientific research? Classically oriented Christian theologians, for their part, may have to concede that the traditional images associated with "the doctrine of the last things" really are not convincing any more because of the dramatic shift in world view, at least in the West since the Renaissance. Moreover, as Catherine Keller reminds us in her essay, Eschatology and Apocalyptic are easily confused in the popular imagination with the result that Eschatology is part of the problem of Evil, not its solution. Finally, and perhaps most especially, orthodox Whiteheadians should feel challenged by many of the essays in this volume to rethink both the strengths and the limitations of Whitehead's metaphysical scheme to undergird a Christian Eschatol-

---

The Far-Future Universe: Eschatology from a Cosmic Perspective, ed. George F. R. Ellis (Radnor, PA: Templeton Foundation Press, 2002).

4. See Steven Weinberg, *The First Three Minutes: A Modern View of the Origin of the Universe* (New York: Basic Books, 1998), 154: "The more the universe seems comprehensible, the more it also seems pointless."

ogy. For, what Marjorie Suchocki has undertaken as a modest reinterpretation and modification of Whitehead's philosophy so as to accommodate traditional Christian belief in life after death for human beings may well be only "the tip of the iceberg." Roland Faber in his essay claims that a major rethinking of Whitehead's categoreal scheme will be required so as to speak convincingly about the end of evil within a process-relational understanding of reality.

In any event, the basic layout of the book is as follows. To begin, a summary of Suchocki's thesis in *The End of Evil* is offered for the reader's perusal, after which Jürgen Moltmann offers a brief overview of the various ways in which evil has been operative in human history. Subsequent essays then take issue with various features of Suchocki's hypothesis, challenging her (and the reader) either to make better use of resources already available in Whitehead's philosophy or, as already noted, to move beyond orthodox Whiteheadianism in the direction of a new metaphysical scheme. The final essay is Suchocki's response to her colleagues and critics. In closing it may be added that the present volume is also intended as an informal *Festschrift* on the occasion of her retirement as Ingraham Professor of Theology at the Claremont Graduate School and the Claremont School of Theology in Southern California. All of the essayists and her many other friends and admirers have been greatly impressed over the years by her creativity and range of thought but above all by her personal warmth and charm. This book, accordingly, is affectionately dedicated to her with all best wishes for the future.

Xavier University   JOSEPH A. BRACKEN, S.J.
Cincinnati, Ohio

The End of Evil

Joseph A. Bracken, S.J.

The End of Evil by Marjorie Suchocki is an imaginative reconstruction of the metaphysical scheme of Alfred North Whitehead with particular attention to the problem of evil: why it arises within the cosmic process and how it can be overcome both within time and in the ongoing divine life.[1] It is a reconstruction rather than simply an application of Whitehead's philosophy to a specific problem area since, as will be noted below, Suchocki consciously modifies Whitehead's categoreal scheme so as to allow for the possibility of subjective immortality for creaturely actual occasions, that is, momentary subjects of experience which in Whitehead's metaphysics are "the final real things of which the world is made up."[2] Hence, her work here could within limits be considered neo-Whiteheadian rather than strictly Whiteheadian even though Suchocki herself is clearly anxious to remain faithful to the spirit, if not always to the letter, of Whitehead's thought. The subtitle of the book "Process Eschatology in Historical Context" makes clear how in her mind Whitehead's analysis sums up a long history of

1. Marjorie Hewitt Suchocki, *The End of Evil: Process Eschatology in Historical Context* (Albany: State University of New York Press, 1988). Subsequent references to this book in the current chapter and in my own essay later in the book will be made simply through page numbers in parentheses rather than with the aid of endnotes.

2. Alfred North Whitehead, *Process and Reality: An Essay in Cosmology,* Corrected Edition, ed. David Ray Griffin & Donald W. Sherburne (New York: The Free Press, 1978), 18. Subsequent references to *Process and Reality* will be inserted into the text enclosed in parentheses.

philosophical reflection on the problem of evil. Whitehead, for example, saw evil (both physical and moral) originating out of a natural tension between freedom and finitude, the self-constituting decision of the individual actual occasion versus the inevitable constraints of the environment within which it is coming to be. As we will see below, Suchocki evidently chose for her historical survey in the opening chapters of the book philosophers who tended to ground their reflections on the problem of evil in one of these two alternatives, freedom or finitude.

Augustine and Liebniz, for example, are counterposed in the first chapter since Augustine believed that all evil, even natural evil, "is the result of sin and its punishment" (6) while Leibniz saw even moral evil as necessary for the pre-established harmony of this world as willed by God: "The total harmony of the whole is the overcoming of the evil of the constituent parts. The good which is served through each particular evil is such that the universe is better than it would have been without each evil" (21). Because of this emphasis on just one pole of the dialectic between freedom and finitude, of course, both Augustine and Leibniz encountered formidable obstacles in their analysis of the problem of evil. Partly as a result of reflection on his own conversion to Christianity, Augustine stipulated that human free will apart from the grace of God is powerless to direct itself back to God once it has fallen away from its proper orientation to God as its Supreme Good (13). But this raises the question whether God gives the grace of repentance to all human beings or only to a few; for, in the latter case God may be held responsible for the existence of evil. Leibniz, on the other hand, emphasized that certain human beings (like Judas, the betrayer of Jesus) freely but inevitably commit serious sin, a condition which God antecedently perceives in their "idea" or finite essence. Yet God chooses to actualize this possibility since, as noted above, the co-existence of good and evil contributes to the pre-established harmony of the best of all possible worlds. For the same reason, Leibniz, unlike Augustine, does not separate the blessed from the damned in terms of heaven and hell but includes the damned within the City of God even as they continue to suffer in punishment for their sins (22). In anticipation of her own (and Whitehead's) metaphysical scheme, Suchocki notes how for Liebniz evil thus paradoxically plays an important role in the final reconciliation of all things within God (23).

Chapter Two continues her exposition of the dialectic between freedom and finitude, this time in terms of the rival approaches of Kant and Schleiermacher to the problem of evil. In *Religion Within the Limits of Reason Alone*, Immanuel Kant distinguished three predispositions of human nature: animality involving the instincts of self-preservation and propagation of the species; humanity, that is, the rational ability to compare oneself with others, and personality, one's accountability to the moral law (26-27). Perversions of various kinds may exist on the levels of animality and humanity; but evil, properly speaking, exists only on the level of personality where the individual has the freedom to obey the moral law or not. Unlike Augustine, however, Kant was wary of the notion of divine grace as necessary for leading a good life. Instead, in his view God as the Supreme Lawgiver shares with human beings the ideal of moral perfection, above all, as manifest in exemplary human beings like Jesus of Nazareth (28-30). Likewise, in the ethical sphere Kant endorsed the notion of an ethical commonwealth or "kingdom of ends" (31) as an ideal for human social behavior. Where Kant saw the moral law as imposed by God upon human nature, Friedrich Schleiermacher saw morality and spirituality as naturally emergent out of the finite conditions of human nature within a world in process of development: "The position of a spiritual creature in the whole of nature is first that of an integral part of the whole; and second, it is that part of creation which, through knowledge, is to bind that creation into a meaningful as well as factual system of interrelationships" in absolute dependence on God (33). Evil arises when human beings yield to the impulses of their prespiritual, sensuous nature and resist the move to "God-consciousness" as exemplified in the person of Jesus who exhibits absolute dependence upon God and interdependence with the rest of creation. As Suchocki comments, Schleiermacher improves upon Augustine in seeing finitude or incompletion not as a fault but as a God-given means for the world's self-development or creativity (37). Here, too, she anticipates what will be a major feature of her own (and Whitehead's) cosmological scheme.

In Chapter Three, Suchocki deals with the more contemporary psychological understanding of evil as alienation or meaninglessness in the philosophies of Hegel and Nietzsche respectively. As Suchocki notes, alienation or estrangement was not considered an evil by Hegel but rather as "an essential means to the realization of the fully self-conscious spirit" (41). Evil occurs only when one fails to achieve full rational self-awareness, that is, awareness of one's dynamic identity both with the Absolute Spirit and with all other finite spirits. The problem, of course, is that many individuals never achieve full self-awareness but remain frozen either at the level of immediate self-awareness in which one is preoccupied strictly with one's own needs and desires or at the level of mediate self-awareness in which one is painfully aware of the otherness of others (including God) but never achieves reconciliation with them through full self-awareness (43-44). As a result, while world history is ideally pictured as a movement of peoples toward freedom in terms of rational self-awareness, in point of fact it is more often a record of successive failures to achieve that exalted goal. Furthermore, God as Absolute Spirit thus appears to be indifferent to the plight of individuals and groups who fall by the wayside (48). In the historical aftermath of Hegel's philosophy, moreover, the notion of evil as alienation from one's ownmost being was a recurrent theme with a growing scepticism about the meaning and value of human life as a result. Friedrich Nietzsche is a classic example of this tendency. For Nietzsche evil is rooted in *ressentiment,* the perversion of the will to power. That is, frustrated in their will to power, individuals take refuge in a moral code which justifies their lack of courage and daring through promises of a better life after death (51) Instead, says Nietzsche, they should acknowledge that this world is all that exists and that they must create meaning and value for themselves in virtue of their own decisions. Thus as Supermen (*Übermenschen*) they will achieve a personal transcendence of the nihilism which follows upon the acknowledgement of the objective meaninglessness of the cosmic process (55-56). Yet, comments Suchocki, why strive to be an *Übermensch* if one's affirmation of life dies with oneself at the moment of death (57)? There is no reason to choose one direction in life rather than another if in the end all life is meaningless.

Finally, in Chapter Four, Suchocki summarizes Whitehead's approach to the problem of evil, noting how freedom and finitude are artfully combined in his philosophical scheme. Freedom is guaranteed by the self-constituting decision of each actual occasion, but finitude is present in terms of the limited actuality which it thus achieves, given the conditions of the world in which it arises, and the limited effect it will have on its successors (62, 68). Evil is thus linked for Whitehead with the loss of actuality in that the actual occasion perishes as soon as it is fully actualized, but also with the loss of possibility in that it can only be actualized one way rather than another here and now and it will undoubtedly be in some measure "negatively prehended" by its successors in their own processes of self-constitution. "Perpetual perishing" is thus the trademark of a world in process (63). At the same time, it is the price to be paid for creative advance since otherwise nothing new would come into existence. As Suchocki comments, "finitude is the locus of value, and that value is achieved by selection. Insofar as entities are open to as yet unrealizable alternatives, novelty enters into existence with its own evolutionary rewards. . . . And yet precisely these conditions of finitude allow evil as well as good into existence" (67). Looked at from another perspective, every actuality in itself is good; every self-constituting decision of an actual occasion is in some sense good. But its longterm value has to be judged in terms of its relationships to other actual occasions and their self-constituting decisions. When a human being, for example, momentarily acts like a pig, that is not evil in itself but only with reference to the individual's own self-esteem and with reference to the impact of the individual's choice on the behavior of other human beings (71-72). Thus good and evil are not to be assessed in terms of isolated events but in the context of the pattern of events unfolding within the Universe as a whole. In *Adventures of Ideas* Whitehead further specifies this pattern in terms of the overarching ideals of zest, beauty, truth, adventure, art and peace (74).[3] God's role in the cosmic process is to note in virtue of the divine primordial nature the best way in which these transcendent ideals can be realized at any given moment within the cosmic process and then via a series of divine initial aims to prompt concrescing creaturely actual occasions to move in that direction within their individual processes of self-constitution. The individual actual occasion, however, always remains free to modify that divine initial aim as it wishes. Thus evil remains an ever-present possibility within a cosmic process which aims at the overall achievement of transcendent good.

3. Cf. also Alfred North Whitehead, *Adventures of Ideas* (New York: The Free Press, 1967), 241-96.

Having completed her historical survey of notable philosophers and theologians who have written on the problem of good and evil, Suchocki in the second half of her book turns to an imaginative reconstruction of Whitehead's philosophy with respect to the problem of evil. In particular, she notes that, while God realizes within the divine consequent nature the ongoing harmony of the transcendent ideals listed above, creatures by reason of their more limited participation in that same cosmic process are not so privileged: for human beings "the overcoming of evil in history is always partial" and unevenly distributed (81). Some suffer far more than others in terms of undeserved evil and never understand how their pain somehow contributed to a higher good. Hence, there must be an overcoming of evil which "lies beyond our immediate experience in the world" if only to support a viable hope for the future (82). The problem, however, is that Whitehead's philosophical scheme does not seem to allow for the possibility of subjective immortality for creaturely actual occasions. An individual actual occasion can be prehended by God and thus incorporated into the divine consequent nature only when its process of self-constitution is completed and it has become objectively immortal as a "superject," an object of prehension both for God and subsequent creaturely actual occasions (83). Suchocki, however, notes that, while creaturely actual occasions prehend their predecessors only in part through a combination of positive and negative prehensions, Whitehead seems to provide for God to prehend creaturely actual occasions in their entirety without negative prehensions. Hence, concludes Suchocki, God must prehend creaturely actual occasions in their subjectivity as well as in terms of their objective characteristics (90-96). But, if God can thus prehend creaturely actual occasions in their subjectivity, then God can give them subjective as well as objective immortality within the divine consequent nature. Creaturely actual occasions are thus "reborn" to ongoing life within God, experiencing themselves both as fully determinate finite actualities and as participants in the infinity of God's own life at the same time (96).

In terms of Whitehead's metaphysical scheme, what Suchocki has done here is to propose a new category to describe the life-history of a creaturely actual occasion. Between concrescence in which the actual occasion is strictly a subject of experience and transition in which the completed actual occasion is a "superject" or object of prehension for subsequent creaturely occasion, Suchocki inserts "enjoyment" or the moment in which the actual occasion is both process and outcome, namely, a creaturely subjectivity experiencing its own completeness (87). This, says Suchocki, is the moment at which God prehends the creaturely occasion in both its subjectivity and objectivity and incorporates it into the divine consequent nature, thus endowing it with both subjective and objective immortality. What Suchocki does not take into account is that she has thereby introduced a type of intersubjectivity into the God-world relationship which Whitehead himself did not anticipate. Whitehead conceived prehension, even divine prehension, along the lines of a subject-object relationship. What Suchocki has done is to convert divine prehension of creaturely actual occasions into a subject-subject or intersubjective relationship. But, at least *prima facie,* there are problems here. How, for example, can God as an infinite subject of experience incorporate into the divine subjectivity creaturely subjects of experience in their subjectivity without undermining their status as ontologically separate realities? In my own contribution to this volume, I will attempt a vindication of Suchocki's innovative proposal by sketching a neo-Whiteheadian metaphysics of intersubjectivity. But for now we will continue with the exposition of Suchocki's own thought in *The End of Evil.*

In Chapter Six, "Finitude and Everlasting Redemption in God: Participation in God," Suchocki first notes that subjective immortality in God is only the beginning of an answer to the problem of evil. For, in that case an actual occasion which experienced severe pain would forever endure pain even in God. The occasion must experience transformation through incorporation into the divine life. To explain how this happens, Suchocki first notes how in terms of her theory a completed actual occasion "enjoys itself as a new value in the world" and at the same time "awaits a confirmation from beyond itself, a valuing of the value which it is" (98). It seeks, in other words, its perpetuation in subsequent actual occasions. Even though these future actual occasions will only partially incorporate the occasion's meaning and value into their own processes of self-constitution, the occasion will in any case find its full meaning and value in some reality greater than itself. The ultimate reality greater than itself is, of course, the divine consequent nature. Hence, in virtue of what Suchocki calls the "transitional creativity" of the actual occasion, it "enjoys its own satisfaction *and*

God's consciousness of it, in the unity of God's now extremely complex subjectivity" (102). Note, however, how Suchocki argues this point. Whitehead himself stipulated that a creaturely actual occasion cannot be aware of its own satisfaction since that would inevitably alter the satisfaction and require a new process of unification of feelings or concrescence.[4] Suchocki disagrees, urging that the transitional creativity of the creaturely actual occasion creates a linkage with the ongoing concrescence of the divine consequent nature. Thus the occasion "experiences itself and more than itself, which is to say, the occasion experiences itself and God's evaluative transformation of itself within the divine nature" (103). The occasion, in other words, is now "governed by God's own subjective aim" toward beauty, harmony, and peace (103). Moreover, existing within the divine consequent nature the occasion experiences its relationship to all other creaturely occasions in a way which would have been impossible in its previous purely finite existence within the space-time continuum. It becomes part of an all-embracing community of creaturely actual occasions which by their dynamic togetherness from moment to moment constitute the ongoing divine satisfaction. God therefore progressively achieves satisfaction in and through the ever-increasing harmony of creaturely actual occasions in community, and the actual occasions achieve a new level of reconciliation with one another within the divine consequent nature (103-6).

The attractiveness of this proposal is that Suchocki can thus also provide for the classical notion of judgment as part of her process-oriented eschatology. "The judgment is multiple: it is a judgment of the occasion as it could have been relative to what it in fact became; it is a judgment of the occasion as a single satisfaction in relation to the communities in which it participated, such as the totality of a living person; it is a judgment of the occasion and, if applicable, its personhood, in relation to the increasingly wider communities of the whole universe; and it is throughout, of course, a judgment of the occasion in relation to God" (106). There is, accordingly, no "cheap grace"; reconciliation for the individual actual occasion is bought at a price,

---

4. Whitehead, *Process and Reality*, 85: "No actual entity can be conscious of its own satisfaction; for such knowledge would be a component in the process, and would thereby alter the satisfaction."

the price of full objectivity about its relation to other creaturely actual occasions and to God. Yet, provided that it freely accepts the truth about itself, the occasion will be "saved"; that is, it will experience "transformation, redemption and peace" (109). Only if it refuses to accept what is in fact the case will it equivalently put itself in "hell," an ongoing state of alienation from God and other creaturely actual occasions even as it remains part of the divine consequent nature (111).[5]

In Chapter Seven Suchocki takes up the related issue of how this eschatological vision wherein Good and Evil are ultimately reconciled in God can and should have an impact on the ongoing redemption of this world. Can Evil likewise be overcome, at least in part, within this world? Here Suchocki appeals toWhitehead's scheme for the dynamic interrelation of the primordial and consequent natures of God in the final pages of *Process and Reality*. There Whitehead talks about the love of God for the world: "What is done in the world is transformed into a reality in heaven, and the reality in heaven passes back into the world. By reason of this reciprocal relation, the love in the world passes into the love in heaven, and floods back again into the world" (115).[6] More specifically, through the ongoing integration of the divine consequent nature with the unlimited vision of possibilities provided by the divine primordial nature, God is able to send initial aims appropriate to all creaturely actual occasions as they arise within the cosmic process (116). But these initial aims are themselves governed by God's own

5. There is, to be sure, a lingering conceptual problem here in terms of the implicit intersubjective relation between God and creaturely actual occasions. Earlier I noted how in God's prehension of the subjectivity of an individual actual occasion there is danger that the occasion's subjectivity will be absorbed without remainder into the subjectivity of God. In Suchocki's description of the divine consequent nature as the "community" of dynamically interrelated creaturely actual occasions (103), there is the opposite danger that the subjectivity of God will be absorbed without remainder into the intersubjective reality of creaturely actual occasions fully reconciled with one another. Is God, in other words, more than "the Immediacy of immediacies, and a Harmony of Harmonies" (106)? Admittedly, it is the subjective aim of God as the ever-concrescing divine subject of experience which allegedly governs the ongoing process of reconciliation among the creaturely actual occasions. But the deeper relation of the divine One to the creaturely Many still remains obscure. It is not enough, in my judgment, simply to refer to God's "extremely complex subjectivity" (102).

6. Whitehead, *Process and Reality*, 351.

subjective aim for the divine concrescence. Given "God's communal nature," as indicated above, it is no surprise that "God's aims to the world inexorably must reflect the value of participating in and contributing to communal richness" (122-23). Thus God prompts individual actual occasions to form societies of ever-greater complexity. But societies often resist further incorporation into even broader social groupings on the grounds that self-transcendence toward a wider goal conflicts with necessary self-perpetuation here and now (124). Yet the divine call to self-transcendence is ever present in the initial aims to the constituent actual occasions of the society in question. Furthermore, present-day evil can always be remedied by future decisions for self-transcendence; no evil is ever final (124).

In the concluding pages of the chapter, Suchocki takes up the issue of freedom within a social context, how freedom and responsibility are exercised within institutions like the state and the church. On the analogy of the soul or dominant set of actual occasions at work within the human body, she argues that governmental officials assume greater responsibility than other citizens for the common good even though all bear some responsibility for the work of the society (128). With respect to church communities, she contends that they have the responsibility to model life in community for the broader civil community: "Insofar as a redemptive community itself models the openness of God's peace, it becomes a concrete lure for the good. It is itself a change in the environment which affects all other finite reality, becoming a force which must be accounted for throughout the larger society" (130). Likewise, by their participation in these civil organizations, church members, sometimes through encouragement and sometimes through confrontation, can help to redress social evils and transform civil society.

In her final chapter, titled "The Metaphysics of the Redemptive God," Suchocki further specifies the understanding of God and the God-world relationship which has been operative throughout the book. Although really no different from Whitehead's own presentation in *Process and Reality*, it has a clarity and definition which in my judgment is lacking in the latter work. She notes, for example, that, while God in Whitehead's scheme is also conceived as an actual entity, the process of concrescence in God is the "mirror image" of the process of concrescence in creaturely actual occasions. That is, while a creaturely actual occasion originates with the prehension of past actual occasions (the physical pole of its existence) and then adds "eternal objects" or structures of intelligibility from its prehension of God's initial aim and the structure of those antecedent actual occasions (its mental pole), God originates in the mental pole of God's existence, the vision of possibilities which Whitehead calls the primordial nature of God, which then becomes integrated with the physical pole of God's existence, the divine consequent nature or God's ongoing prehension of what is happening in the world (136-37). In this sense, the creaturely actual occasion moves from an initial multiplicity of prehensions to the unity of its own finite self-constitution and resultant "satisfaction" in what it has become (138-39). God, on the other hand, moves from an initial unity, the vision of possibilities in the primordial nature with its satisfaction in the conceptual order, to an integrated multiplicity in terms of the divine consequent nature: "The primordial satisfaction directs rather than concludes God's concrescence" (141). In this way, God is both complete and incomplete at the same time. At evey moment an integration of the primordial and consequent natures in God is actualized and a deeper satisfaction in God's engagement with the world is realized, but in the next moment a new integration of the two natures and a further satisfaction will be achieved (142). There is thus an awareness of succession within the divine consciousness but no real seriality, no sequence of different subjects of experience as in the created order, since one and the same divine concrescence is everlasting (150). God is the wholly transcendent actual entity always in process of concrescence through interaction with creaturely actual occasions originating in space and time. "The only real requirement is that the future, when it occurs, will be conformable to God's aim, but this is just what has been eternally assured in God's primordial satisfaction" (152). Precisely in this way, there is indeed a guaranteed End of Evil.

"Deliver Us from Evil" or Doing Away with Humankind?

Jürgen Moltmann

1. The Fascination and the Banality of Evil

The most pleasant way to deal with Evil is to be found in one's favorite detective stories. I read them eagerly with much excitement and find them relaxing as evening entertainment. The criminal is both incorrigible and increasingly sophisticated. His criminal energy is colossal and most impressive. His criminal activity is somehow both overblown and fascinating, at least for himself. Yet the detective who is on his trail is nevertheless a little more clever than he and — through "adding things up" after the fashion of Sherlock Holmes or with comparable analysis of life in St Mary Mead with Miss Marple or "with license to kill" as with 007 (James Bond) — is always hot in pursuit. In the end Justice triumphs. Evil is rooted out, the criminal is brought to justice and therewith "all the details of everyday life are restored to their rightful place" (Catherine Keller). Sherlock Holmes is at leisure once again; Miss Marple tends her garden; and 007 indulges once more in his favorite activity.

The detective stories from Agatha Christie to Donna Leon both awaken and satisfy our curiosity as to Evil. The craftiness of Evil and its entanglements captivate our interest; yet in the end everything is resolved quite satisfactorily. All for the best, since from the beginning

Translated by Joseph A. Bracken, S.J.

of our reading or watching TV we suspected that it would so work out. The best detective stories have been written by women. For with them Evil is subtle and not so brutal as with men. Thus we relax, knowing that these horror stories are fiction, entertaining diversions.

Unhappily, this is not real Evil. For Evil has laid our world in ruins and proceeds, with hatred and murder, lies and destruction to heap up the "killing fields" of human history and to make our personal lives miserable. We cannot catch up with this real (non-fictional) Evil as in the detective stories. In real life there is no happy ending. New forms of Evil arise out of old, and those who contest Evil slip all too easily into a strategy based on Evil and indirectly propagate it rather than root it out or at least limit it. World history does not read like a detective story, either for us or even less so for God.

Is there a fascination with Evil? At the present time, the theme Evil has broad currency in Protestant and Catholic academic circles. For the moment, that is, in the age of a "postmodern world." Does it reflect an interest in the gruesome because the modern world has become so boring? Do human beings cynically amuse themselves with the misfortunes of others? Are we moved simply by intellectual curiosity? We have explored outer space and unlocked the secrets of the human genome. Now shall we also explore the negative terror of Evil so as finally to come to grips with it? Or is something else involved?

There is, as psychoanalysts concede, a de facto fascination, a power of attraction, which evil, cruelty and the destruction of life and happiness for human beings can exercise. Experiences with Evil which human beings bring about can also transfer them into a power-trance. Someone who is capable of inflicting brutal force on a helpless victim, like a torturer or rapist, feels "like a god," a "lord of destruction," a "Master over life and death." To be sure, he cannot do anything constructive, but he can destroy; he cannot love anything but he can hate everything; he cannot give life but he can take it; he cannot initiate anything but only end things. He is the "Terminator," the "Wrath of God," the Rider of the Apocalypse, the Power of the End-time, the Fury of Annihilation *(Verschwindens)*.

In the postmodern world, to be sure, human beings rarely have immediate elementary experiences. Most of their experiences are filtered and given meaning through the media; many remarks are pure cliches. In such a "virtual world" of computer games the demand for immediate experience and one's own direct action can become quite strong. At that point we seek avenues for spontaneity in life and we hunger after reality. Because within our well-established world and well-insulated social environment we can bring about nothing new and original, we are captivated by the force of destruction: "Let it burn!" Not without reason satanic cults and black masses rage in the affluent countries of Europe, for example, in Norway; likewise, the temptation grows to burn down churches and refugee asylums. Fascination with Evil in a comfortable welfare state? Child pornography and pornography loaded with violence and murder are offered on the Internet and obviously sought after.

The banality of Evil? Many generations of Christians have imagined World History as a grandiose struggle between God and the Devil and between Good and Evil. On the one side there is the light-filled Kingdom of God and on the other side the Counter-Kingdom of Satan shrouded in darkness. On the one side there is the superior Providence of God and on the other side the Master-Plan of Evil with calculated disruptions and intentional acts of destruction. Both Kingdoms, that of Light and Darkness, of Good and Evil, of God and the satanic Anti-God, of Christ and the Anti-Christ, are preparing for the final conflict over world supremacy. Religious Apocalyptic expected and tried to hasten the Final Conflict in the valley of Armageddon. Secular Apocalyptic shouted out: "Peoples, pay attention to the warning-signs; on your feet for the final battle." Contemporary Christian, Jewish and Muslim believers in Apocalyptic still think the same way and look forward to the approaching End. At some point and somehow the ambiguous history of this world with its deviant ways and violence must come to an end: They say: "Better an end with violence than such violence without end!" Moreover, they do not shrink from [the possible use of] poison gas and Intercontinental Ballistic Missiles to bring this history to a close.

But the struggle with Evil is so glamorous only in our theatrical fantasies. In reality Good is not here; Evil over there. Here, the Kingdom of God; there, the Kingdom of Satan. God has a name; Evil has no name: "Its name is legion." That is, it is anonymous and pseudonymous, not nameable, indefinable, not specifiable. Evil in us and in our world has many sources and many faces. It constantly generates itself anew and grows in strength. If we cut off the head of the hydra, nine new heads grow. Evil is in reality like a tangle of roots that follows no order, with no beginning or end, that submits to no regulation even from Hell. Rather, it reproduces itself chaotically and remains unconstrained. It positions itself in the middle of stability and order. Admittedly, there are always extraordinary evildoers (Hitler, Stalin, Pol Pot, Pinochet, Saddam, and others), but it is more our anxiety that fixes upon evil in such perverse individuals. In reality Evil is to be found in well-heeled bureaucracies of desk-job-criminals who on the surface only "did their duty" (like Eichmann in whom according to Hannah Arendt the banality of Evil appears as something of secondary importance, unassuming, of little prominence, virtually overlooked). There is no fascination with Evil to uncover in the behavior of the Concentration Camp killers. But they also had no guilty conscience for doing evil. They did the "dirty work" assigned to them and drank Vodka. Is Evil attractive? No! In this context, Evil is disgusting.

"Deliver us from Evil." If Evil is not an exciting detective story, if it has no compelling power to fascinate, if it is hard to determine and yet everywhere present, if it is so banal that it can poison everything, then we should not step forward to a moral struggle with the Evil in ourselves, or to a political struggle with the Evil to be found in others, or to a religious struggle against Satan and the cohorts of Hell. Rather, we should ask God finally to deliver us from Evil. It is better, one says, to light a candle in the darkness than to do battle with the ghosts of the night. Only in the light afforded us by redemption do we recognize what Evil really is, where it is and how its seductions have appeared to us.

In the Biblical texts human beings are really not called to do battle with Evil; much more they call out to God to "rescue" them from Evil as from a sea in which they are about to drown. "Miserable man that I am," complains Paul, "who will deliver me from this mortal body?" (Rom. 7:24). For, as he confesses in the name of all human beings, "I do not do the Good that I want, but I do the Evil that I do not want" (Rom. 7:19). He puts his trust in Christ, who "rescues us from the present evil age in accord with the will of God" (Gal. 1:4). Clearly for those who speak thus, the swamp of Evil is so bottomless, so boundless, that they cannot like Münchhausen pull themselves out of it by the hair of their heads nor can they otherwise contend with the swamp without sinking deeper into it. Only God, who calls Being into existence out of Nothingness and proposes new beginnings for human history gone astray, can "deliver" from Evil. And he delivers us inasmuch as he pulls us out of Evil rather than purifies us from Evil. We have to distance ourselves from Evil, not vice versa, since Evil is not something distasteful for us who are otherwise good. Rather, Evil is so deeply rooted in our very being that the atmosphere around us is poisoned by it. Seeing things this way, we are not pessimists obsessed with our sins, but optimists preoccupied with salvation since we have hope not only for a more humane world but for more humane human beings.

2. What Is Evil? "Sin, Death and the Devil"

When I was confirmed in 1940, I received a lofty commission at the same time: "Fight the good fight by having faith and a good conscience" (1 Tim. 1:18-19), in line with Dürer's portrayal of the Knight against Sin, Death and the Devil. I became no great fighter, neither morally nor militarily. I only remember the traditional distinctions which we once used to categorize the different kinds of Evil. The philosopher Leibniz had the following threefold distinction:

1. physical defects (*Übel*) — sickness, death
2. moral evil — sin, guilt
3. metaphysical Nothingness (*Nichts*) — the Devil, destruction.

Physical Defects

We cannot call the physical ailments which we suffer like sicknesses, disabilities, accidents and dying "evil" since the viruses and other sources of sickness are not evil. Perverse drives and various forms of mental illness are very debilitating but not evil. "Death" (*Tod*) means the end of the unsteady, sickness-prone, transitory condition of human existence in which we are created. Unquestionably the physical disabilities which we suffer influence often enough the moral evil that we inflict upon others. But is Evil for that reason to be identified with a physical disorder? And if it were such, can it be healed? At the end of this essay we will return to this point in distinguishing and evaluating the various kinds of Evil. For now we will simply distinguish between physical disability and moral evil.

Moral Evil (Böses)

We must on the other hand distinguish moral evil that came into the world through human beings and has ever since been propagated by them from metaphysical Nothingness *(Nichts)* that in all forms of destruction opens up like an abyss. Evil is not destiny, fate or tragedy. As little as we can make the Devil responsible for our sins, thus not holding ourselves accountable, so little is eternal Nothingness as the abyss of emptiness *(Verschwinden)* responsible for the acts of destruction which we, above all in the twentieth century, have suffered. There go forth from this Nothingness enticements such as Dostoyevski described in his "Demons," to be sure, but Nothingness is not Evil and Evil is not yet Nothingness but the reversion of Good into its opposite. If we speak of Evil, then we remain in the world of human beings who move toward inhumanity when they behave in an inhuman way. They behave in an inhuman way when they turn truth into a lie, good into evil, overpowering instead of loving [another], and turn love for life into a death wish.

3. Catalog of the Appearances of Evil

The first and for everything else foundational insight is that Good and Evil are not symmetrical and equal to one another like positive and negative, plus and minus, but unequal. Good can exist without Evil, but Evil cannot exist without Good. For this reason we describe Evil on occasion as un-good or no good *(das Ungute).* "He did not do well." Try once describing Good in this manner: is it a lack of Evil *(das Unböse)?* No, that does not work. A lie is an untruth but truth is not a failure to lie *(die Unlüge).* For this reason since the time of Plato philosophers have readily designated Evil, *malum,* as loss of good, *privatio boni et veri.* Good is Being, that which is and is affirmed; Evil is the negation of Being as good and affirmed. Quite properly Mephisto in Goethe's "Faust" names himself the personification of negation:

I am the Spirit of ongoing negation and that quite rightly,
for what value if what comes into being collapses?
Accordingly, it would be better that nothing came to be.
Thus everything that you call sin, destruction, in short, Evil,
Belongs to me.

Evil is the reversal of Good; a lie is the reversal of truth; hatred is the perversion of love; the ugly is the distortion of the beautiful. That means, however, that Evil, lies, hatred and death are nothing in themselves, have no power of their own against the Good, the True, the Beautiful and Being, but are only their perversions. The Devil does not create a counter-world. For he can create nothing but only reverse and destroy, bring the Good in the world of creation into disarray.

Hidden in every form of Evil is a distorted Good that must be redeemed. Hidden in every lie is a warped truth which must be brought to light. Hidden in every act of hatred or criminal energy is an enormous love-energy which must be freed from its perversion and brought back to its source. Not only must evil people, the destroyers, those in denial, and sinners, be redeemed as individual persons, but Evil itself and these terrible powers of destruction must be redeemed and converted into something positive.

A Lie Is an Untruth

I can rely on the truth. Whoever tells the truth can be trusted. Yet, "whoever tells a lie cannot be trusted even when he tells the truth." Whoever speaks the truth and gives witness to the truth through keeping his promise creates trust on which one can rely. Without the guarantee of truth-speaking there is no life together. Trust generates life and freedom. When we lie, however, we falsify the truth and make everything unreliable on which others lean. We deceive them in that we abuse their trust. Where nothing can be counted on, then one treats everyone with distrust and cannot spend time with anyone. But if one cannot spend time with anyone, then in fact one cannot continue to live. Lies poison the atmosphere with distrust. Yet since we are expected as part of community life to trust others and to be ourselves trustworthy, every liar can exploit that trust as pure naivete. All liars in the world of politics exploit the trust of the populace so necessary for life together. All liars in the world of advertising exploit the desires of people for what is good, true and beautiful. Lying destroys along with trust life itself, not only the life of the one lied to but the life of the liar himself. Why then do we lie?

As I see it, there are three motives. We lie to other people to deceive them and to exploit their trust for our own purposes. For we promise "pie in the sky" with no intention of keeping it. We assure people of things that we neither can nor want to give them. That is lying with a deceitful intention.

Most of the time, however, we lie out of anxiety, either out of anxiety about an unpleasant reaction from others or out of concern for others, to protect them. Perhaps with men self-centered motives prevail, and with women other-centered motives. When we thus lie, we don't expect the truth either from ourselves or others. Thus, while deceitful lying is readily recognized as a malicious reversal of the truth, what is one to say when on the basis of a good intention to protect the other I lie to him about the truth of his fatal illness and substitute the illusion of an attractive future? Is the compulsion for truth-telling to everyone in every instance and under any and all circumstances good or evil? Am I in the face of murderers (the Gestapo, the Stasi or however else these devil's minions in dictatorships are called) obliged to tell the truth or should I not lie to liars in order to save human life? What is to be said about "white lies"? That lies are the conversion of truth into untruth and that the Devil according to the Gospel of John is "the father of lies" (8:44) is certainly true, but what the truthful life concretely is in a world full of lies is not nearly so clear.

Evil Is Knowable in Relation to the Good That It Corrupts

Evil is thus always measured in terms of the Good. If we no longer know what is Good, then we can no longer say what is Evil. What then is Good? As already mentioned, Good is what is true; Good is what is loved for its own sake. Good is to be present, to exist in harmony with others, to be alive in relation to other forms of life. For life is communication in and through communion. If relations break off, then we experience a curtailment of our lives. If people die whom we love and by whom we are loved, then part of our life is lost. We can in general say: the Good is life lived robustly, with warmth, and in communion with others. The Good is primarily and over and above everything else to be together with God, the source of life, to experience his love which affirms us where we are and accepts us as we are, and draws us back when we stray.

If essentially this is what is meant by Good, then Evil is the reversal of this good and worthwhile existence: unhappy life in common, disappointed love, a craze for destruction of life, both one's own, that of the other and of life shared with the other. Just as love is the communication of life, so Evil is experienced in the breaking off of what is necessary for life. Just as life begins with the Yes of God and the Yes of the other, so Evil starts with a No to God, to the other and to oneself. Evil in human life is always linked with death somehow. In breaking off a relationship, I threaten another with "social death" (mit dem sozialen Tod) and create for myself deep loneliness. Through unloving behavior, I spread hatred and close doors which should be open. With jealousy and envy I deprive others of due respect and seek to humiliate them. In virtue of malicious gossip I defame them behind their backs. With murder and vicious assault human beings take the lives of others directly and their own lives indirectly. Every diminishment of a life that is reliant on trust and affirmation is evil.

Why do such reversals of Good into its opposite take place? If we possess free will, why do we do it? If it is an illness, why don't we find a cure? Is it our anxiety in the face of nothingness (Nichts) that makes us so crazy? Somewhere deep in our psyche something must have gone wrong, something unfortunate must have happened, that expresses itself in so many small and occasionally big misdeeds. Clearly we do not have this power of Evil under control, and we feel ourselves burdened and guilty because of what this power of negativity accomplishes through us.

When Evil is nothing more than Good turned into opposite, then salvation from Evil consists in converting Evil back to its original state of goodness, hatred back to love, envy back to respect, and revenge back to forgiveness.

The Diabolical Circularity of Evil

Lying, malice, hateful deeds and death wishes are not phenomena limited to the behavior of individuals nor are they simply located in an individual's conscience. Rather, they permeate the political, social and cultural structures of society in which individual persons participate, sometimes in a more active way, more often passively and through acquiescence. I recently read in a Swedish detective story that there are no evil human beings but only evil circumstances that compel or at least seduce them into employing force. "We would be good rather than uncouth, but circumstances do not allow it," wrote Berthold Brecht in his "Three Penny Opera." But that cannot qualify as a personal excuse.

When we can locate Evil in individual persons, then we see it clearly: the liar, the rapist, the child-molester, the murderer. When, however, Evil happens in a massive way, as in wars at Verdun, Stalingrad and Hiroshima, then it overwhelms our power to grasp it. We don't see individual victims but only read numbers. One cannot imagine 6 million Jews who were gassed in Auschwitz. The mass murders under Pol Pot in Cambodia and the massacres in Rwanda are incomprehensible for us. Likewise, we lose the appropriate concepts, when we move out of the restricted, easily comprehensible sphere of private life into the much larger social and political circles within which private life is carried on.

Herbert Haag, who wrote about his "Departure from the Devil" in 1971, found Evil in the everyday life of little people as something modest and relatively rare. Evil was, strictly speaking, the exception, Goodness the rule. As a rule, human beings fulfil their duties every day and do what is right. He even claimed: "We have less time for Evil than we have for Good." Goodness gives us pleasure; Evil is by nature distasteful to us. I agree although I also note that Herbert Haag is a Swiss citizen and thus never experienced the pain of the Second World War and its aftermath. If one, moreover, looks beyond the limits of life as a private individual into the broader circle of political and economic powers which control such a life, then often the Goodness of everyday existence is revealed as the pointless fulfilment of duty in the service of a greater Evil. I think, for example, on my youth during the Second World War. Ordinary soldiers occupied France, Denmark,

Poland, the Balkans and Russia. They did their duty as soldiers so as consciously to do good and avoid evil. Heinrich Böll said disarmingly: "I was always a decent human being." Women back home produced grenades and built defenses likewise in good conscience. And all of us were in the service of Evil: I myself as an anti-aircraft assistant and soldier, my future wife in the Basig munitions factory in Berlin under siege. We contributed to the mass murder of Jews and brought enormous pain to the peoples of Europe.

In the circles of private life at that time anyone who refused service in the war effort was deemed a coward and traitor to the Fatherland. In the context of the broader powers of Evil and in the light of subsequent history the conscientious objector is viewed as a true resistance fighter from the first moment since he refused to become a general or a soldier in the service of Satan.

In today's world, we go about our daily duties, work in the industrial nations of the North and consume the bounty of the South. We do not do anything wrong and we moreover willingly give money to "Bread for the World" and "Caritas." Yet an unjust worldwide economic order with its equally unjust price-fixing brings it about that we are co-responsible for the oppression and exploitation of the Third World. It would be too simplistic for this reason to eat every banana with a feeling of guilt and to experience pangs of conscience with every bite into Argentinian beef. For it is not only a personal problem that can be solved through adopting an alternative innocent lifestyle. It is also a structural problem linked with injustice on the basis of rapid globalization.

Yet we are not helpless. These broader structures are not immune to personal and social alternatives but instead — as advertising makes clear — quite vulnerable to public protests. The campaign of the Protestant women's organizations to "buy no fruit from Apartheid" was not so unsuccessful as various objections to individual women would lead one to believe, but in fact contributed significantly to the overthrow of unjust structures in South Africa. Likewise, the conscientious objectors during the Second World War were not without impact. For not without reason did the German High Command execute more than 24,000 of them, more than any other army in any other war that we know of.

It is of course true that the sinister workings of Evil within corporate structures become over time self-sustaining. Such structures are initially created by human beings but gain an objective power over those same individuals and thereby leave them no alternative. In this way perpetrators become slaves of Evil. Is there a collective guilt for those who acted collectively?

"Resist the beginnings" is a good motto. In 1933 much would have been possible to avert the dictatorship of Hitler, which a few years later was no longer possible. To see through and unmask the conditions generated by Evil is one more step in gaining freedom from them. The personal fearlessness of the crowds in Leipzig and Dresden brought down the GDR like a house of cards in 1989. Taboos associated with Evil, the idols of force and the lies of the ruling powers can be done away with, even when such attempts are life-endangering.

4. Clarifications and Value-Judgments about Evil: Open Questions for Discussion

Is Evil the Price to Be Paid for Human Freedom?

"A human being is created free even if he or she is born in chains." Only with respect to living creatures with free will can one speak of Evil. The lion who kills its victim does nothing evil but follows its instincts. We do not protest if it doesn't eat straw, at least not yet. On the other hand, if a human being is equipped with free will, then he always stands before the choice between Good and Evil. If he chooses Evil instead of Good, then he is the cause of Evil and he is accountable for Evil. For that which he does not cause or does not willingly do, he is not accountable. So runs the depiction of Evil as a moral problem. Thereby one recognizes Evil as a possibility within the range of human activity and one overcomes it through an appeal to human free will and decisiveness. If a human being can avoid doing evil, he should do so. "You can; therefore, you should," as Kant instructed us. Unfortunately, real human beings find themselves again and again at a crossroads. But they don't feel like Hercules, who can be counted on to make the right decision, but rather like Sisyphus: "He who has the choice feels the pain." Are we humans then as free as on the day of our creation? Our life-history burdens us with so many antecedent sequences of events (*Vorgängen*) and decisions already made that our range of possibilities is not absolute and our decision-making power not so great as we would like to think. More realistic is Paul when he confesses: "The willing is ready at hand, but doing the good is not" (Rom. 7:18). Is that an excuse? Am I lacking in moral accountability when I claim full or partial innocence of guilt?

So much for the subjective side of Evil within the realm of moral freedom. From the objective side, one recognizes that things never go as one anticipates and desires. For there are unexpected problems arising from within things (*Die Tücke des Objekts*), "dumb accidents," an unhappy linking of circumstances, so that in the end we often say: "That isn't what I wanted even though I did it." Or we say: "I didn't do it even though I wanted to do it." Who is at fault? Has the Devil double-crossed our good intentions? Are we being "tricked by reason"? Does the Providence of God come into play here? For it is not only that our good intentions often go awry. Sometimes it is the other way around. "You planned something bad, but God turned it to good," says Joseph to his evil-minded brothers who had sold him into slavery in Egypt without knowing that God sent him there to care for them in their time of famine.

When all Evil in the world is the fault of human beings or more precisely when only that can be counted as evil which human beings do with free will, then the responsibility for Evil is shifted eventually to their Creator. If God has endowed humanity with free will and thereby with a capacity for Evil, is God then not responsible for an evil world which human beings have created? "God made men and women good but weak," confesses Herbert Haag. But that in the end implies: "God wanted a sinful world." Thus the question recurs. If Evil is the price of human freedom, is that not too high a price to pay? One need only think of the mass murders and the massive destruction of the twentieth century to awaken doubt and a sense of hopelessness in human beings about themselves and God.

Is Evil a Sickness? Are Human Beings Driven to It?

If we accept this perspective, then we trace the Evil that affects human beings back to a malice in their natural makeup. In the conflict between human beings and Evil, then court-appointed doctors and psychotherapists have the last word. We acknowledge the inner turmoil of mental patients and those with compulsive behavior. They need medical assistance, not punishment. They are not accountable for their actions and thus are not guilty of a crime. But is every act of stealing thus a case of kleptomania and every murderer driven to the deed? If we then reduce Evil to physical disabilities such as inherited dispositions or genetic mistakes, would we not be in line to do away with humanity, at least the humanity known to us? If Evil is a sickness, then we can heal it. If it is a sickness that cannot be healed, then we must protect ourselves against these sick people or eliminate them from human life, for example, through castration whereby their reproduction and further proliferation can be cut short, or through prenatal diagnosis to avoid their birth at all. Yet, even if we can in this way root out Evil, we still have to deal with the question of the evil that is associated with this repressive activity or extermination.

If we in the future could so change the human genome that nothing evil would ever again happen, then we would have deprived human beings of their free will. They would all function well and do what was prescribed for them, but who would dictate what is to be done? If we could somehow genetically engineer a totally good or a totally evil world, we would not know the difference between good and evil. A world in which one cannot distinguish between good and evil might well be the "brave, new world" of Huxley and Orwell, but would such a painless and innocent world be one worth loving?

Is Evil Sin? How Do Sinners Win Freedom from Their Sin?

In Biblical terms, Evil is not only the opposite of Good and not only a violation of law, but sin, that is, a deviation, literally, a "separation" from the living God and his covenant with life. Human beings become in their personal lives set apart, sinners, before they commit this or that sinful act or sin by omission. If sin is thus a breakdown or accident in one's relation to God, then it must be understood as transcendent of morality. The immorality of Evil or moral self-justification follow upon sin in this sense. If human beings have lost God, then they always try, albeit despairingly, either to be what they are and thus assert themselves in their abandoned state, or refuse to be what they are and make themselves small and unassuming (in their own eyes). Out of the "flight from God" (Augustine) follows either pride, the desire to be one's own lord and god, or timidity, the willingness to be less than fully human. Men tend to make themselves greater than they really are; women on the contrary, less significant than they truly are. Both men and women, however, become diminished human beings, much as Luther portrayed the sinner, or they become self-preoccupied narcissists, as Sigmund Freud with his love for classical antiquity analyzed the individual. Out of this inner disposition proper to godless and godforsaken sinners follows then the evil that they do or permit or that happens to them. Whoever objects on moral grounds to a sinner does not help him but only "reduces him to zero." One who as a therapist offers the sinner medication likewise does not help him but makes him into a "poor mental case."

From a biblical standpoint Evil is sin and must be healed in terms of one's relation to God. Only when God, from whom the sinner has departed, has mercy on him or her, much as a mother has compassion for her children or as the rejected father takes back the prodigal son with open arms, are sinners redeemed from their abandonment. This mercy of God we call "forgiveness of sins" or "the acceptance of sinners," that is, the godless and godforsaken. To sinners previously shipwrecked in their relations to God a "new beginning" is conferred in which like newborns they can begin life free of constraint. Forgiveness of sins relieves for sinners the burden of the past. Rebirth to a lively hope opens for them a new future in life.

This unconditional love of God, into which those who strayed and wandered away now know themselves to be forever received, changes their entire life. The young Luther said tellingly: "Sinners are beautiful because they are loved; they are not loved because they are beautiful." For God's love is creative; it makes unfortunate sinners good, just and beautiful, so that they do not have to reproach themselves any more.

The person in whose fate humanity was both true and real is Christ. In the crucified Christ were gathered all the sins of the world and he took them on himself from us. "You who bear the sins of the world." In the risen Christ opens up the complete fullness of eternal life in [and through] the love of God. This same love of God pours itself out over us in the power of the Spirit and fills us with unexpected new vitality. "Why should he not give us everything with him?" Yet such an experience leaves us with open questions: Does Christ carry all the pain to be found in this world, thus not only sinners, but the victims of sin as well? When will God have mercy on this dangerously threatened world of ours? When will God's justice triumph, so that murderers no longer exult over their victims? The blood of victims continues to cry to the heavens!

Eschatological Visions

Robert Cummings Neville

Marjorie Hewett Suchocki is surely the most important American liberal theologian to take eschatology seriously.[1] To be sure, she is not as colorful as Thomas J. J. Altizer for whom the whole of Christianity is purely apocalyptic eschatology.[2] But then Altizer is a radical, not a liberal, theologian; I'll return to the relation of eschatology to apocalyptic below. Nor does Suchocki go so far as Wolfhart Pannenberg to make the very witness of Christianity depend on eschatology.[3] But then Pannenberg is a confessional theologian, albeit far more philosophical than most, not a liberal theologian.

"Liberal theology," at least in this context, is the project that takes very seriously the need to develop models of God, of the religiously important aspects of the human condition, and of the relations between God and the world, that are accountable on two fronts.

1. See her *The End of Evil: Process Eschatology in Historical Context* (Albany: State University of New York Press, 1988).

2. For the record, among Altizer's directly apocalyptic eschatological writings are *The New Apocalypse: The Radical Christian Vision of William Blake* (East Lansing: Michigan State University Press, 1967; reprint edition Aurora, CO: The Davies Group, 2000); *History as Apocalypse* (Albany: State University of New York Press, 1985); *Genesis and Apocalypse: A Theological Voyage Toward Authentic Christianity* (Louisville, KY: Westminster/John Knox Press, 1990); *The Genesis of God: A Theological Genealogy* (Louisville, KY: Westminster/John Knox Press, 1993); *The Contemporary Jesus* (Albany: State University of New York Press, 1997).

3. See Pannenberg's *Systematic Theology* in three volumes, translated by Geoffrey W. Bromiley (Grand Rapids, MI: Eerdmans, 1991, 1994, and 1998).

28

One front is making normative sense of the religious tradition, especially its ancient origins; "liberal" Jewish, Muslim, Buddhist, Hindu, and other religious theologies are possible as well as liberal Christian theology of Suchocki's sort. "Normative sense" means saying what is true in the traditions, not just what they mean. The other front of accountability for the models is all the elements of contemporary imagination, knowledge, and culture that might affect the plausibility and credibility of the models. Furthermore, liberal theology maintains that how one reads the religious tradition is dependent on implicit or explicit models of the religiously relevant matters. Thus the tradition itself is only a partially independent front for accountability, with the result that theology is in constant fallible dialectical motion, not a hermeneutical circle but a normative circle. Paul Tillich is an outstanding example of a twentieth-century liberal theologian in this sense, despite the fact he shared with Barth the credit for founding Neo-orthodoxy in Christian theology.[4] I believe the liberal program is right.

Suchocki's models famously derive from Whitehead with creative modifications, as outlined succinctly in Joseph Bracken, S.J.'s, introductory essay here in this volume. The process theology derived from Whitehead has taken many forms, and Suchocki's is perhaps the most serious and detailed in addressing the first front of accountability, the tradition. Even more than her eschatology book, *The End of Evil*, the earlier *God-Christ-Church* carefully elaborates her process model in terms of the traditional "loci" of Christian doctrine.[5] Suchocki is a genuine church theologian, one who places great emphasis on eschatology.

I have been blessed with a long friendship with Marjorie Suchocki, in the course of which she has argued that my theology does not place enough emphasis on eschatology and has kindly offered to amend my models of God, the world, and the human condition so as to support a proper doctrine of last things.[6] My metaphysi-

---

4. See Tillich's *Systematic Theology* in three volumes (Chicago: University of Chicago Press, 1952, 1957, 1963).

5. See her *God-Christ-Church* (first edition; New York: Crossroad, 1982; new revised edition: New York: Crossroad, 1989).

6. See her fine article, "Neville's Theology: A Feminist and Process Dialogue," in *Interpreting Neville*, edited by Nancy Frankenberry and J. Harley Chapman (Albany: State University of New York Press, 1999), pp. 205-221. In that article she also criti-

cal views are sufficiently close to Whitehead's as to make this a plausible friendly amendment.[7] Nevertheless, I decline to accept the suggestions and in this essay will draw out the contrasts between her eschatology and mine, two eschatological visions. Several questions will draw out the contrast.

1. What Is the Ancient Form of Eschatology?

The biblical notions of eschatology have to do with "last things," the end of the world, with related notions of final judgment on individuals or groups, the resurrection, heaven and hell, and eternal life.[8] Scholars have distinguished two broad eschatological theories or thematic approaches in the New Testament, a future-historical eschatology and a realized eschatology.

The future-historical eschatological theme treats divine judgment as a future event, with heavenly rewards and hellish punishments to follow. Often this is taken to be a future time in which the world as we know it comes to an end. The earliest New Testament eschatological writing is probably St. Paul's first letter to the Thessalonians where, in the 4th and 5th chapters, he addresses the concerns of members of the congregation about those who had died before Jesus returned. Paul and his community expected Jesus to return momentarily and bring those who are "in Christ" to God.

> For since we believe that Jesus died and rose again, even so, through Jesus, God will bring with him those who have died. For this we declare to you by the word of the Lord, that we who are

---

cizes my theology for thematizing masculine and feminine symbols in religion, the topic of another discussion.

7. Moreover, she is right that in my book she discussed, *A Theology Primer* (Albany: State University of New York Press, 1991), I had not sufficiently dealt with eschatology, and should have. The topic received a book-length treatment in *Eternity and Time's Flow* (Albany: State University of New York Press, 1993).

8. Alister E. McGrath, in his influential and helpful glossary in *Christian Theology: An Introduction* (second edition; Oxford: Blackwell, 1997), defines eschatology as "the section of Christian theology dealing with the 'end things,' especially the ideas of resurrection, hell, and eternal life," p. 569.

alive, who are left until the coming of the Lord, will by no means precede those who have died. For the Lord himself, with a cry of command, with the archangel's call and with the sound of God's trumpet, will descend from heaven, and the dead in Christ will rise first. Then we who are alive, who are left, will be caught up in the clouds together with them to meet the Lord in the air; and so we will be with the Lord forever.... For you yourselves know very well that the day of the Lord will come like a thief in the night. When they say, "There is peace and security," then sudden destruction will come upon them, as labor pains come upon a pregnant woman, and there will be no escape. But you, beloved, are not in darkness, for that day to surprise you like a thief; for you are all children of light and children of the day; we are not of the night or of the darkness. So then let us not fall asleep as others do, but let us keep awake and be sober; for those who sleep sleep at night, and those who are drunk get drunk at night. But since we belong to the day, let us be sober, and put on the breastplate of faith and love, and for a helmet the hope of salvation. For God has destined us not for wrath but for obtaining salvation through our Lord Jesus Christ, who died for us, so that whether we are awake or asleep we may live with him. (1 Thessalonians 4:14-17, 5:2-10)

Many of these themes are found in Jesus' teachings as reported in the synoptic gospels, for instance in Matthew 24–25. The themes include the coming to earth of God (or Jesus, in Paul's case), cataclysmic destruction and transformation, martial metaphors for the steadfastness and wakefulness of the faithful, and judgment separating the righteous from the unrighteous, for Paul those who are in Christ from those who are not. The Book of Revelation intensifies these themes to apocalyptic proportions.

The theme of realized eschatology is that within this life Jesus has already overcome the world (John 16:33) and that, because of this, Christians have a kind of dual existence. On the one hand they are already buried with Jesus in his baptism and raised with him in resurrection, even now joined with him in the divine presence. On the other hand at least some Christians are still alive and continue to have to face the problems of historical existence. As the author of Colossians wrote his readers:

For in him the whole fullness of deity dwells bodily, and you have come to fullness in him, who is the head of every ruler and authority. In him also you were circumcised with a spiritual circumcision, by putting off the body of the flesh in the circumcision of Christ; when you were buried with him in baptism, you were also raised with him through faith in the power of God, who raised him from the dead. . . . So if you have been raised with Christ, seek the things that are above, where Christ is, seated at the right hand of God. Set your minds on things that are above, not on things that are on earth, for you have died, and your life is hidden with Christ in God. When Christ who is your life is revealed, then you also will be revealed with him in glory. Put to death, therefore, whatever in you is earthly: fornication, impurity, passion, evil desire, and greed (which is idolatry). On account of these the wrath of God is coming on those who are disobedient. (Colossians 2:9-12; 3:1-6)

A similar view is expressed in Ephesians, say at 2:4-10. John's gospel makes the strong point, in chapters 14–17, that Jesus' true home is in God, that he is going to prepare a place for his friends whom he will bring into God, and that meanwhile in his absence from ongoing historical life he will send the Holy Spirit to guide those whom he loves through persecutions and trials. Whereas the future-historical eschatology speaks of God or Christ coming to Earth to transform it, the realized eschatology does not necessarily promise a transformation or ending of history, only continued vicissitudes within history. For the realized eschatology historical life needs to be read in terms of the larger reality of God which is our true home; to think of historical life only in its historical dimensions is to miss its true nature.

These New Testament symbols are extraordinarily intense. Each symbol is surrounded by other symbols, and the families of symbols do not always mesh. Perhaps the future-historical eschatological symbols can themselves be read as metaphors for a non-historical kingdom of God, as in the realized eschatological themes. And the realized eschatological passages do not preclude life after death in a transformed state even though that does not have as much eschatological significance as the already realized transformations. The distinction between future-historical and realized eschatologies is not clear-cut in the New Testament. Suchocki's model addresses both the future-historical and realized eschatological themes.

Chapter 7 of *The End of Evil*, "Freedom and Temporal Redemption: The Historical Community," building on her interpretation of Whitehead's theory of evil in chapter 4, presents her model of how God redeems history in time. Suchocki's future-historical eschatology is markedly different from that of the New Testament in its basic symbols. The New Testament, in the synoptic gospels, Paul's letters, and the Book of Revelation, says that history as we know it will come to an end. God will enter history to establish his kingdom subjecting everyone to judgment distinguishing the sheep and the goats. Paul and the Book of Revelation go so far as to say that the historical world itself will come to an end and that God will be directly represented by Jesus. Suchocki does not attempt to represent the end of history but supposes, with Whitehead (and most of the rest of us), that history will continue indefinitely, brought to a close only by natural processes such as long-term entropy, cataclysmic stellar events, or human foolishness. Moreover, she does not attempt to represent anything like a second coming of Jesus within history. Rather, for her the historically objective memory of Jesus, steadied by the divine lure, maintains a continuous, not apocalyptic, influence on history.

Apocalyptic can best be understood as an intensification of anticipated historical judgment and punishment. In Isaiah, for instance, beginning in chapter 14, there are a series of oracles about nations surrounding Israel — Moab, Damascus, Ethiopia, Egypt, Tyre — predicting in each case that they shall suffer from famine or the sword, from marauders or the disruption of their trade; all these are historical calamities. Suddenly in chapter 24 through 27 the historical calamities are exchanged for cosmic ones — the earth is laid waste, the windows of heaven open to destroy all life, the foundations crumble. Whereas the earlier oracles could be understood in historical terms alone, the apocalyptic turn relativizes history within the ontology of the creation and flood stories. So it is with the New Testament apocalyptic. Whereas Jesus in the synoptic gospels might have been expecting only a divine intervention to bring about justice within history, with appropriate rewards and punishments, Paul's vision and even more so that of the Book of Revelation indicates that the historical plane is taken up in a larger reality. Apocalyptic remains a future-historical eschatology because it says the transformation of the earth will come in future time, and is thus distinct from realized eschatology. Suchocki's eschatology is future-historical because it deals with the promotion of justice and redemption within time. But it is resolutely not apocalyptic. The divine judgment she allows for operation within historical time is the sort revealed in the lures shaping each event, not a separation of sheep from goats. Moreover, she does not suggest that justice will triumph within history, only within God.

The second part of Suchocki's eschatology is realized. The model she presents is her most creative extrapolation from Whitehead's cosmology. In it, as analyzed in several papers within this volume, she provides a categorical way of understanding the subjective continuity of individual consciousnesses within God after the death of the individual. Like John's Jesus saying that he shall bring the disciples into God, where he is going to prepare a place, for Suchocki, people come to a true and full realization of themselves only within the divine life. Only within God can they see the judgment upon them in all the connections of their life. And within God all can be reconciled. The engine of reconciliation is the dipolar conception of God. On the one hand the consequent nature of God registers all the people and their circumstances, and this part of the divine life is as temporal as history. On the other hand the primordial nature of God is eternal and provides for every time the conceptual resources for reconciliation and harmonization of all things temporally prehended. This is a realized eschatology because not only at death but at each moment of life every person is subsumed into God in judgment, reconciliation, and harmony.

Certain aspects of the ancient biblical symbols for eschatology are different from those registered in Suchocki's model.

First, she makes little attempt to attribute eschatological consequences to Jesus, except in the sense that he remains an abidingly influential teacher. The symbols of the atonement, by which Jesus' life and death acquire justice for really unjust sinners, or by which his blood pays the penalty for unrighteous sinners, or by which his paschal sacrifice wards off the angel of death from those who deserve it, do not get much play within her system.[9] I suspect that like many lib-

---

9. I have analyzed the atonement symbols at some length in my *Symbols of Jesus:*

eral theologians (though not myself) the atonement symbols have little eschatological significance for her.

Second, a very powerful eschatological motif for Suchocki is the theme of comforting the victims of the world and bringing them justice. One of the chief motives for her doctrine of subjective immortality is that for a great many people there is no justice in this life. Suffering is not redeemed in this life. Therefore, the dwelling of victims within God is required if God's reign is to be just. I see very little of this theme in the biblical eschatological symbols. Jesus, of course, advocated kindness and the obligation to relieve suffering — feeding the hungry, clothing the naked, and visiting those in prison. But this was not an eschatological theme. For biblical eschatology, especially of the future-historical sort, salvation is for the righteous and damnation for the unrighteous, and those who are merely suffering are not mentioned in the eschatological context except where that means bearing up so as to come through the trials with righteousness. Furthermore, whereas Suchocki provides much metaphysical representation of divine righteousness, in accord with the biblical model, her God is much too kind to have the fiery wrath so obvious in the New Testament God.

Return to the question of what a metaphysical model is for. If it is merely to give reconstructed representation to the biblical symbols, including doctrines, worship practices, basic texts, and so forth, Suchocki has given a remarkably successful account of some of the main themes of both the future-historical and realized eschatologies. Yet she downplays the eschatological role of Jesus as well as the divine wrath, and introduces the theme of making things up for the victims of suffering that is not to be found strongly expressed in the Bible. Assuming that her model is successful in representing what she wants, by what principle does she pick and choose among the biblical symbols for those that need representation? Is it merely that in our time we cannot stomach bloody atonement symbols and can't believe that a good God would leave those who suffer with no compensation except according to their righteousness? I think not.

A Christology of Symbolic Engagement (Cambridge: Cambridge University Press, 2001), chapter 2.

2. What Problem with Ultimacy Does Eschatology Address?

An intermediate step is required to address the question of which ancient symbols deserve to be reconstructed with a contemporary metaphysical model. We need to appeal to a theory of religion that shows how religious symbols engage us with whatever is ultimate. A theory fit for all religions would keep to the language of ultimacy. A theory specified to Christianity (and the other monotheistic religions) would see the religion as a complex of ways of living before God, practically as well as in terms of beliefs. Religious symbols shape the practices and beliefs. Although the symbols have their literal content, a theological analysis can show that they function to engage people with the ultimate in various ultimately important questions. I have argued, for instance, that the symbols of the atonement engage some people with the ultimate in judgment regarding blood guilt; the symbols of the Cosmic Christ engage people with regard to whether human beings have a home in the cosmos; the symbols of Jesus as Second Person of the Trinity engage God with reference to how people can come into relation with God; the symbols of the historical Jesus engage the question of how Jesus can be living and normative for his followers after his death and ascension; the symbols of Jesus as friend have to do with how Jesus can be incarnate in us and our contemporaries.[10] With respect to what fundamental human problem relating to the ultimate do the eschatological symbols engage us?

I propose three inter-related ways of answering that question: how does life relate to death? How do communities and individuals stand in ultimate judgment? How does life have meaning, if it does?[11]

Regarding life and death, many non-ultimate aspects of that question exist, some of which are morally interesting, such as how to

---

10. See *Symbols of Jesus.*

11. These are taken from Paul Tillich's analysis of three types of anxiety in *The Courage to Be* (New Haven: Yale University Press, 1952), chapter 2. The issue of life he thought predominated the ancient world, so that eschatological symbols have to do primarily with surviving or overcoming death. The issue of moral righteousness and condemnation became predominant in the middle ages and reformation period, and so sparked Luther's concern with justification. The issue of meaning Tillich thought was the way of asking the eschatological question in the late modern period.

define death within a coma, how to weigh the cost of life versus death with terminally ill patients, and so forth. In the ancient world many people believed in reincarnation, life after life. As the Indian religions argued, this was not an achievement but the ultimate problem: not to be able to die as an individual so as to become non-dual with Brahman is the fundamental human predicament for many forms of Hinduism. In the ancient West Asian religions, however, including Christianity, life meant being close to God, and death was a fading away because of distance from the divine presence. According to the New Testament book of Hebrews, one of the functions of Jesus was to be the priest who presents even us sinners to God, being both the sacrificer and the sacrifice. For Paul, life in Christ gives Christians victory over death. As in the 1 Thessalonians text above, those who live in Christ will be taken up into fullness of life in God. The rest either stay spiritually or physically dead or, on interpretations assuming the natural immortality of a separable soul, go to everlasting punishment. Suchocki's model of subjective immortality within God directly addresses this concern for life overcoming the mere ending of death. She is insistent that people maintain their individual identities within the larger life of God, so that immortal life is the way of being ultimately real. For her, everyone gets that immortality by metaphysical necessity, not as a reward for righteousness or for being in Christ, as it was for Paul and many others.

The question of ultimate judgment adds a dimension to that of life, showing that freedom is one of the things that distinguishes life in its subjectivity from the death of being merely past. Moreover, the question of judgment is the summary question of how we stand before God, in ultimate perspective. Many non-ultimate forms of judgment exist, especially in the moral realm. But the ultimate dimension to the question is how it all adds up for us, collectively and individually. Suchocki has brilliant ways of showing the complexity of judgment on individuals and groups, each having something of a life of its own but in wider contexts. In some contexts a life might be good, in others evil. How can these be summed up? Suchocki points out that only within the infinite conceptuality of God can these be harmonized so that a summary judgment can be made; she argues that individuals in God can experience this judgment.

The question of whether life is meaningful only intensifies the other forms of eschatological thought. As Tillich pointed out, when cultures no longer believe in immortality, or in a cosmic reward system for righteousness and evil, they can still believe in the meaningfulness of life that comes from the ontological courage to be.[12] This dimension of the eschatological question was expressed in the ancient world by the claim that the world belongs to God, is God's kingdom, and is meaningful because it is created through God's word. For the New Testament writers, it was God who made the world meaningful with, first, the law, and second, Jesus' actions to make anyone who puts him on a part of the divine kingdom. Suchocki addresses the question of meaningfulness in a thoroughly modern way, not claiming that history by itself is meaningful, admitting full well that many people are so brutalized as to have virtually meaningless lives, but arguing that all people and conditions have meaning within the harmony that is the divine life.

Is it possible to give contemporary answers to the eschatological question in these three forms without a significant ontological role for Jesus, without the wrath of God, and with a non-biblical concern to make things right for the victims of suffering? Obviously Suchocki has done that in the ways mentioned just above. The price paid for abandoning a strong atonement doctrine is that the concerns for immortality and judgment are not particularly Christian, in her view. Good enough: other religions ought to have ways of addressing the eschatological issues without the Christian symbols. Can she do without the wrath of God? The price paid is a kind of pallid urgency about the ultimate dimension of life and judgment. Can she legitimately insert the concern for making things right for victims of suffering? I think many would argue that a world in which that is not done at some level is not truly meaningful. For her, an ultimately unjust world would not be meaningful.

In the end, Suchocki's eschatological vision rests on a conception of God that requires ultimate harmony and balance. For her God is good, not in any syrupy way but in cosmological ways, and by necessity not choice. She affirms with biblical and metaphysical warrant that God preserves human life everlastingly, that judgment is made with appropriate rewards, and that the whole is meaningful primordi-

12. *Op. cit.*

ally in eternity and consequently in everlasting history. This vision is a classical Christian theology, with the qualifications mentioned concerning her departures from biblical themes.

3. Is Suchocki's an Adequate Eschatological Vision?

The imaginative world of the New Testament symbols is very far from our own. We no longer share the metaphysical view of the many-layered cosmos implicit in that ancient imaginative world. Most in that world assumed an immortal soul, and therefore had to imagine some place for it to go after death, either rebirth or an afterlife in a new dimension. For many, the assertion of the Lordship of God or Jesus meant that the afterlife would have to be arranged justly, with rewards for righteousness and punishments for wickedness, inattention to the divine, or impurity. With modern science we no longer can imagine the depths of the Earth to be a living hell nor outer space to be a living heaven. Because we now understand life to be so tied to biological conditions, belief in a separable immortal soul is counter-intuitive within our imagination; not that many people do not believe in immortality, but that they have to suspend their scientifically shaped imagination to do so.

One of the functions of theology is to examine the relations between the ancient imagination within which the symbols of the faith arose and our own imagination within which they need to be effective if we are to be faithful and engage God by their means.[13] Metaphysics is the instrument that reveals the gaps between the now-incredible imagination of the ancient world and our own that defines the boundaries of credibility. A metaphysics that is viable and plausible on all the contemporary fronts to which it is accountable might be able to give a reconstructed meaning to the ancient symbols. With a reconstructed meaning, it might be possible to engage God, the human condition, and the relations between God and world in our time just as they did in the ancient time. The meanings as parsed by the ancient and late or post-modern imaginations might be different, as measured by differences in metaphysics, although the engagements might be the same. A sophisticated semiotic theory about religious symbols is

---

13. This thesis is defended and illustrated at length in *Symbols of Jesus*.

required to make this case in detail.[14] The great power of Whitehead's metaphysics is that it reconstructed many of the classical Christian symbols relating God and the world for the late-modern imagination within which scientific causality defines the way things work. Whitehead's metaphysics recognizes the immensity and eternity of the cosmos, alien ideas to the ancient imagination, and does not require miracles in the Enlightenment sense of setting aside natural law. Suchocki has been the most thorough of Whitehead's successors to trace out the power of his metaphysical system for reconstructing ancient Christian symbols, and the question here is how that fares regarding the eschatological ones.

What is the point of the ancient eschatological symbols? What engagement with God do they mediate? Suchocki's answer to this, I think, would be two-fold. On the one hand is a concern for continuing life after death. On the other is a concern that those people who suffer in this life find "redress and reconciliation beyond that offered by history."[15] Moreover, often she represents as one of the chief reasons for the first the fact that the second requires a transhistorical resolution.[16] Although she explicitly rejects a "pie-in-the-sky-by-and-by" sense of redress and reconciliation, she does believe that for many people, redress and reconciliation cannot happen in this life objectively speaking and so would have to be enjoyed subjectively in a continuity of subjective life beyond the historical plane. For her, this is a continuing subjective life of individuals within God in which they witness the redress and reconciliation accomplished by means of the divine primordial nature harmonizing anything the consequent nature can present. Whitehead's doctrine of God does not allow for this, and so she ingeniously modifies that metaphysical conception in ways discussed in several of the essays in this book. I'm not concerned here to assay the metaphysical cogency of that but to ask whether she has addressed the heart of what eschatology is about.[17]

14. I have attempted this in *The Truth of Broken Symbols* (Albany: State University of New York Press, 1996). See also *Religion in Late Modernity* (Albany: State University of New York Press, 2002).

15. See her "Neville's Theology," p. 214.

16. Like most process theologians, Suchocki takes history so seriously as to be a future-historical eschatologist with almost no admixture of realized eschatology.

17. I do believe it is impossible within even remotely Whiteheadian categories

My hypothesis is that the deepest question of eschatology is to address the relation of human life to God in light of the difference between time and eternity. The ancient background assumption, articulated clearly by Augustine and others before him, was that God is eternal and creates a temporal world; various metaphysical systems ancient and more recent have articulated what this might mean. The temporality of human life might well be interpreted in the three ways Tillich described: anciently as concerned for continuous life after death, medievally as the moral judgment of such life continuing after death, and modernly as the questionable meaningfulness of life that is nothing more than the limits of one's biological vitality. So we in our time need to say what temporality means to us.

I say that the temporality of human life can be understood only within the categories of eternity. The temporal years of living that count, and perhaps the only ones that exist, are those from birth to death. But our identities as small children include not only our brief pasts and present quasi-responsible creative moments but also all the dates of our future, which is likely open-ended and interwoven with the futures of vastly more complex processes than human individuals. A child's future is constantly shifting its real possibilities as events happen, including the child's own choices. As middle-aged people with long responsible pasts laying obligations on us now to determine the future for better or worse, we have a seemingly constant stream of present decisions to make, capitalizing on our advances and trying to undo our mistakes but mainly coping with the morally freighted events over which we might have influence; we look to the fairly well laid out future for serious possibilities for action. As old people with little future that depends on what we do, with little to do in our present moments but to maintain life and make sense of our past, we come to see our past and that of our environs as itself constantly having been changed by subsequent events: what seemed so attractive at the time turned out to be less than it seemed, and what seemed incidental in the long run took on great significance. Three senses of dy-

---

to say that finite creatures prehended within God can have the subjective capacity to witness, that is, freely to prehend, new relations for themselves within the divine life. So long as God is conceived as temporal the subjective creativity of creatures must be external to the subjective creativity of God. That's the whole point of the process defense of human freedom and divine non-culpability in evil.

namism integrate the three modes of time: the future is constantly shifted by what happens; the present is a constantly shifting date of active and humanly decisive creativity, and the past is the growing actualization of value-laden possibilities whose values are so intertwined that the significance of the past is always shifting in multiple patterns.

What is human temporal identity? European modernity has attempted to reduce it to present existence; the present filling of inner sense, said Kant, is the definition of existence. Whitehead and process theologians, including Marjorie Suchocki, have tended to go along with this, saying that the future is real only in present anticipation and the past real only in being prehended by a subsequent present entity. The debates between Whiteheadians and Hartshorneans often revolve around how to keep God wholly present relative to a successive temporal world.

But I say that human identity is the sum of the dates from birth to death where each date has all the dynamic shifts it had as future, all the decisiveness of its present happening, and all of the dynamic accretions of its past. Who we really are in ultimate perspective is never only who we are on one day, but who we are in all our days. Identity at any one date is always abstract. Ontological identity is who we are in all our days as future, present, and past together. Of course, as process thinkers have pointed out so well, our identities are not isolated like substances but constituted in continuities with a vast network of things around us, perhaps in organic fashion; so our identities are bound up with the identities of all those other processes with their dates as future, as present, and as past. The full ontological togetherness of our future, present, and past dates is not a temporal togetherness; their togetherness at any point within time is but an abstraction from the whole, freezing the dynamic of our real lives into the specific future, present, and past for that moment. The full ontological togetherness of our temporal lives is in eternity. Eternity is the dynamic within which all the dates of our lives, and the cosmos, are together in their shifting characters as future, as present, and as past.

On the classical view of God as eternal creator of a temporal world, *ex nihilo*, with which I agree, the creative act is eternal, creating not all at once (as if in a totum simul present), not at a first date (as if in the past), nor even in the future (*pace* Lewis Ford and the Platonists). The created world is the terminus of the eternal creative act, and as temporal it has all the freedom and indeterminacy we note from positions within time. But the sum of the temporal created world is the togetherness of all its dates, all in their future dynamism, all in the present existence, and all as contributing to an actual past whose significance is constantly shifting. The eternity of the unfolding temporal world is the life of God, which is not temporal or in any time. Eternity in this sense is not like Whitehead's eternal objects — static — but is an infinitely more fulsome dynamic than can be laid out from the perspectives of any one point within temporal flow.

The deep eschatological question, I suggest, is how our temporal lives add up eternally and how this relates to the dynamic eternity of God. In some respects our lives are individual and in other respects bound up with our communities, and both senses have the eschatological question. How we add up in eternity has many dimensions. One comes from the fact we are very pricey beings; our evolution cost thousands of species, our filling of our habitat diminished many others, our metabolism consumes millions of calories of life, our organized family lives require repressing brute instincts, and our civilized life requires policing our natural affinities and hatreds. How can we present ourselves to God in eternity so blood guilty? That's what the classical atonement symbols address. Another dimension of how we add up is to have a home in the universe, which we know now to have no center, no intentional beginning, no meaningful entropic end; Christ the King, present to us in the Logos of existence, is nevertheless the beginning and the end. By what human form can the eternal life we enjoy through our days relate to the eternity of God's immense creation? The life of Jesus shows that form as the human incarnation of the Logos defining process, time, and eternity. How should we live our temporal lives in light of their eternal significance, and that of the divine life itself? The historical Jesus started a movement shaped by a community of love and that can be shaped today by imagining its normative continuity through the symbols of the risen and ascended Christ, judge and lover. How can we individually come to love the eternal God who created for us a world of suffering and death? By befriending Jesus, lover of our souls. An imaginative confrontation with Jesus can redeem the worst sinner and show how to live the normative way, the truth, and the life eternal through the trials and tribulations of ordinary existence. At least this is what I have argued at length, showing new applications for many of the classical symbols.[18]

Behind the differences between these two eschatological visions, Marjorie Suchocki's and mine, lie more profound differences about the nature of God or the ultimate. These differences are so close to the level of native intuitions as to be almost incapable of being articulated. I think that she belongs to the group of theologians who believe that the rock-bottom affirmations about God or Ultimacy have to do with divine symmetry, wholeness, harmony, and goodness.[19] It is better, for her, to sacrifice traditional claims about divine creation and omnipotence than the symmetrical perfections of God. On this "symmetrical" view, if I might adopt that as a label, to leave the suffering of brutalized people unassuaged would be a greater offense than to limit divine power. Eschatology must be the bringing of everything into the perfection, harmony, wholeness, and symmetry of God. I, on the other hand, find my affinities with "asymmetrical" theologians for whom the act of divine creation proceeds from no predetermined unitary or good divine nature but creates all things, including such symmetries, harmonies, wholeness and perfection as are to be found in the world.[20] The creative act itself is arbitrary, singular, resulting in a tilted cosmos all of whose elements have value (being harmonies) but are often unfairly located; some people are just born to advantage and others to disadvantage, as some parts of the cosmos support life and other parts are sterile. The eschatological point for the asymmetrical view is how, in our finite search to achieve at best temporary and fragile harmony, we relate to the eternal singularity of Willful Yahweh. What a great wonder it is that we have the crucified Jesus to guide and establish that relation, because nothing says it has to be that way! (Perhaps other religions pick up on other ways to relate to the singularity of our eternal identities and God's.) For me, eschatology must

---

18. In *Symbols of Jesus*. The theory of eternal divine creation expressed here is explained at greater length in *God the Creator* (Chicago: University of Chicago Press, 1968; revised edition, Albany: SUNY Press, 1992), and in *Eternity and Time's Flow*.

19. In different ways, the neo-Platonic lovers of the One, Thomas Aquinas, and Leibniz (as well as most Buddhists) would be among this distinguished group.

20. These would include the creation *ex nihilo* tradition, Duns Scotus, and Descartes (as well as the Buddhists who refuse to ontologize). I would claim the Bible, with its view of God as particularly willing, as having asymmetrical affinities.

be the intensification of wonder and love for the eternal tilted act of creation that gives us this tilted world in which we have our eternal identities with their irrevocable suffering folded into the divine life. I think God is not whole or perfect, but holy and lovable (with difficulty) as one who creates with frightening, fruitful abandon.[21]

Surely the eschatological truth should encompass both visions. Can they be integrated without losing the heart of each?

21. I owe the distinction between symmetrical and asymmetrical theologies to Wesley J. Wildman and discuss it in *Symbols of Jesus*, pp. 30-32.

The Mystery of the Insoluble Evil:
Violence and Evil in Marjorie Suchocki

Catherine Keller

> There exists a control, an imperialism in the name of good, capable of killing lives. This is the reason why we have to say once again that good and evil live off of one another and that there is no way to root out the bad growth from the good.
>
> Ivone Gebara, Out of the Depths

> There is a fundamental ambiguity to existence, with good and evil interwoven.
>
> Marjorie Suchocki, The End of Evil

Seeking some sustainable decency, we try to root out the bad growth from the good. In the process it seems we damage the root system of the good. The ambiguity becomes an acute paradox when suffering and the fear of more suffering invoke the language of "good and evil."

If we think of "good" and "evil" as relative to each other, we weaken the incentive to resist evil — to take the risk that every struggle against injustice must entail. This complacency drifts blandly toward accommodation of an oppressive system into which we are interwoven.

If we do *not* think of good and evil as relative to each other, we strengthen the otherness of the evil. But the distance does not hold. For in the very risk undertaken against a perceived threat to our "good," we dance with the enemy. We mimic the enemy's brutality. We roll toward an absolute ethic. In the domain of Christian culture, that means a specifically messianic indignation, the apocalypse that in naming the other as "evil" lays claim to the preemptive prerogatives of the good: the messianism that blurs so grandly, so oxymoronically, with imperialism.

But how would we avoid the risk of the messianic — that the earth was made for an all-embracing delight and not for an elite brutality? Here, in the root of theology — and of all western radicalism — the risk and the hope are inseparable: that the heart of the cosmos pulses not indifferently, but in harmony with this "good."

Is this the hope encoded as the "end of evil"? Or does such eschatological code only dig us deeper into a paralyzing paradox?

I do not propose in this paper to offer a neat third way — neither the cool consuming relativism nor the hot conquering dualism — which from the messianic viewpoint would come out lukewarm, anyway. I am however grateful for the opportunity to think a bit more directly about evil and its possible "end," or at least *"eschaton,"* and specifically to do so in the inspiring company of Marjorie Suchocki and her interpreters. The specific brilliance of her contribution to process eschatology and to the doctrine of sin will be crackling through this whole volume. Suchocki recognizes the danger of either direction: of relativism or of absolutism in relating "good and evil." For evil like good "follows from the fragility of interdependent existence." The ambiguous relativity flows from the vastly intimate connectivity comprising, to the core, all creatures. But the possibility of good and evil actualizes itself only among the humans.

What I will propose might seem, perversely, to counter *The End of Evil*. It does not. In solidarity, if not unity, with Suchocki's arguments concerning the evil in history, I want to entertain the proposition: "there is no end of evil." To do so let me begin with the microphenomenology of "evil."

Terms of Evil

Evil: how should one define it, when every specific declaration of "evil," every revelation of an Other as evil, moves toward and begins to mimic the evil? Does the very word "evil" not in itself attract, with its implication of a mystery? "Evil" cannot be reduced to a failing or even a falling, but suggests, if not a proper devil, an inhuman force of iniquity, a motive force, an appetite. This enmity not only hurts me but somehow thrives in the hurting, indifferent to my difference, numb to our shared humanness. That positive force of evil — the glint in the eye, the hint of malevolence, the whiff of pleasure in inflicting pain — this is not definable as violence, or even as disproportionate destruction. Massive violence is part of the natural universe to which no morality can be attributed. It might be bad, but not what in English is called "evil." "Evil" moves in an aura of greater dignity and terror than the merely "bad," the wrong, the ill, the mistake, the lack.

What spins the head on the shoulders (as in *The Exorcist*) is this realization: the positive energy of the evil, far from the pleasure of a demon, who enjoys evil as such, may gleam with moral certainty. *They may be as sure of my "evil" as I am of theirs.* This circularity is as appalling as evil itself.

Shall we call a moratorium on the term? Certainly it would be best to circumscribe it, to use it sparingly, with the expectation that it will ricochet back against us. "Bad" (and the romance languages cannot distinguish between evil and bad, *"mal"*) has the great advantage of a wide spread of meanings, some lacking any moral sense — a bad knife is not evil, just dull. Bad things happen to good people; but a book called *Evil Things Happen to Good People* would be unpublishable, eclipsing the whole range of suffering that is caused by accident, ambiguity or nonhuman nature, which is only I believe misleadingly called (by Whiteheadians as well) "natural evil." However, just because of its breadth, "bad" does not capture the avoidability and thus the intentionality of what we call evil.

Shall we talk of "sin" instead? Suchocki persuasively attempts in *The Fall to Violence* to define sin as "against the creation" and only thereby against the Creator. I agree, but want to stay for the time being with "evil." For despite her and every other progressive attempt (mine included) to speak of collective, systemic or structural sin, I fear that the signifier "sin" willy nilly reinforces the traditional privatization of morality. To say "sin" outside of a tightly disciplined community of discourse conjures a perfume of "sex" — morality wrapped like the serpent around Eve's naked body. Sorry, but I think there is no definitional solution. Within the context of the church, I will keep using the word "sin" and working — as I will below — to resignify it. But it will not solve the semantic problem of "evil."

There is something in the term "evil" that the peoples of the book, at least, seem to need, something that dignifies both the suffering of its victim and the brutality of the oppressor. Its ill seems at once more and less than human, and therefore liable to tales of the supernatural, or similarly, diabolizations of whole groups. It is precisely the systemic injustice that creates this effect: a system is both more and less than human, and organizes its components to a larger end. The systemic evil has a *quality*, not just a sociology.

Suchocki suggests we read "evil" as the wider aggression or violence, as Whitehead indicates, and "sin" as its character once it becomes avoidable. This is helpful, if it does not contribute to the naturalizing of evil. In order to drain away some of the circling, self-righteous excitation of the rhetoric of "evil," without forfeiting its semantic intensity, let me suggest a defining substitute, if not a synonym. What we call evil signifies *violation;* and more precisely, violation as *a humanly avoidable brutality.* This is something like what Suchocki means by "sin against the creation" as "unnecessary violence." But by calling it "violation," which is by definition always unnecessary, always internalized, we enunciate the internal relatedness, the intimacy, of the betrayal. Violation as a term extends beyond violence to include the evils of smoothly internalized injustice. It addresses thereby the range of *needless suffering*, of which only a part is caused by needless violence. To violate is to obstruct the becoming of a subject in its otherness, its agency — to *subject* it without regard for its own genesis. Such appropriation is often accomplished without violence (which I want to reserve for its literal meaning, for the materiality of destruction — which may be imperial or intimate, a bomb or a voice, but intends to overwhelm the agency of an Other as organism). The violence by which certain systems are achieved and maintained (a *pax romana* or *americana*) does not have to be often performed. But such a system remains oppressive, "evil" (though not only evil, of course), even when it runs nonviolently. Violation is never far from violence, but signifies the more inclusive term.

Violation captures both the character of a violence that is no longer justifiable as natural aggression. For it could have been avoided.

And it captures also the routine forms of evil in which violence is largely unnecessary, such as the subjection of women to marriages, or religious covenants, in which no violence is used but male dominance is unquestioned, and female agency violated; such as the unquestioning participation of the U.S. public in patterns of consumption violating the integrity of the ecosphere and its most vulnerable populations. Violation thus can operate systemically, unrecognized as such, almost indistinguishable from innocence, but for the willed character of the ignorance ("what I don't know can't hurt them").

Violation evinces a habitual character: an isolated spontaneous act of violence does not count as evil. It is not clear that an evil singularity exists. Violation requires repetition. It has been received and rehearsed through patterned systems of violation, which suddenly gain momentum. But the term "violation" also preserves a certain edge of aggressive intent — often self-righteously motivated — that cultivates its cruelty. If violation renames the *activity of evil*, brutality signifies the *quality of evil*. Brutality — with no reference to animals, brutes — suggests the repetitive, habitual character that runs systems of injustice on the socioeconomic as well as the intimate level. The culture of brutality infects discourse: as Derrida distinguishes from violence "the brutality in a discussion, in an argumentation, the dogmatic fiat."[1] In other words Christian theology, born in opposition to the "evil" of its heresies, bears special responsibility for the brutality of discourse. And it will confess only its own evil as "sin."

"Sin" would then signify, in the present microphenomenology, not evil as such, which is intercreaturely, but rather the *transcreaturely* brutality that we may understand as *violation of God*. All of our relations comprise *ipso facto* relations to God. "Sin" designates the violation of the divine-human relation — but precisely, with Suchocki, as an evil against the creation, not as some uniquely religious transgression, like unbelief or heresy. "Sin" rightly frames every violation of the *creature* as a violation of the *creator* (and not — and this is key in Suchocki's argument — the other way around). In process panentheism, violation is acute, it penetrates the divine nature, it has *consequence* for God. And as this God lacks the brute power of omnipotence

---

1. Jacques Derrida and Maurizio Ferraris, *A Taste for the Secret* (Cambridge: Polity, 2001), 91-92.

— *preemptive violation,* let us call it — the effects of any evil ripple out indefinitely.

But *endlessly?* Why would one not hope — in good faith — for evil's end? Would it not be a kind of sin in itself, not to trust in God's capacity and will to put an end to evil?

Original Sin, Prevenient Violence

While *The End of Evil* is a highly abstract analysis, speculating freely about the inner life of God, it is helpful to read first the later work of Suchocki. Her agenda for a process eschatology receives in each of her subsequent books a fresh actualization. Especially the *Fall to Violence* moves with pastoral passion to concrete sites of needless suffering. In her revisiting of the question of evil, now under the category of violence, she concerns herself little with the divine mind. But she reorients the notion of sin so that it ceases to function as an excuse for sin among Christians: that is, as a way of focusing on their relation to the Creator in abstraction from their relation to the creatures. By positively redefining sin as violence against the creation, she closes the great theological loophole out of which Christian responsibility for the living world has been so effectively sucked.

If sin signifies "needless violence," violence, explains Suchocki, becomes needless in the context of "self-transcendence." She claims "that without the ability to transcend our violent tendency, there may be evil, but it is not yet sin."[2] That is, it is only as we become capable of avoiding violence, and therefore of unnecessary violence, that we can refer properly to "sin." This is the point at which the species sustains "a degree of self-transcendence," by which she means transcendence of self-identity "by empathic recognition of other-identity." (I would not make the distinction between sin and evil in quite that way, implying that evil can happen without human responsibility. I am calling "evil" what she calls "sin," but am glad, as noted above, to absorb the language of "sin" as a theological rhetoric highlighting the relation of all our relations, i.e., the God-relation.) Her notion of transcendence is close to that of the recognition of the face of the Other in

2. Marjorie Suchocki, *The Fall to Violence* (New York: Continuum, 1994), 94.

Levinas. But he lacks, along with any feminist sensibility, a relationalist reading of empathy, which as a mode of (theological) *transcendence* may be unique to Suchocki. She has the "breath of life" that makes the hominid becoming a *human* occur at the point of empathic transcendence.

I implied that by broadening the definition of evil/sin as needless violence into violation, we include the suffering inflicted by smooth, internalized systems of power/knowledge, the Foucaultian discipline, by which women for instance see themselves as several pounds larger than they are, inner city children see themselves as stupid, a class, race or nation sees itself as inferior. Both this systemic violation and more overt violence display the quality of brutality at the point of Suchockian transcendence, the moment in which empathic recognition of the Other is possible — and so systemically repressed. This transcendence marks at once the specifically human and therefore the *inhuman*. Not the *nonhuman:* brutality characterizes neither the animal nor the divine. And yet process theology reads human specificity against the grain of the standard dualisms by which the difference between the animal and the human is secured — as though our brutality represents a slide back down to the "brute." But the nonhuman animals, however violent, do not violate.

So how would we draw such a clear boundary around "evil" as a specifically *human* potentiality? Suchocki makes an indispensable move here: she allows us to distinguish between stages of the human, and therefore blurs from the rear any pristine separation of the human transcendence from its own prehuman relations. Original in Suchocki's analysis — at least for Christian thought about original sin — is Marjorie's serious engagement of theories of evolution. She claims that human beings have a "propensity toward violence." "The capacity for violence," she avers, "is built into our species through aggressive instincts related to survival."[3] When she claims that we are "by nature an aggressive species with a history of physical and psychic violence," one might proffer predictable objections of biological essentialism. One might assume that she has neglected the social construction of violence. On the contrary, social constructivism — including its feminist forms — tends to neglect the biological and environ-

3. Suchocki, *Fall,* 85.

mental forces in and out of which cultures construct themselves. It worries that any acknowledgment of natural aggression will legitimate it, will "naturalize" injustice. Similarly, theology outside the influence of Whitehead has avoided serious consideration of evolutionary science in the understanding of sin. It worries that any acknowledgment of a creaturely bent toward violence may shift the onus of evil toward the creator. But however well motivated by anti-reductionism and the desire to cover God's back, neither the denial of our animality nor the biology of our aggression has managed, it would seem, to lower the all-over level of our species' violence.

The theories Suchocki prefers argue not for a genetic determinism but rather for a history of adaptations to conditions such as the droughts at the end of the Pleistocene period, which did not allow the vegetarian hominids to survive, but favored the hunters. Moreover, she draws from Eibl-Eibesfeldt not just the case for the universality and physiological basis of aggressive instincts, but at the same time evidence for a countervailing bonding instinct shared with higher primates. She builds upon his hope that the "instinct toward bonding might increasingly be the antidote that controls the more destructive instinct toward aggression."[4] So the moment of self-transcendence constitutes the possibility of the relational cure. One thinks of the most primal rites of tribal community-building, of the most global abstractions of "the law" as the bond building a universe. And one recognizes — with Suchocki and with Paul — that only with the law is sin possible: only in the sustained awareness of the bonds of community can the survival-habits of violence be recognized as problematic and therefore subject to alternative strategies. For Suchocki, the originality of sin roots in this sense of an alternative: instincts of aggression already, before we can be responsible for them, incline us toward violence that we nonetheless recognize as unnecessary and therefore as sinful.

A perplexity adheres to the case for "original sin," however. For if it is the aggressive bent, or even instinct, that inclines us to violence, then how can it be *sinful?* The response would be, I think: not inherently, but after the fact, when it can be transcended. Nonetheless there is a bit of a slide here: "the condition of original sin, then, in-

---

4. Suchocki, *Fall*, 93.

volves aggressive tendencies within our humanity that naturally incline us toward violence." The verb "involve" is carefully ambiguous: do the "tendencies" partly (combined with social structures of institutionalized violence) *comprise* original sin? After all the aggression is what makes the sin collective, inherited and therefore "original" in the first place. Sin, she says, is "rebellion against creation" — against our own creaturely interdependence with other finite creatures within the relational structures of the creation. I share her assessment of the collectivity traditionally encoded in original sin. However, it begs the question of the role of the "original" aggression in making the *sin* original. One still hovers close here to a demonization of nature; indeed to call anything in nonhuman nature "evil" — though not sinful — suggests the traditional displacement of evil and of sin onto "nature." But her intention is rather to emphasize that this species has still the opportunity to mature, that it is an incomplete creation, that we still vehemently struggle with an aggressive disposition that is not our own "fault." Suchocki makes here a crucial contribution.

If we emphasize that in her reading original sin "involves" natural tendencies but is not caused or defined by them, then the very prevenience of these species' aggressions belies the "originality" of sin. There is always already the animal Other in the human self, and it will neither explain our evil (away) nor itself be transcended. The empathic transcendence dips into our animal sympathies as well as our aggressions. And of course it is the bonding instinct that has morphed, presumably, into the empathy of empathic transcendence — and that makes us so knowing in our brutality. The boundary between the violative and the merely violent can be no more clearly drawn than can that between animal altruism and human ethics. But its fluidity does not make it less significant. Without its edge, we will not call each other to account.

"They found/Pieces of flesh,/Erased by men's wrath,/Bearing no messages from the deep." So laments the Chilean poet Marjorie Agosin.[5] The edge of evil maps the watery zone of human discourse, where we

5. Marjorie Agosin, "Idioms," in *Sargazo/Sargasso: Poems*, trans. Cola Franzen (Fredonia, NY: White Pine Press, 1993), 29.

rewrite the messages from the deep, in the metaphor of the Chilean poet. And in which we also erase each other's significance. Elaine Scarry has well documented the ultimate brutality of torture and war, of the flesh violated to the point of illegibility, the reduction of the incarnate human to a speechless body. So in theology we must also return — as has Suchocki so powerfully — to the wounds. It is not God who rubs out the marks of evil but "men's wrath," rewriting history for the benefit of the killers — they who violate with heroic self-esteem, blaming the other, naming the evil; who betray their self-doubt there where they erase the traces of their murders.

In the opening epigraph of this essay, Gebara notes that good and evil feed off of each other. Evil is not a one-way parasitism, or an Augustinian lack. Like Suchocki, she stresses the radical ambiguity of existence: she is "creating an understanding of the dynamic of life and its oppositions, with what actually constitutes us and keeps us alive. Without evil we would not know what is good: without sickness we would not know what health is. Without evil we would not know how to give thanks for the good." One must realize that Gebara, unlike Suchocki or this author, writes from within the base Christian liberation network of Latin America, from within daily struggles with routine, systematic brutality. So her (implicit) refusal of the standard liberation messianism, in which good and evil enter into apocalyptic opposition in history, is a work of great courage. I draw Gebara into conversation with Suchocki here as a kind of test, as her theology emerges really from below, the below of the southern hemisphere, its poor, its women — and its convergence on the most urgent matters of suffering and evil with process theology suggests not only a strand of influence (McFague) but the growing resonance of process thought with the world where speculative abstraction can rarely be afforded. Like Suchocki, Gebara is pointedly "not implying an ethical relativism that would allow killing for profit or stealing people's rights through a privileged exercise of authority."[6] But she has seen too much evil done in the name of the absolute good — of a religious or a political hierarchy. Also similar to Suchocki, she derives the relativity of good and evil from a more general feminist anthropology of relatedness: "if we look at relatedness, we can move be-

6. Ivone Gebara, *Out of the Depths: Women's Experience of Evil and Salvation* (Minneapolis: Fortress, 2002), 137.

yond the model of humanity perceived as a male body, for example the body of the male Christ, in which the function of every man and woman is in a line of subjection that maintains a hierarchy." She consistently contextualizes her relational anthropology as cosmology. "Relatedness opens the way of an interdependent justice, an ecojustice, that is, justice that includes the ecosystem."[7]

If Gebara draws from a closer range of women's oppression, indeed deriving her reflection from the stories of women, it is this dense experience of her religious practice among the poor that produces her own sense of the complex multiplicity of evils. So Gebara understands evil *as suffering* — combining then both "natural" and "ethical" evil. For these sufferings can never in their diversity be neatly parcelled into the "good" and "evil" piles, and there is no point at which our natural condition can be separated from cultural good and evil. Among her main examples is the story of Isabel Allende's daughter, who died of a disease. That disease was neither caused nor exacerbated by any social or perhaps even ecological imbalance; nor was the suffering increased by virtue of any social contextual indicators. (Allende was by this time a famous author.) This sort of illness and premature death causes suffering of the most intense sort, it is personal tragedy, it is a wretched torment for both mother and daughter, it is certainly not "fair." But I still must ask: does it help to call it 'evil'? Gebara freely calls the illness, the suffering and the death "evils," against which the mother struggles on behalf of life just as intensely as she struggled against the Chilean dictatorship. However, Allende herself does not characterize the illness as "evil" — as unbearable, as a torment, as unfair, violent, as certainly "bad" (of course, in Spanish also *mal* would cover both, a difference between romance languages and the Anglo Germanic, a difference between bad/evil, *schlecht/böse* that this essay cannot begin to contemplate).

At least in English, let me hold out for the distinction between humanly and "naturally" caused suffering as a fluid and always to be contested boundary (the sociolinguistic, the specifically human, goes *almost* all the way down; and would go all the way down, were there a

---

7. Gebara, *Out of the Depths*, 143. Earlier, in *Longing for Running Water* (Minneapolis: Fortress, 1999), Gebara unfolds a version of McFague's body of God, as the Sacred Body.

bottom!). All cries of suffering erupt "out of the depths." Thus in their nondualistic, feminist and cosmological sensitivities, Suchocki, though less than Gebara, and for philosophical, Whiteheadian reasons perhaps more than solidaristic ones, is also tempted to use the language of "natural evil." But the possibility of struggling (with Gebara) against the causes of (with Suchocki) the "needless violence" — human violations of both human and nonhuman life — requires, I am insisting, that we cease to blame nature.

Or, by implication, God. As neither does. But whenever we correct the dangerous dualism of good/evil by naturalizing evil, we implicitly give God responsibility for the evil in nature, the ultimate "evil" being death itself. Finitude then appears as a punishment, not part of the good nature, to be cured by God in the *eschaton*. This is a profound biblical tradition, created in Paul and John of Patmos, though otherwise alien to both testaments. And it runs counter to both Suchocki's and Gebara's feminist, liberation and processual rejections of divine omnipotence. Gebara lets go of any divine person, and therefore of any logic of theodicy, as well as any speculation about the internal workings of the divine.

Suchocki, on the other hand, holds out for the God developed in Claremont Whiteheadianism whose personal goodness has replaced omnipotence. But within the depths of Godself, the "messages from the deep" are immortally inscribed. She goes further however. She wants the brutality of the world to cease: at least within the "nature" of that good-natured God.

Evil's End?

There is not and there will not be an end of evil: this proposition warrants repeating. I do not mean to be making a gloomy forecast. For I believe we should not even hope for such an end: neither as termination, nor as telic end, i.e., purpose, no overriding aim that justifies evil while allowing it to deliver some eschatological fruit — *o felix culpa*. There may be much good harvested from rotten violated trees. There may be much sin, or much activity that seemed in the rhetorics of its time "sinful," for which we may be grateful, sooner or later — whether or not we invest our hope in the dogma of Christ's incarnation as the great good that happens only in response to human sin. But these positive outcomes of bad initial conditions would not comprise "the end of evil" — nor would Suchocki claim that they would. Evil would not in any of these cases be the cause of the good, nor would it be erased by the good. This "no end of evil" does not step into opposition to Suchocki's "end of evil."

I am trying to say only something rather simple, and to say it as clearly as I can: there is no final end of evil. And that is "good." In other words that there will be no termination of evil in the universe is not something we should regret. Because if there were it would mean the termination of what we call "good." For as Suchocki concludes: "the very structure which yields evil is precisely the structure which yields redemption."[8] The possibilities for good in the world are actualized by the finite and free creatures who may also choose evil, but whose ability to choose evil is actually enhanced by their ability to choose the good. For these creatures come "interwoven" with each other in a fragile web of interdependency as ambiguous as the choices of the creatures who comprise it. Yet she does in fact find through Whitehead a way of affirming a certain "end of evil," precisely in view of this radical ambiguity:

> The end of evil is its continuous transformation in God beyond all history, which then provides possibilities for particular transformations in time.

Does this magisterial concluding proposition, the theological crux of her philosophical argument, actually claim that there is a termination? Not in history, and therefore not at any endpoint of any sequence of events. Or is the "end" therefore a "purpose" after all, suggesting that evil has served its purpose by getting transformed in God? I think not, though her own carefully ambiguous sentence does allow this reading. She of course wants us to think with her of the "consequent nature of God" as the "kingdom of God," already eternally realized in God. Such may be the case. But it seems to me a way of gently indicating that in fact evil, like history, is *not* going to end — whatever

8. Marjorie Suchocki, *The End of Evil* (Albany: State University of New York, 1988), 154.

cataclysms may attend human history or the future of our particular planet. However, the proposition can all too readily be (mis)read as an oddly Whiteheadian acquiescence in classical Christian *Heilsgeschichte*, in which the apocalypse and final judgment bring about an end of evil, if not of history itself: an end never conceived as a temporal endpoint, but rather as the consummation of time in eternity.

Furthermore, it *does* suggest a radical cleansing of evil from the insides of God. Whitehead's sense of the divine "completion" at any moment suggests the union of temporal occasions "with their transformed selves, purged into conformation with the eternal order which is the final absolute 'wisdom'."[9]

Does this purgation install a sanitation department within the divine mind? Then the evil would at every moment remain outside the (open) gates of the sparkling city, like the apocalyptic New Jerusalem. For Suchocki God *is* that eternal city, so how we understand its civic order will be mirrored directly in our collective attempts to live out an image of God. Instead of the apocalyptic binary of good inside/evil without, can we imagine God the City as a space in which evil is judged as such but not thereby eradicated ("the tender judgment of a care . . .")? As she beautifully elaborates, that judgment adjusts itself, and thus the universe, toward the new wave of possibilities, the lure for the next moment. . . .

Immortal and Unfree

Suchocki acknowledges that the experience, the immediacy, of the occasion is not necessarily affected as it is taken into God: its "immediacy in this concrescence does not necessarily imply any change to that immediacy." But then she worries that "there is the danger that whatever has been experienced in finitude as unmitigated evil will continue to be experienced in such a fashion through all eternity."[10] It would be thus experienced by God according to Whitehead. She is however making at this point her case for "subjective immortality." So the jeopardy is multiplied: the evil would be experienced by those it originally involved,

---

9. Alfred N. Whitehead, *Process and Reality* (New York: Free, 1978), 347.
10. Suchocki, *Evil*, 101.

perpetrators and victims, endlessly. "Such an eschatological 'heaven' might well be described as 'hell', since it would amount to a freezing of all time into the multitudinous instances of satisfaction." God's process would go on, but the finite occasion would be forever frozen in this tormented state. "Better that the immediacy were not retained," she insists, "than that it be retained with no transformation." For her the solution entails a twofold adjustment of Whitehead's intuition: (a) a subjective immortality in harmony with Christian individualized eschatology is added; (b) and so that the everlasting subject may not persist in everlasting hell, the transformation is accomplished by what can only be divine fiat. "The occasion is therefore not free to accept or reject its completion within God, for freedom belongs with the concrescing subject." And at this point that subject is God: "the occasion's freedom was exercised in its finite process of becoming, and was exhausted in that process." Whitehead would agree.

The question is the endowment of that exhausted occasion with an immortal subjective life in God. It now lives in its unfreedom, incorporated "into the freedom of God."[11] If it had lived "in conformity with God's own desires for it, then the occasion's experience of God's freedom would be experienced as an extension and fulfillment of its own freedom: insofar as its finite decision was contrary to God's purposes, the experience of God's freedom would be felt as the restriction of its own." Unlike any kind of subjectivity Whitehead conceived, this kind does not *become*. But doesn't this unbecoming subjectivity sound like the realm of the immortal shades? Or indeed even a bit like the heaven and hell we thought we abandoned when we became process theologians? To be sure, it lacks the truculent imaginary of the torture chamber, which miseries the saved can savor from above (presumably as "needed contrast," so they can appreciate their bliss). But doesn't this view of a dual unfreedom — an enforced "peace" for the good and everlasting "restriction" for the wicked — remind one of the standard stasis of immortality: a boring heaven for those who got it right, and a punitive hell for those who didn't? Does the suspension of subjective freedom within a living subject (which Whitehead never does, as the immortality is objective only) not echo the Reformation paradoxes of human freedom as bondage to God's freedom, the only freedom

11. Suchocki, *Evil*, 111.

which ultimately matters? Actually, of course, Suchocki's hell is really purgatory. Invoking Whitehead's "apotheosis of the world," she joins the generous minority tradition of the universal redemption: "here the judgment is a transformation which moves from the experiential knowledge of one's effects to the inexorably required and purgative participation in God's own life."[12]

The fantasy of a tutelary self-knowledge brought on by participation in the divine vision suits my own sense of justice: neither the too cheap grace of a merely imposed divine "justification" and forgiveness of the wicked, nor the morally too costly vision of a place of permanent torment (even Karl Barth found the notion of an eternal hell — subsisting even when God is "all in all" — subchristian). However, what I cannot get my mind around is any such notion of forced salvation, of ontological improvement inflicted by divine power.[13] This is precisely the dilemma with most concepts — graciously intended, and always at risk of hereticization — of *apokatastasis ton panton*: the agency, the freedom, of the creature is violated if that creature did not already choose God's will freely. That is, if the creature is saved no matter what, as a subjective life, then the myriad forms of resistance against the divine will are overriden. For the creature, the end of evil is the end of freedom. Since I follow Suchocki in a certain Methodism, let me mention that this problem occurs also for John Wesley, in whom the doctrine of the cosmic new creation as total reconstitution undermines the divine-human synergy of salvation, which at the same time so promisingly distinguishes his theology from the Reformation *sola gratia*.[14] The process synergy of salvation can it seems even within process theology get violated at the level of "heaven."

12. Suchocki, *Evil*, 113, citing *Process and Reality*, 348.

13. I find that my speculation resembles much earlier and more elaborate work of the editor of this volume, who argues that salvation is so linked with "the development of human potentialities in this life," that "one and the same process of personal growth spans both time and eternity." In other words, heaven and hell are not a matter of divine reward and punishment, something done to us, but simply the eternalizations of our choices. See Joseph A. Bracken, S.J., "Salvation: A Matter of Personal Choice." *Theological Studies* 33 (1972): 410-24.

14. Cf. my "Flows of Salvation: A Constructive Feminist Wesleyan Eschatology," forthcoming in *Quarterly Review*. Suchocki's work on Wesleyanism figures prominently.

In Whitehead himself, the problem hardly arises. The subject without freedom gets produced only by squeezing the living waters of a subjective immortality from the rock of a merely objective immortalization. I do not — in some fit of late modern grumpiness — wish to discard the attempt, as a meaningful Christian thought experiment, valuable to the church and those within it who struggle to reconcile process cosmology with the more personal afterlife expectations that for them mean "salvation." (If it does not convince me, it is not anyway the sort of argument designed to convince, but rather to strengthen belief.) But in fact what matters more to Suchocki is what matters to Whitehead (and to the present author): the unfolding adventure of human history in the living — and dying — universe, in which cooperation with God "saves" what is salvageable. The divine recycling of the remembered dead as nutrients for their own future neither requires nor excludes their subjective afterlife.

Evil in God (the City)

If for Suchocki "the reconciliation of all things in God" means that "finite freedom, exercised within the ambiguities of history and in cooperation with God's unfailing aim, makes dim reflections of that divine city possible in our own histories," I take no exception. Her identification of God with the heavenly city — either Augustine's city of God or Kant's commonwealth — offers a beautiful metaphor of the divine as complex social interaction rather than mere One — or Three. This move, harmonious with Whitehead's own identification of "the kingdom of heaven" with the consequent nature of God, contributes an immense and needed amplification of the sociality encoded in the classical Christian trinity. That is, the promising perichoretic relationality of the trinity has tended to get locked inside of the *trias,* before, over and above the creation (even in Moltmann). By contrast, Suchocki's metaphor of the divine city exists to unlock the logic of that sociality, so that its internal relations come flowing into civic history. The figure comes at the culmination of her reflection on freedom and temporal redemption in human sociality. While she does not make explicit in this philosophical prolegomenon the affinity to a certain trinitarian complexity within God, she has offered a needed bridge between the "completion" of God in the consequent nature, and the initial aim for the next moment.

"Like a great intensity of light striking a prism and breaking into many colors, the harmony in God is reflected to myriad standpoints in the nascent world as so many definite possibilities for modes of mutual relating in the world which is about to be."[15] This is an invaluable, indeed prismatic, contribution to process theology. In this way the intradivine relationality is never separated from the relation between God and world. For the intradivine relationality is the redemptive relation to the creature, not a secret divine brotherhood of three. Thus "the initial mode of the redemption which occurs in God provides the possibilities for redemption in the world." This argument works with or without the postulate of subjective immortality, if I am not mistaken. And it allows her to thereby offer Whiteheadian "ground to the hope for an enriched and enriching world community, as 'what is done in the world is transformed into a reality in heaven, and the reality of heaven passes back into the world.'"[16] (Thy will be done — an imperative not directed, as is usually assumed, at God — as in "do it, God!" but to us, who pray.)

To return to the matter of evil within "the reality in heaven." I am resisting understanding that *civitas dei* as a sanitary space, a sort of supremely high and urban milieu in which none of the complex mess of history shows up. If existence is comprised, as Suchocki puts it well, of an ambiguous interweave of good and evil, how would the city retain its complexity — which after all makes it a city — if the evil could be purged from it? I do not want to step outside the protective gates, however, of divine goodness — a doctrine which process theologians, including Suchocki, have so brilliantly guarded against the implicit immorality of divine omnipotence. Rather, I am trying to think a complex goodness, an open-ended goodness — which is not in fact offering a positive lure for every occasion. Or for any occasion. The specific lure, as the initial aim of every occasion, need not be understood as encoded with a particular, father-knows-best (even if he is not all-powerful) sort of content. It carries rather the condition of the possibility of well-being for that event, which is at the same time a

15. Suchocki, *Evil*, 121.
16. Suchocki, *Evil*, 134.

limit of what is possible. (One thinks of Derrida's play on "the (im)possible" as the just, that which "comes," the messianic without the messiah.) The lure is not a voice saying here, do this, this is my will — let us leave such specific guidance to fundamentalists. It may rather sound something like the still small voice that whispers — without words, with the signifiers of wind, in a hint of hope, a rush of potentiality — look here, beneath this bush, beneath this rock, this relationship, this dream, this metaphor: here *you* may find the possibility you need.

"Insofar as a redemptive community itself models the openness of God's peace, it becomes a concrete lure for the good."[17] God, for Suchocki, would in other words not tell us but *model* how in the midst of war to make peace. The concrete or positive lure is not a divine revelation but rather a work of social justice — of "social holiness" in Wesley's mature understanding of the kingdom as fully public work. God's peace as a paradigm of openness to the Other does not contradict its own openness by offering customized directions to the world: God is as Suchocki emphasizes often radically open to the way in which we will incarnate God in the world. It is not a matter of "here, take this, this is my lure." And if you don't "get it," here comes the next. I am arguing not with Suchocki, but with misunderstandings of process theology produced by attempts (mine included) at simplification.

The lure is the individuated relation of the divine eros to a specific creaturely becoming. Given that it pervades the possibly infinite universe, we cannot credibly maintain a "me and my God" sort of account of this I-thou. But we can nonetheless, as Buber put it, "say thou to the universe," and appropriately fulfil our humanity by humanizing — without anthropomorphizing and anthropocentering — this cosmic desire, even as it humanizes us. Even as it animalizes itself in relation to animals, mineralizes in relation to minerals, vegetates in relation to vegetables, and urbanizes in relation to cities. So actually I am only underscoring Suchocki's point that "the redemptive society labors with God, increasing the possibilities for redemption in the world."[18] That labor gives birth to an ever new creation. But that creation is always already scarred and damaged, and on our little

17. Suchocki, *Evil*, 130.
18. Suchocki, *Evil*, 130.

planet, it may be mortally wounded. Even as possibilities for redemption do indeed increase in the world (a scale of global peace movement, for instance, and awareness of our responsibility for the non-human earth, unimaginable even a few decades ago), so it seems do the mechanisms of annihilation (which seem endlessly resourceful in trumping resistance). We seem to be heading toward some decisive climax. But so have we seemed to apocalyptic populations countless times before. No one knows the (next) outcome. It is not written. We have reason to sit on the edge of our chairs.

Mitigating not Terminating

The contrast of good and evil has a dramatic character — hence the hyperboles of eschatological poetry describe a divine perspective we might indeed ascribe, with no literalism, to the consequent nature. I do not imagine God's mind, as it prehends human evil, transforming it into good, or as erasing it from the good. I imagine it in perfect focus, heightening the contrasts. Not as a telescope focused parentally on us, but as (literally) a *pano*rama immense beyond our comprehension, putting our delinquencies not only "in perspective," but of course transcending all perspectives, as the perspective immanent to all perspectives, and to which all perspectives are immanent. So our evil would be at once *judged* as such, exposed in its contrast to the wiser possibility, and at the same time, as a contrast amidst all the contrasts of the universe, utterly *relativized*. If the City of God *is* God, this play of oppositional contrast within a vast pluralism of potentialities might indeed resemble the life of a great — truly cosmo-politan — city.

God, in the consequent nature, may *see* how "what in the temporal world is mere wreckage" might get constructively recycled. But it does not *do* it. If I may switch from an urban to a theatrical metaphor: the consequent nature does not make tragedy into comedy (in the classic sense of an edifying happy ending). It dramatizes the tragic. In disclosing the evil as what it is, the tragedy becomes "good" in the way *Hamlet* is "good" — aesthetically. And the goodness of the work of art is precisely not good vs. evil but good vs. bad. *Hamlet* is such a "good" play it captures the "fundamental ambiguity" of being (or not), while at the same time it exposes acts of true violation as such.

God would thus see *in beauty*. God would see the brutality — beautifully: not indifferently, but within the immense, *prismatic* panorama.[19] This goodness is not achieved by violating the decisions, good, bad, really evil, trivial, or indecisive, of the creatures. Whitehead's "God is a little oblivious as to morals." This does not make God less but *more* sensitive to our suffering, viewing both the suffering and the perpetrators of suffering with compassion. But the compassion does not entail fixing us, even *within* the consequent nature of God: that would be bad theatre and bad love. God would "hear no evil, see no evil." Yet great theatre does not leave the evil raw and victorious: if good does not triumph, neither does evil. The sophic vision at any given moment counters the evil by contrast not only with the good it violated but with everything else in the universe. With this unique combination of judgment and relativism, wisdom loves friends and enemies. But differently — as befits their own choices.

In other words I do not imagine evil being terminated in God but *mitigated* — as it then might be in the world. Good is brought out of it through precisely the process of "rhythmic responsiveness" that Suchocki delicately traces.

"The world moves toward its redemptive completion in God, adding thereby to the completion of God."[20] I would adjust this only to make sure that the conventional sense of eschatological completion does not overwhelm the radical Whiteheadian insight into the "everlasting process" of the world. Completion must not connote an ultimate victory of good over evil, or a historical endpoint of final consummation, or even — though Whitehead can be read differently — an "end of evil" as a timeless consummation transcendent of the temporal process. If the notion of timeless consummations leaves one (me) cold, the *time-full* and ambiguous ones of history do suggest altogether nonlinear modes of temporality, close to what has been too abstractly marked as "eternal."

19. G. Vattimo has commented on the "overabundance of forms, lights, and colors, as if the revelation (according to the etymology of apokalypsis) of salvation at the end of time was not so much a destructive catastrophe as a transfer of things on the plane of phantasmagoria, a dissolution of the real in 'secondary' qualities bound with the perception of the senses." Gianni Vattimo, *After Christianity* (New York: Columbia University Press, 2002), 52.

20. Suchocki, *Evil*, 152.

So by claiming that "there is no end of evil" I am not countering Suchocki's analysis of the way evil works in history. I am countering the risk that her eschatology could harmonize with the history of ahistorical Christian triumphalisms, in which things are sweet in heaven even if they are unbearable here. Given how often and perhaps even increasingly they are unbearable, a dogma of unambiguous divine goodness contributes to the case against process theology as unduly sanitized. I am convinced, however, that the charges of process sanguinity remain poorly founded. If the divine nature *takes in* the radical otherness of evil, not as its own evil, its "left hand," but as an alterity to which the divine self is internally related, it has already taken upon itself the risk of evil: as Jesus in the desert of temptation, as YHWH gambling with Satan's torment of Job. Then God seems capacious enough to accommodate the wild ambiguities of the universe, without controlling them. But still, in the midst of the most insidious violence, the divinity who dwells among us and in whom we dwell, would not be diminished in goodness, a goodness that is laced with beauty — the beauty of mortal creatures, always in some measure a "tragic beauty," the beauty of the "great sea monsters," seen as evil from another biblical perspective.[21] I am still elaborating only upon Suchocki's sense of the ambiguity at the root of good and evil.

The ambiguous but utter "it is good" takes on the interpersonal face of the universe — the Sophia, Elohim or Christ figure appears in the human struggle with human evil. We have tried to hold this God responsible for our species' suffering. And we must continue to struggle on behalf of this God, whose face hardens into brutality only in our deification of our own brutalization. If within these monotheisms the divinity comes free of the brutality of omnipotence, and yet at the same time capacitates free creatures to struggle meaningfully against brutality, we will still not find an end of evil. For we then anticipate no moment in which "good" and "evil" could be cleanly separated. We anticipate no timeless *eschaton*. And the chaff will leave its residue on the wheat.

Might we then not best abandon the discourse of "evil" and its

21. I distinguish systematically between "tehomophobic" and "tehomophilic" biblical traditions, as two different moods or styles of response to the *tehom*, or primal chaos. Cf. *Face of the Deep: A Theology of Becoming* (London: Routledge, 2003).

"end" to those who perpetrate ever greater brutality in the name of the end of evil (as Kristol claims President Reagan showed we can)? Perhaps such an abandonment would undermine our struggle against the violation of life — so much of which is perpetrated in the name of putting an end to some Other's "evil." But I suspect to the contrary that by disengaging a discourse that has led only to ethical failure and despair, we might renew our hope. We release new energies for resisting the machine of violation. For "evil" — the word and what we name with it — still, despite all the risk of its discourse, will not have the last word. Brutality will be passed on through the wounds. It *brutalizes*. But it can be constrained and transformed. Its effects can be healed. The "bonding impulse" can bring forth good from the wound, if only the wound is recognized. Our own species' creativity — with its wildly canny nomadisms, aggressions, individualities, its differentiation, defiance and sass — would be inconceivable apart from the possibility of evil.

More directly: if we cannot come close to evil repeatedly, hoping for some fresh good (and I do not know of much good that has come without the risk of some serious, and ipso facto needless, suffering), then not much good will come of us. All messianic impulses take this risk — and routinely outdo, as does indeed the Book of Revelation, the violence of their various Beasts and Harlots. Perhaps if we are not to surrender the messianic altogether, and with it the passion for justice, the best we can do is to teach the ambiguity of our interdependence with that which terrifies us. Once we demonize the Other, we participate in the demonic. The violations we perpetrate in the passion of the good will be mitigated only by the rigors of an impartial compassion. This is not a pollyanna politics, but the ultimate political realism — as the dance of terrorism and empire has manifested. We can only hope that the exposed and instantaneous interdependence of the postmodern planet will constrain the diabolical messianisms of both conquest and terror. But the healthiest ethical alternatives — and this would be true at the level of intimacy as well as globality — would never have been, and will never yet be, without terrifying risk to ourselves. We can pick up the cross of this risk knowingly — or continue to nail others onto it.

A gamble that risks the good we have, and so the very boundary of the good, answers to the lure of life, at least so the morally ambiguous parable of the stewards, in which the one who fails to risk all loses all, would suggest. And if as process theologians argue, the potentiality of good is proportionate to that of evil, it is as predictable as anything in a probabilistic universe could be, that when the potentiality for evil exists, evil will continue — sometimes — to take place. God, process theology clarifies, wills the risk, but not the evil. But God is not clueless about likely, indeed inevitable outcomes. (Hence we may have to be a bit more respectful in our reading of classical Catholic distinctions between divine foreknowledge and omnipotence.)

Insoluble Mystery

The risk marks the shadowy area of uncertainty, the indeterminacy that edges every moment (*eschaton* in Greek means "edge," or rim, in space as well as time). So a process eschatology might shift focus from the *end* to the *edge*, where the wider good must be negotiated. Complexity theory speaks of "the edge of chaos," and a theology of becoming discerns not just one good choice and many lousy ones at that edge, but a probabilistic haze of many-hued possibilities. There is therefore always evil at the edge of chaos, though the evil is never strictly speaking the chaos — the *tehom* — itself. Theologically, the edge of chaos signifies that indeterminacy cannot now, in the future, or in "heaven" be reduced to ontological certainty. Indeterminacy characterizes the cosmic creativity itself — and the uncertainty, however well organized into however many universes, remains bottomless. *Tehom*, the bottomless indeterminacy, remains "beyond good and evil." It remains the source and mystery, in its spontaneities, of both. It demands an apophatic response, yet "messages from the deep" drift into our awareness. The unknowable edges the known.

This bottomlessness is not mysterious because God has not revealed it to us, or because it is off-limits, but because it remains indeterminate within God. God does not master this mystery. It is the mysterious itself. Indeed, *the mysterium fascinans et tremendum* could even characterize the dual nature of the process God (who often seems to lose mystery in the interest of a metaphysically assured goodness): the God who fascinates/attracts/lures and empathizes/judges/encompasses. But this divine mystery is not then contained within a personal agency, but rather marks the uncontainment of God: as the edge of the impersonal out of which the metaphors of an (inter)personal deity configure.[22] The divine mystery and the mystery of human evil mingle dark (but not evil) waters at that very edge, where we partake — by divine invitation — of the bottomless uncertainty. So indeed the origins of suffering and of evil lie in "mystery" — but precisely not in the sense usually meant: that God's intentions transcend our understanding. The *mysterium iniquitatis* lies indeed in the "transcendent" origin of evil — but in precisely Suchocki's sense of the empathic transcendence whereby humans (at their own creative risk) respond to one another.

A final thought about the mystery, a rather silly little thought it had seemed, is haunting me. I said we should not even hope for an end to evil on the earth. And I have been thinking how I love murder mysteries. This might be just a bad habit, and I should read Shakespeare instead. However, I realized during the most recent U.S. war how oddly comforting it was to read or view a British murder mystery: just one, or a handful, of murders — and whole communities snap into action, to see with vigilance, lawfulness and intelligence that justice is done. The genre presumes — almost utopically — that a single life matters ultimately. I now realize that I wouldn't even want to be part of an earth where murders never happen. It would be a social order without chaos. Too much passion, diversity and turbulence would have been repressed. The wild uncertainties of our species' creativity would have been traded against security. It could seem worth it, after too much violence. But no more murders would mean that the boundary between avoidable and inevitable violence would have been rigidified. The boundary between good and evil would have been fixed; and this is in itself an evil, entrapment in the unacknowledged paradox.

I *would* want, however, to be part of an earth organized against every kind of needless suffering: that is, a planet where *wars*, recognized as mass murder, have become obsolete, where the death of 50,000 children a day from avoidable causes belongs to a barbarous

---

22. Bracken has done groundbreaking work on the relation of the impersonal Godhead of the mystical tradition to Whitehead's creativity. See *The Divine Matrix: Creativity as Link Between East and West* (Maryknoll: Orbis, 1995), 59.

past, where natural disasters can be met with humane skill, and where we are healing rather than destroying the carrying capacity of nonhuman nature itself. I *would* want to be part of a planet where individual murders are the worst evils. This seems, just barely, as practical utopia, imaginable. And there would still be enough danger to obviate boredom. We would mobilize our most adventurous talents in the struggle to prevent all preventable suffering, and to heal and mitigate the suffering that could not be avoided — while protecting the dangerous freedom from which violations flow. This would be democracy — which can when you read this, I hope, still be imagined.

Our history is unfolding inside of a divine mystery. We are privileged to take part in its splendor. Our moment is infinitesimal. But we get to be part of something infinite. We, with our brutalizing systems, may yet — as Suchocki suggests — have a chance to mature as a species. Is it worth the effort? Every effort will itself ripple endlessly through the ocean of the divine indeterminacy. If we don't imagine any end of evil in God — not in one who interacts intimately with human history and is saturated by all of time — we can still imagine every violation fading into the past of some future moment. Its wound healed, its drama written. Its mystery unsolvable.

Subjective Immortality in a
Neo-Whiteheadian Context

Joseph A. Bracken, S.J.

As already noted in my introductory essay, Marjorie Suchocki makes clear the basic inadequacy of Whitehead's eschatology in dealing with the problem of human pain and suffering. That is, while God through "his vision of truth, beauty, and goodness" as given in the divine primordial nature can basically be at peace with "the revolts of destructive evil, purely self-regarding" (*Process and Reality* [PR] 346), which cause so much pain and suffering within this world, the creatures themselves are not so privileged. For human beings in particular, "the overcoming of evil in history is always partial" and unevenly distributed. Some suffer far more than others and many more never understand how their pain and personal suffering contribute to a higher good beyond themselves. Hence, argues Suchocki, there must be an overcoming of evil which "lies beyond our immediate experience in the world" if only to support a viable hope for the future (82). Yet her own revision of the Whiteheadian metaphysical scheme so as to allow for subjective immortality for human beings and indeed for all finite creatures is flawed in my judgment because it is not thorough enough. As mentioned earlier, she fails to see that her own revisions logically require a rethinking of Whitehead's philosophy in the direction of a metaphysics of intersubjectivity. In the following pages, accordingly, I will first summarize what I consider to be the shortcomings of her argument and then elaborate how a neo-Whiteheadian metaphysics of universal intersubjectivity would indeed remedy those shortcomings and strengthen her overall argument for the possibility of subjective immortality within a process-relational approach to the God-world relationship.

Basic to Suchocki's argument is the contention that God prehends finite actual occasions at the moment of "enjoyment" when they are both subject of experience and superject, that is, when they have completed their process of self-constitution and are concomitantly aware of what they have just become. In this she is consciously modifying Whitehead's own statement that "[n]o actual entity can be conscious of its own satisfaction; for such knowledge would be a component in the process [of self-constitution] and would thereby alter the satisfaction" (PR 85). In response, she argues that, properly understood, Whiteheadian creativity is involved not only in the actual entity's subjective process of self-constitution but in its objective outcome, the latter understood as its active "givingness" rather than simply its passive "givenness" to successor actual entities (87). Whitehead, in other words, in his abstract analysis of the self-constitution of an actual entity, separated out what should have remained dynamically one, namely, process and outcome as a continuous reality. Instead of the "satisfaction" of the actual entity being separate from its process of concrescence as Whitehead himself maintained (PR 84), the moment of satisfaction is rather its fullness and completion. Satisfaction is the entity's active enjoyment of what it has become and in that sense the ontological basis for its active self-presentation, its "givingness," to future actual occasions.

The second stage in her argument is that God can prehend finite actual entities in this moment of "enjoyment" and thus in their subjective immediacy as well as in their objectively prehensible characteristics because, in Whitehead's view, God's conceptual vision is infinite with no limitations or negative prehensions (PR 345). That is, unlike finite actual entities which can incorporate only selective features of their predecessors' existence and activity into their own limited process of self-constitution, God can incorporate into the divine consequent nature the fullness of another entity, even its subjective immediacy in the moment of "enjoyment," without thereby losing God's own distinctive identity in the process. But, she claims, if God can thus fully incorporate creaturely actual entities into the ongoing divine concrescence, then by the same token God can bestow on creaturely actual entities subjective as well as objective immortality.

Instead of being simply objects of thought within the divine mind, actual entities can co-exist with God, share the divine life forever. Admittedly, fully to co-exist with God, an actual entity must undergo transformation; it must "experience itself and God's evaluative transformation of itself within the divine nature" (103). In effect, it must see and accept itself in its true relation to God and the world of creaturely actual occasions out of which it arose and to which it somehow contributed, whether for better or for worse. It must experience judgment, but a judgment which, if accepted, eventually brings a sense of redemption and peace as the actual entity takes its rightful place within the cosmic process (109).

Given the *prima facie* attractiveness of this proposal for a Christian understanding of "the last things," there is, as mentioned earlier, a latent problem with its conceptual presuppositions. Whereas Whitehead himself clearly conceived prehension, both divine and creaturely, in terms of a classical subject-object relationship, Suchocki's proposal just as clearly presupposes a subject-subject or intersubjective relationship between God and creaturely actual occasions. For, if God prehends an actual occasion in its subjective immediacy as well as in its objective characteristics, then God and the actual occasion must somehow stand over against one another as mutually exclusive subjects of experience. But, if this is the case, how can God incorporate the subjectivity of the creaturely actual occasion into the divine consequent nature without undercutting its ontological status as an independent subject of experience, in effect reducing it to simply an object of thought for the divine mind? Suchocki, to be sure, further argues that God needs to incorporate the created subjectivity into the divine consequent nature; for, otherwise, the created actual entity would add nothing new to the divine life since all objective characteristics of that same actual occasion are eternally given as potential forms of existence and activity within the divine primordial nature (93). But such a line of thought, as I see it, indirectly reinforces my own contention that there is a dramatic difference between God's prehension of an objective possibility which has here and now become actualized and God's prehension of a created subjectivity which exists in its own right as a rival subject of experience and thus as much more than simply an object of thought for the divine mind. The created subjectivity cannot, in other words, truly co-exist with God, undergo transformation with God's active assistance as Suchocki proposes (111), unless it continues to exercise its own independent subjectivity, albeit in a new and different way.

Still another feature of Suchocki's rethinking of the God-world relationship which remains obscure is her contention that finite actual occasions constitute a community once they have been assimilated into the divine life: "The unity of God, retaining the immediacy of each prehended occasion, is community, an ultimate and transforming togetherness which confirms and redeems finite reality" (103). Granted that in virtue of their incorporation into the divine life created actual occasions undergo transformation, that is, experience in a new way their relatedness both to God and to one another, one still must ask what is God's relation to this community. Is God likewise a member of the community or does the community of created actual occasions effectively constitute the reality of God in terms of the divine consequent nature? If the former be the case, then once again an unacknowledged intersubjective relation between God and created actual occasions comes into play. On the other hand, if God is represented as simply "the Immediacy of immediacies, and a Harmony of harmonies" (106) within the community of transformed creaturely actual occasions, then God's own reality as a transcendent subject of experience seems to be absorbed into the community of created subjects of experience. Suchocki, to be sure, claims that the subjective aim of God as the transcendent subject of experience guides the initial creation and ongoing renewal of this community of finite subjectivities: "The harmony of each finite satisfaction as it completes another finite satisfaction through intensification of meaning, whether through contrast or similarity, takes place through God's mutuality of subjective form, or God's own feeling of how each of the occasions taken into the divine nature relates to all of the others" (105). But then the question posed above logically returns. If God is indeed an independent subject of experience, then what is God's relation to the community of creaturely actual occasions within the divine consequent nature?

In fairness to Suchocki, it should be noted that this is not only her problem but Whitehead's as well. That is, Whitehead never really thought out the proper relation between the two dimensions of the divine being, namely, the divine primordial nature and the divine consequent nature. As Lewis Ford has pointed out in his careful analysis of the development of Whitehead's metaphysics, God's role in the cosmic process was initially that of a principle of order and limitation for the scope of creativity within the cosmic process; only in the final stages of the composition of *Process and Reality* did it occur to him that God's existence as a separate transcendent entity was required for the unity and direction of that same process.[1] Thus in *Process and Reality* the divine primordial nature is represented as an unlimited vision of possibilities proper to God alone and not shared with creatures. Yet simply as a primordial valuation of possibilities, the divine primordial nature is deficient in actuality and unconscious (PR 345). Thus, in order for God to become fully actual and conscious, the divine primordial nature must be integrated with the divine consequent nature. But what is the divine consequent nature but God's ongoing prehension of the ever-increasing community of finite actual entities constituting the cosmic process? Likewise, what is the reality of the world apart from God as the sole transcendent entity, the only entity which survives the passage of time? Two possibilities present themselves, neither of which is in my judgment fully satisfactory. Either the world is progressively absorbed into God or God is ultimately absorbed into the world. Whitehead, of course, would have one believe that God and the world are equally real and equally necessary to one another within the cosmic process: "God and the World are the contrasted opposites in terms of which Creativity achieves its supreme task of transforming disjoined multiplicity, with its diversities in opposition, into concrescent unity, with its diversities in contrast" (PR 348). But, in point of fact, one is logically subordinate to the other, depending upon one's antecedent religious convictions. If one is a theist, then the physical world comes into existence at every moment only to be absorbed into God as the sole enduring reality. If one is an atheist or secular materialist, then "God" exists only as the personalized principle of order and limitation within the ongoing cosmic process.

Accordingly, Suchocki's project to legitimate traditional Christian belief in life after death for human beings and indeed all sentient beings (finite actual occasions) within the context of Whitehead's

---

1. See Lewis S. Ford, *The Emergence of Whitehead's Metaphysics, 1925-1929* (Albany: State University of New York Press, 1984), 227-29.

process-relational metaphysics is a notable achievement for theistically minded Whiteheadians like myself. But, as I see it, it still falls short of its long-term goal in that it fails to critique Whitehead's scheme with sufficient thoroughness. Whitehead, after all, was primarily a philosopher with an interest in the reality of God only as a necessary function within his cosmological scheme. Suchocki, on the contrary, is a theologian whose primary agenda is a rational justification of traditional Christian beliefs in the reality of God, Christ, Church, redemption, grace, personal immortality, etc. Hence, one should expect to make certain adjustments in Whitehead's metaphysical scheme so as to take account of what one believes to be true on other grounds, e.g., divine revelation. On the other hand, this does not have to be seen as a capitulation of reason to revelation. Given the ultimately provisional and incomplete character of all philosophical schemes, it may well turn out to be the case that the adjustment in one's antecedent philosophical conceptuality in order to account for what one believes to be true on other grounds will in the end result in a philosophical system better grounded in common human experience. Thomas Aquinas, for example, introduced the category of existence (over and above that of essence) into the metaphysics of Aristotle, largely because for him as a Christian the existence of the world was not a "given" as it was for Aristotle but a gift, the gift of a Creator God. But, in so doing, he expanded the notions of act and potency to include still another level of philosophical reflection. He offered a plausible solution, in other words, to the basic philosophical question: "Why is there something rather than nothing?" The answer to that question may not necessarily be belief in a Creator God, but in any case it does raise a legitimate philosophical question which presumably never occurred to Aristotle.

In similar fashion I will at this point first indicate how Whitehead's metaphysical scheme can be represented as a metaphysics of universal intersubjectivity, provided that one is willing to rethink what he meant by a "society" as the byproduct of successive generations of actual occasions in dynamic interrelation. In brief, my argument will be that a Whiteheadian society should no longer be conceived as an aggregate of actual occasions with a "common element of form" (PR 34) but as a structured field of activity, a law-like objective context, for those same momentary subjects of experience in their dynamic interrelatedness. Afterwards, I will show how this intersubjective rethinking of Whitehead's metaphysics solves the problems alluded to above in Suchocki's own efforts to justify belief in subjective immortality for all sentient creatures within a process-relational world view. God and the world will be seen as co-existing within a common space or "divine matrix," to the ongoing structure of which both God and creatures contribute through their dynamic interrelation.

To begin, then, why is the understanding of a Whiteheadian society as a structured field of activity for its constituent actual occasions so important for the rethinking of the latter's philosophy as a rudimentary metaphysics of universal intersubjectivity? As I have indicated in a recent book,[2] there is a necessary vertical as well as a horizontal dimension to any understanding of intersubjectivity. That is, by their dynamic interrelation subjects of experience inevitably create a space between them which serves as the necessary context for further interaction. Equivalently, it is the intermediate vertical dimension to their ongoing exchange on a horizontal plane. This, as I see it, is what Martin Buber basically had in mind with his enigmatic notion of "the between" (das Zwischen).[3] That is, within the context of transcendental subjectivity as elaborated by Immanuel Kant and the German Idealists, there is no way to posit the Other as genuinely Other than oneself; one inevitably reduces the Other to a dialectical moment in one's own process of self-realization. Hence, one must presuppose that in the moment of genuine communication with the Other as Other a common space is created wherein each can both be itself and at the same time affirm the Other as genuinely Other than oneself. This common space, moreover, is ontologically, even if not temporally,

---

2. Cf. Joseph A. Bracken, S.J., *The One in the Many: A Contemporary Reconstruction of the God-World Relationship* (Grand Rapids: Eerdmans, 2001), 109-30.

3. Cf. Martin Buber, *I and Thou*, trans. Walter Kaufmann (New York: Scribner's, 1970), esp. 37-72; also by the same author "What Is Man?" in *Between Man and Man*, trans. Maurice Freedman (New York: Macmillan, 1965), 203-5. Admittedly, Buber conceives the "Between" as a necessarily transient reality (just like the passing experience of the Other as "Thou") which devolves into the "It" of the objective social world at every moment. In point of fact, the "Between" must be both objective and intersubjective at the same time if it is to function as a mediating reality between opposing subjectivities, as I shall indicate below.

prior. That is, the common space does not pre-exist the two subjectivities but rather co-exists with them as the necessary *precondition* of their intercommunication Without the logical antecedent possibility of this common space, *bona fide* interpersonal communication *(das Zwischenmenschliche)* could never take place. Human beings, says Buber, would remain fixated in I-It *(Ich-Es)* relationships which are ultimately solipsistic in that each subjectivity implicitly reduces the Other to an object of thought or desire in its ego-centered world.

What, however, is the connection between Buber's notion of the Between and Whitehead's category of society? In my judgment, a Whiteheadian society is an instance of the Between, existing no longer simply between human beings in rare moments of genuinely interpersonal communication, but between all actual occasions as they prehend one another and thereby internalize their relations to one another. They thereby create a common space between themselves which is their objective reality as a society. Unfortunately, as noted above, Whitehead conceived "prehension" in terms of a subject-object relationship. In this way, by his own admission, "the ultimate metaphysical truth is atomism. The creatures are atomic" (PR 35). Each actual occasion incorporates the world into its self-constitution. But it remains itself alone, ontologically speaking. Thus, when he came to speak of societies as enduring realities, the equivalent of "substance" in classical metaphysics, Whitehead had no recourse but to think in terms of aggregates of actual occasions, some of which, to be sure, had a "regnant" member and thus were capable of further internal organization as a "structured society" or society made up of subsocieties (PR 103). If, on the other hand, he had expanded upon his rudimentary remarks about the nature of societies in *Process and Reality* and *Adventures of Ideas,* then he would have had the logical starting-point for a metaphysics of universal intersubjectivity and, in principle at least, a new way of conceiving societies as other than aggregates of actual occasions.

In *Process and Reality,* for example, Whitehead seems to think of societies as "environments" for their constituent actual occasions:

> Every society must be considered with its background of a wider environment of actual entities, which also contribute their objectifications to which the members of the society must con-

> form. . . . But this means that the environment, together with the society in question, must form a larger society in respect to some more general characters than those defining the society from which we started. Thus we arrive at the principle that every society requires a social background, of which it is itself a part (90).

In my view, "field" could be substituted for "environment" in this context without loss of meaning. Moreover, "field" should be understood not as a convenient mental fiction or purely logical construct but as an objective reality with a law-like structure necessary for the ongoing self-constitution of its constituent actual occasions. As Whitehead himself comments, "in a society, the members [constituent actual occasions] can only exist by reason of the laws which dominate the society, and the laws only come into being by reason of the analogous characters of the members of the society" (PR 91). A Whiteheadian society, in other words, exhibits a continuity of form and function over time only because successive generations of actual occasions mutually prehend the same "common element of form" (PR 34). But where is that "form" located when one generation of actual occasions has ceased to exist and another is still in process of concrescence? Whitehead himself seems to think that each new generation of actual occasions recovers that form through a process called "transmutation" whereby each individual actual occasion retrieves the form proper to its predecessors in their conjoint existence and activity (PR 250-52). But, as I have explained at length elsewhere,[4] a much simpler explanation is to postulate the existence of societies as structured fields of activity for their constituent actual occasions. These structured fields of activity perdure over time as successive generations of constituent actual occasions come and go. Each new generation of actual occasions prehends within the field(s) to which it belongs both the objective pattern of interrelation between its predecessors an instant ago and the subjective form or "feeling-tone" arising from that pattern (PR 23).[5] Societies, in other words, while derivative from the

---

4. See Joseph A. Bracken, S.J., "Proposals for Overcoming the Atomism within Process-Relational Metaphysics," *Process Studies* 23 (1994), 10-24.

5. Judith Jones in a recent book argues that subsequent actual occasions within a given society are strongly influenced in their own self-constitution by the feelings of their predecessors, above all, their immediate predecessors (see Judith A. Jones,

dynamic interplay of actual occasions at any given moment, neverthe-less possess their own objective ontological reality as enduring con-texts or "environments" for the law-like succession of generations of actual occasions over time. As Whitehead himself comments in *Adventures of Ideas*, "[a] society has an essential character, whereby it is the society that it is, and it has also accidental qualities which vary as circumstances alter. Thus a society, as a complete existence and as retaining the same metaphysical status, enjoys a history expressing its changing reactions to changing circumstances."[6]

Thus understood, Whiteheadian societies may be suitably com-pared to the notion of "system" within the philosophy of Ervin Laszlo and other systems-oriented thinkers. Laszlo defines a natural system as a "nonrandom accumulation of matter-energy, in a region of physi-cal space-time, which is nonrandomly organized into coacting interre-lated subsystems or components."[7] Laszlo's focus here is not on the components as such but on the system or social totality resulting from their dynamic interplay, just as I draw attention to the way in which Whiteheadian societies are the enduring social realities while individ-ual actual occasions come and go. Furthermore, in his systems-approach to reality, Laszlo sees the relation of systems to one another in terms of interlocking and hierarchically ordered fields of activity.[8] Hence, as I have argued elsewhere,[9] it should be possible to combine

---

Intensity: An Essay in Whiteheadian Ontology [Nashville: Vanderbilt University Press, 1998], 3, 8-14). While I fully concur with this hypothesis, I believe that it is better ex-plained by way of my own theory of Whiteheadian societies as structured fields of ac-tivity for their constituent actual occasions and thus as carriers of both form and feel-ing from one generation of actual occasions to another. What I find ambiguous in Jones's theory is the alleged presence of a past actual occasion in its successor. The feeling-tone of the past actual occasion is certainly present in its successor(s) but, as I see it, not the subject itself as a self-constituting reality here and now; see on this point *The One in the Many*, 151-54.

6. Alfred North Whitehead, *Adventures of Ideas* (New York: The Free Press, 1967), 204.

7. See Ervin Laszlo, *Introduction to Systems Philosophy: Toward a New Paradigm of Contemporary Thought* (London: Gordon and Breach, 1972), 30.

8. *Ibid.*, 47-53. See also his most recent book *The Connectivity Hypothesis: Founda-tions of an Integral Science of Quantum, Cosmos, Life, and Consciousness* (Albany: State Uni-versity of New York Press, 2003) in which the link between "fields" and "systems" in his cosmology is much more explicit.

9. Bracken, *The One in the Many*, 132-37.

the metaphysical insights of Laszlo and Whitehead, with Whitehead accounting better for the ultimate components of systems and Laszlo better accounting for the systems or objective social realities which result from the ongoing interplay of these ultimate components at different levels of existence and activity.

In any event, it should be clear that Whitehead's philosophy taken by itself cannot be used in defense of a metaphysics of intersubjectivity wherein a subject-subject relation rather than a subject-object relation is paramount. A subject-object relation, to be sure, is compatible with Whitehead's metaphysical atomism in which individual subjects of experience constitute themselves as microcosms of the world out of which they are emerging but are related to one another only analogously; each actual occasion is thus its own world of experience. A subject-subject relation, however, as noted above, logically demands a common space or "Between" within which the two subjectivities can simultaneously affect one another. Yet in Whitehead's scheme contemporary actual occasions are causally independent of one another (PR 61); hence, there is no common space or Between within which they can simultaneously affect one another's self-constitution. In principle, then, only Whiteheadian societies can be mutually present to one another and affect one another's self-constitution in this way. But how is one then to reinterpret the standard Whiteheadian understanding of society so as to allow for such a common space or "Between" between societies?

In terms of my own scheme, two personally ordered societies of actual occasions, when understood as structured fields of activity for those same actual occasions, can merge to create a common field of activity as the basis for their ongoing intersubjective relation to one another. They have co-created a "Between" or common ground of existence and activity which gradually becomes more and more structured by their joint activity. In and through this common field of activity which is structured by their ongoing mutual interaction, the two subjectivities (or, in Whiteheadian terms, personally ordered societies of actual occasions) are influencing each other's self-constitution. That is, in both cases the latest member of the society, namely, the newly concrescing actual occasion, prehends a past world constituted not only by the decision of its own predecessors but in large measure by the decisions of the predecessors of the newly concrescing actual occasion in the other society. Through the common field of activity, in other words, not the individual actual occasions but the societies to which they belong are simultaneously affecting each other's ongoing self-constitution. The societies thus possess a genuinely intersubjective relation to one another.

At this point, we are in a position to re-evaluate Suchocki's thesis in *The End of Evil*. Suchocki stipulated that God prehends finite actual occasions in the moment of "enjoyment" when they are simultaneously both subject of experience and superject or objective actuality capable of prehension by successor finite actual occasions. In this way, says Suchocki, God can incorporate these finite actual occasions in their subjective immediacy into the everlasting divine consequent nature. This assures the subjective immortality of the occasions in that they now live the divine life, experiencing themselves and their relation to God and one another with a completeness that was impossible for them within the limiting conditions of earthly life. But, as already noted, there are conceptual problems here with the way in which a created subjectivity can be incorporated into the divine subjectivity without loss of its own identity and with the way in which God as a transcendent subject of experience relates interpersonally to the community of created subjects of experience within the divine consequent nature. As I see it, both of these problems can be solved if one concedes that Whiteheadian societies are structured fields of activity for their constituent actual occasions. For, as already noted, in that case the fields of activity proper to separate Whiteheadian societies can combine or merge so as to create common fields of activity in which the ontological independence of the different subjectivities (Whiteheadian societies) can be guaranteed. Such a scheme, as I will explain below, works best with a strictly trinitarian understanding of God in which the three divine persons can be said antecedently to share a common field of activity even apart from creation. But, as I also indicate below, it can likewise be extended to the unipersonal concept of God to be found in the writings of both Whitehead himself and Charles Hartshorne.

For example, each of the three divine persons of the classical doctrine of the Trinity in Christian theology can be represented in Whiteheadian terms as a personally ordered society of actual occasions whose field of activity is totally unlimited and therefore infinite.[10] These three infinite fields of activity, accordingly, merge to form a single conjoint field of activity from three interrelated perspectives much as in the trinitarian theology of Thomas Aquinas the three divine persons are "subsistent relations," three interrelated ways to possess numerically one and the same divine essence.[11] Within this conjoint field of activity or "divine matrix," a finite subjectivity or a society of finite personally ordered actual occasions can exist as itself and yet at the same time relate itself to each of the divine persons according to a pattern already fixed by the dynamic relations of the divine persons with one another. In brief, the finite subjectivity links itself with the "Son" in the "Son's" ongoing relationship to the "Father" in the power of the "Holy Spirit."[12] In line with the Pauline vision in the Letters to Ephesians and Colossians, Jesus Christ as the incarnate Son of God thus becomes the mediator between heaven and earth, that is, the divine community and the cosmic community of all finite actual occasions as these are further organized into various subcommunities or subordinate fields of activity. Key here, however, in terms of my problematic in this essay is that each finite subjectivity remains itself within its own field of activity even as its field of activity is incorporated first into the much broader field of activity proper to creation as a whole and then into the field of activity proper to the three divine persons. Subjectivities, in other words, cannot merge without loss of individual identity but their respective fields of activity can merge to create a common space or "Between" for the ongoing interplay of those same subjectivities.

Furthermore, as I see it, this field-oriented approach to the God-world relationship can still be fruitfully employed if one conceives God in strictly monotheistic terms. For example, if one follows Charles Hartshorne in thinking of God as a personally ordered society of divine actual occasions,[13] then the enduring reality of God can be

---

10. Cf., e.g., *Society and Spirit: A Trinitarian Cosmology* (Cranbury, N.J.: Associated University Presses, 1991), 123-39; *The Divine Matrix: Creativity as Link between East and West* (Maryknoll, N.Y.: Orbis, 1995), 52-69; *The One in the Many*, 126-30, 146-51.

11. Thomas Aquinas, *Summa Theologiae*, I, Q. 29, a. 4 resp.

12. See *Society and Spirit*, 140-60.

13. See Charles Hartshorne, *Creative Synthesis and Philosophic Method* (La Salle, Ill.: Open Court Publ., 1970), xv; by the same author, "Whitehead's Idea of God," *The Philosophy of Alfred North Whitehead*, 2nd ed., ed. Paul Arthur Schlipp (New York: Tudor

considered a superordinate field of activity which overlaps and encompasses the field of activity proper to the world along the lines of a soul-body metaphor. That is, God as the "soul" of the universe is omnipresent to all finite societies of actual occasions in their respective fields of activity and orders them to one another and to God's own self.[14] The task is somewhat more difficult for someone who adheres to Whitehead's own conception of God as a transcendent actual entity whose process of concrescence is never-ending. For in that case the field proper to God as the transcendent actual entity would logically have to be what Whitehead calls the "extensive continuum," that is, "one relational complex in which all potential objectifications find their niche. It [the extensive continuum] underlies the whole world, past, present, and future" (PR 66). Insofar as God and all finite actual entities in Whitehead's view share a common world (PR 65), their common field of activity must be the extensive continuum. Likewise, insofar as "God and the World are the contrasted opposites in terms of which Creativity achieves its supreme task of transforming disjoined multiplicity, with its diversities in opposition, into concrescent unity, with its diversities in contrast" (PR 348), one must presuppose a common field of activity for God and finite actual entities in their dynamic interrelation.

Yet, as indicated above, a trinitarian understanding of God from within a process perspective has a distinct advantage in setting forth a field-oriented approach to the God-world relationship. By their dynamic interrelation the three divine persons of the Christian doctrine of the Trinity co-create the primordial field or "divine matrix" within which the fields proper to societies of finite actual entities can be hierarchically ordered. One has, in effect, created a conceptual scheme in which there are structured fields of activity or "systems," as already noted, at all levels of existence and activity. But there is still another advantage to be gained in employing such a trinitarian approach to the

---

Publ., 1951), 549-50; also David R. Griffin, "Hartshorne's Differences from Whitehead," *Two Process Philosophers: Hartshorne's Encounter with Whitehead* [AAR Studies in Religion, no. 5] (Tallahassee: American Academy of Religion, 1973), 36.

14. See Charles Hartshorne, "The Compound Individual," *Philosophical Essays for Alfred North Whitehead*, ed. F. S. C. Northrup (New York: Russell & Russell, 1936), 218-20; likewise, *Man's Vision of God and the Logic of Theism* (Hamden, Conn.: Archon Books, 1964), 174-211.

God-world relationship: namely, the way in which it helps to solve the second conceptual problem within Suchocki's scheme. Suchocki stipulated that upon incorporation into the divine consequent nature finite actual occasions aggregate into a cosmic community, "an ultimate and transforming togetherness which confirms and redeems finite reality" (103). But if this community of redeemed finite actual entities constitutes the divine consequent nature, what is the relationship of God as the primordial or transcendent actual entity to these finite actual entities? Is God, as Suchocki claims, "the Immediacy of immediacies, and a Harmony of Harmonies" (106) for their dynamic interrelation, in which case "God" seems to be only a collective term for the reality of the community? Or if, as Suchocki likewise claims, God's subjective aim governs the way in which the finite actual entities relate to one another so as to make up a genuine community rather than simply a discordant aggregate of clashing finite subjectivities, then what is the relationship of God as such an independent divine subjectivity to these created subjectivities?

To resolve this ambiguity in Suchocki's (and, as we have seen, likewise in Whitehead's own) understanding of the God-world relationship, I make appeal once again to my own trinitarian scheme in which the world of creation, that is, all the interlocking and hierarchically ordered societies of finite actual entities, takes its rise and continues to exist within the divine matrix or structured field of activity proper to the three divine persons. For, on the one hand, this means that the three divine persons are ontologically independent of the world of creation; they do not require an ongoing relationship either with this world or with any other world in order to exist as a divine community. But, on the other hand, this also means that the world of creation is an objective reality in its own right, sustained by the power of God in virtue of the divine matrix but still ontologically independent of the three divine persons for its own existence and activity. The three divine persons and all their creatures, in other words, must be said to co-exist within the divine matrix. The divine matrix is the power of being in the first place for the three divine persons. But in the second place by reason of a conjoint decision on the part of the divine persons to bring finite subjectivities into existence, the divine matrix is the power of being for all finite subjectivities in their relations with one another and with the divine persons. The divine matrix, accordingly, is the common ground where the three divine persons and all their creatures can intersubjectively be engaged with one another without loss of individual identity or ontological integrity.

This is unquestionably a significant departure from orthodox process philosophy and theology. Within the metaphysical schemes of both Whitehead and Charles Hartshorne, for example, God is seen as the only enduring reality. Actual occasions are progressively incorporated into the divine consequent nature according to Whitehead and acquire thereby objective immortality. But the world of creation is by definition new at every moment and therefore subject to "perpetual perishing" (PR 340). For Hartshorne, God as the "soul" of the world likewise serves as the living memory of events past within the world process, but the world as the "body" of God is never the same from moment to moment. In her laudable efforts to legitimate belief in subjective immortality at least for human beings, if not for all finite subjectivities, within a process-relational frame of reference, Suchocki took a dramatic step forward in proposing that God prehends finite actual occasions in their moment of "enjoyment" and confers on them subjective immortality through incorporation into the divine consequent nature. But, as I have tried to make clear in this essay, her hypothesis is still too timid, insufficiently critical of the work of her philosophical mentor, Alfred North Whitehead, and other Whiteheadians. My aim here, accordingly, has been to develop further what was only hinted at in Suchocki's own work, namely, to reconceive Whitehead's subject-object approach to prehension of other actual entities in such a way as eventually to allow for a subject-subject relationship between societies of such actual entities and therewith by degrees to transform Whitehead's philosophy into a *bona fide* metaphysics of universal intersubjectivity.

One further point can be made before concluding. For, there is still another conceptual problem with Suchocki's scheme which I believe can be remedied by recourse to my own reinterpretation of Whitehead's philosophy. In fidelity to Whitehead's dictum that "the final real things of which the world is made up" are actual occasions (PR 18), Suchocki provides for the subjective immortality of individual actual occasions within the consequent nature of God, as indicated above. But this raises the problem of the so-called "million Marjories." Each actual occasion enjoys its own sense of transformation and peace within the larger ontological reality of the divine consequent nature. Yet how are all these individual actual occasions linked to one another so as to constitute the unitary reality of the redeemed human person in God? For that matter, how are the actual occasions constitutive of the human body and other societies of actual occasions, both animate and inanimate, thereby incorporated into the divine consequent nature so as to enjoy in their own measure eternal life? From a Christian perspective, what is at stake here is both the classical belief in the resurrection of the body as opposed to the simple immortality of the soul and the equally strong belief in the redemption of the material order, the new creation (Rev. 21:1-4), at the end of the world. A full treatment of this topic would require still another article.[15] But the link with the intersubjective metaphysical scheme which I have laid out above can be briefly set forth here.

If one treats Whiteheadian societies as structured fields of activity for their constituent actual occasions and if these structured fields of activity endure as individual occasions or sets of occasions come and go, then what is incorporated into the divine matrix or divine field of activity from moment to moment within the present temporal order is not the individual actual occasion or momentary nexus of occasions but the field with its structural pattern and feeling-tone, as noted above. For, what is important for the self-identity of the society in question (e.g., the human soul or mind) is not the individual occasion or momentary nexus of occasions but the field to which the individual occasion or nexus of occasions contributes both its structural pattern and feeling-tone. There must always exist, to be sure, an individual actual occasion or nexus of such occasions within the field so as to give a subjective focus to the field here and now and to keep adding to its overall structure and feeling-tone. But, in the final analysis, the individual actual occasion or momentary nexus of occasions is simply the latest actualization of the field, the latest member of the society in question.

Given this line of thought, then the problem of the "million Marjories" disappears and one has the theoretical basis for affirming the resurrection of the body and therewith the progressive redemp-

15. See my article "Intersubjectivity and the Coming of God," *Journal of Religion* 83 (2003): 381-400.

tion of the material order. For, in terms of the personally ordered society of actual occasions constitutive of the soul or mind of a human being, one can then say that, while during the entire lifetime of that same human being on earth the field proper to his/her mind or soul was progressively being incorporated into the divine matrix, only the actual occasion occurring at the moment of death would realize that this has indeed taken place and for the first time take full possession of the field to which it belongs within the divine matrix. It would for the first time become fully conscious of its self-identity in God and thereby experience, as Suchocki claims for the individual actual occasion, "transformation, redemption and peace" (109). That is, the occasion would forever remain what it chose to be at the moment of death. But it would never stop growing in its appreciation and acceptance of what God accomplished through it and its predecessors in the same personally ordered society within the broader cosmic process.

In similar fashion, one can logically affirm that the body of that same human being as a highly complex structured society of sub-societies of actual occasions will likewise possess a final nexus of actual occasions at the moment of death when bodily integrity dissolves. These actual occasions, while not experiencing self-awareness in the manner available to the actual occasions constituting the mind or soul, will nevertheless become aware of their bodily self-identity in a new way. That is, they will experience themselves as the natural culmination of a growth process which is reflected both in the structure and feeling-tone of the finite field(s) of activity to which they immediately belong and in the structure and feeling-tone of the divine matrix into which they are now incorporated. Only the final actual occasions constitutive of the body at the moment of death, therefore, will experience this transformation, but such a transformation or "resurrection" will inevitably involve a strong sense of bodily integrity from the first moment of conception to the final moment of death. Furthermore, by the same logic all the final actual occasions constitutive of animate and inanimate societies which for whatever reason have ceased to exist anywhere within the created order will experience some limited sense of "transformation, redemption and peace" as they take their rightful place within the divine matrix. In brief, then, while all the structured fields of activity proper to the world of creation are without exception continuously being incorporated into the divine matrix, only those occasions proper to the final moment of a given society will experience this transformation into the divine life. The transformation of the material universe through incorporation into the divine life is thus a reality both "already" and "not yet" achieved. As Whitehead himself claimed at the close of *Process and Reality*, "[w]hat is done in the world is transformed into a reality in heaven, and the reality of heaven passes back into the world" through the continuation of a cosmic process which has not yet reached its final end (PR 351).

God's Advent/ure: The End of Evil and the Origin of Time

Roland Faber

Marjorie Suchocki's eschatology *The End of Evil* is truly an astonishing fulfillment of the endeavor to formulate process eschatology.[1] Within a framework that does not know of any "end" of the world, at least a world as we know it, she speaks of the *Eschaton* of the world and in an important sense of the Eschaton of *all* worlds, characterized by one of its most prominent hallmarks: the "end of evil."[2] The "eschatological world" — whatever else it might be — will not be defined by "evil": the "end of evil," hence, is the end of *any* "world" we can imagine in the series of cosmic epochs that is delineated by what we consider to be the basic features of "world": time, inheritance, and decision. Nevertheless, it will be a *world*, that is, not purely identical with God or vanish into nothingness.[3] Although there will remain a unified plurality of actualities, it will be freed of evil.

However, we ask: What might this eschatological world be like

---

1. Cf. M. Suchocki, *The End of Evil: Process Eschatology in Historical Context* (Albany: SUNY, 1988).

2. For process theology's basic problems with the "end of the world" cf. J. B. Cobb and D. R. Griffin, *Process Theology: An Introductory Exposition* (Philadelphia: Westminster Press, 1976), 111-127.

3. The problem of the "identification" of God and world or the "disappearance" of their difference arises in Pannenberg and Altizer, although for different reasons. Cf. Th. J. J. Altizer, "Theology and the Death of God," in Th. J. J. Altizer and W. Hamilton, eds., *Radical Theology and the Death of God* (Indianapolis: Bobbs-Merrill, 1966), 95-112; W. Pannenberg, *Wissenschaftstheorie und Theologie* (Frankfurt: Suhrkamp, 1987), 111f.

so that it, while deprived of evil conditions (probably even of the possibility of being in evil conditions) and the ability to carry out evil acts, still is to be named "world"?[4] What kind of world could we think of as being without time, inheritance, decision, and freedom?[5] The end of evil, indeed, is a challenge to a process framework.[6] In following some of the most interesting insights of Suchocki's eschatology, I intend to explore the possibility and theological importance of the "end of evil" by explaining *the* Eschaton to be the *origin* of time (becoming and perishing), inheritance (causation), and decision (freedom of choice and determination) rather than to appear as their (world-destroying) "end."[7]

1. The End of Evil

In Suchocki's eschatology, five important theological conditions and metaphysical presuppositions shape her proposition of an "end of evil." First, Suchocki's God essentially is eschatological reality.[8] Similar to Lewis Ford's, Wolfhart Pannenberg's, and Jürgen Moltmann's God of the future, God reveals Godself as "power of the future," relating itself to the world *from* its future or more precisely: its *eschatological future*.[9] Other than in Ford, Suchocki's God is not ever-future creativity, pluralizing itself into present occasions, themselves passing into past occasions, but a primordial superject that, with regard to the world, offers itself as their possibilities. Other than in Pannenberg and Moltmann, the "power of the future" endlessly receives the past world

4. For the contemporary background of the eschatological question for the "end of the world" cf. D. Fergusson, "Eschatology," in C. Gunton, ed., *The Cambridge Companion to Christian Doctrine* (Cambridge: CUPress, 1997), 226-244.

5. Cf. P. Fiddes, *The Promised End: Eschatology in Theology and Literature*, Challenges in Contemporary Theology (Oxford: Blackwell, 2000).

6. Cf. D. R. Griffin, *Evil Revisited: Responses and Reconsiderations* (Albany: SUNY, 1991), passim.

7. Cf. R. Faber, *Gott als Poet der Welt: Anliegen und Perspektiven der Prozesstheologie* (Darmstadt: Wissenschaftliche Buchgesellschaft, 2003), 230-244.

8. Cf. Suchocki, *End*, 135-152.

9. Cf. W. Pannenberg, *Systematic Theology*, vol. 3 (Grand Rapids: Eerdmans, 1998); J. Moltmann, *The Coming of God: Christian Eschatology* (Minneapolis: Fortress Press, 1996); L. S. Ford, *Transforming Process Theism* (Albany: SUNY, 2000).

into God's eschatological nature without ending the series of cosmic epochs in a final event named Eschaton.[10] Suchocki's eschatological God is an eschatological process that captures the world in its agony, thereby transforming the world into God's reality — everlastingly growing by the world God saves.

Second, the Divine structure that allows for Suchocki's eschatological God is the *reversal of the poles*.[11] In Whiteheadian terms, God is bipolar: God provides the world with its possibilities out of the wealth of God's primordial infinitude of possibilities that, in God's creative process of valuation, is God's primordial nature. And God preserves the outcome of the becoming world (in the infinite creation of ever-new actualities) by God's encompassing receptivity that, in God's just valuation of the decisions of the creatures, is God's consequent nature. God is provision for the world and preservation of its becoming.[12] While, in a certain sense, every occasion begins with its mental pole but really becomes from its reception of its world that it inherits by the physical pole, God in an absolute sense begins with God's mental pole, God's primordial nature.[13] This is the "reversal of the poles."[14] God's mental pole is the *origin* of God beyond any world and independent of all worlds. In God's primordial nature, God's primordiality is infinite and un-preformed by anything except God who *decides* the infinite chaos of possibilities as process of valuation; that is God's subjectivity. In Suchocki's assessment of the reversal, the primordial nature in being the origin of God sheds light on the *alterity* of God's process as not only originating in the infinite mental pole but, thereby, having the unconditioned ability to comprise the world in God's physical prehensions.[15] Because of God's infinite subjective process of self-valuation, God's receptive process — the transforma-

---

10. Cf. M. Suchocki, *God — Christ — Church: A Practical Guide to Process Theology* (New York: Continuum, 1995), 183-226.

11. Cf. Suchocki, *End*, 137-139.

12. Cf. Suchocki, *God*, 28-36.

13. Cf. A. N. Whitehead, *Process and Reality: An Essay in Cosmology*, corr. ed., ed. by D. R. Griffin and D. W. Sherburne (New York: Free Press, 1978), 36, 75, 87, 224, 345, 348.

14. Cf. M. Suchocki, "The Metaphysical Ground of the Whiteheadian God," *Process Studies* 5/4 (1975): 237ff.

15. Cf. ibid., 237-246.

tion of the world into God's consequent nature — can be all-inclusive, all-perceptive, and just.[16] Because of the reversal of the poles, God's eschatological nature can face, suffer, transform, and heal the evil of the world.[17] This consequent nature (in the reversal of the poles), indeed, is the "end of evil" and — what Whitehead calls — the everlasting "kingdom of heaven" beyond the characteristics of any world in the series of cosmic epochs: their time (becoming and perishing), inheritance (causation), and decision (freedom of choice and determination).[18]

Third, God saves the past world into the "presence" of the kingdom of heaven by the gift of *subjective immortality* as the state of every occasion in God's consequent nature.[19] Subjective immortality — other than the objective immortality of which Whitehead speaks regarding the relevance of past occasions in the becoming of other occasions in the world[20] — means that God saves every occasion from being purely lost in the history of the world. In God's eschatological nature, immortality is *subjective* because God revives the occasions *themselves* in their immediacy in the memory of God rather than only valuating their "pastness" as being important for other occasions' becoming — and be it in God's collection of the "perfect" world.[21] In being subjective, the immortality of an occasion reconciles its immediacy with the value it has gained in its perishing as "perfect" superject of its existence. Hence, its "being" in God is not just that of an "object" for God's prehension but also that of an "immediate superject." This paradoxical state is the status of the occasion's redemption: that it is a *superject* whose becoming is finished and whose being is "perfect," that is, devoid of time and any further causation and decision, *and* that it, nevertheless, exists in a certain mode of subjective imme-

---

16. Cf. H. Maassen, *Gott, das Gute und das Böse in der Philosophie A. N. Whiteheads,* EHS, vol. 20/236 (Frankfurt: Peter Lang, 1988), 143-149.

17. Cf. R. Faber, "Messianische Zeit: Walter Benjamins 'mystische Geschichtsauffassung' in zeittheologischer Perspektive," *Muenchner Theologische Zeitschrift* 54 (2003): 68-78.

18. Cf. Whitehead, *Process,* 350, cf. 346. Cf. Suchocki, *God,* 199-216.

19. Cf. Suchocki, *End,* 81-96.

20. Cf. Whitehead, *Process,* 29, 60, 82, 223.

21. Cf. L. Ford and M. Suchocki, "A Whiteheadian Reflection on Subjective Immortality," *Process Studies* 7/1 (1977): 1-13.

diacy in which it enjoys itself as a prehension of God's kingdom.[22] Indeed, in this state, a redeemed occasion is "itself" — even more "itself" than it was as long as it was in becoming — and, hence, is not an "occasion" of the world anymore. An occasion in its subjective immortality *lives* beyond its becoming and being, beyond itself and all others; it exists in "ex-static self-transcendence" that, at the same time, is its final identity.[23]

Fourth, Suchocki allows for a new interpretation of salvation as *self-transcendence* by understanding the heavenly kingdom of the consequent nature as *transpersonal emptiness*.[24] Because redeemed occasions exist in "self-transcendent identity," God transforms their "essence" (relationality) from their settings in the "creative order" of societies and personalities in the world of their becoming into a transpersonal peace.[25] By the deconstruction of the societies and personalities, which are the battlefield of order and novelty, becoming and perishing, inheritance and decision, good and evil, God really *transforms* the world into the Eschaton.[26] The transpersonal transformation is the eschatological process by which the world "becomes" the kingdom of God and every occasion "is itself, all other occasions, and God."[27] This eschatological process harbors the overcoming of the world by ending all evil that has haunted the world in its intercommunicative structures. In God, the redemptive process transcends all structures (and their inherent evil) into a trans-structural immediacy of all occasions with themselves, all others, and God. As eschatological peace, this transformation into God's self-transcendent emptiness is *life beyond "becoming"* (as in the series of the cosmic epochs), but also without inhibition of universal communication and mutual immanence.

Fifth, these features of Suchocki's eschatological God ground in

22. Cf. Whitehead, *Process*, 350f.

23. Cf. R. Faber, "Zeit. Tod. Neuheit. Gedaechtnis — Eschatologie als Zeittheologie, part 1: Zeit und Tod," *Freiburger Zeitschrift für Philosophie und Theologie* 49/1-2 (2002): 189-213.

24. Cf. M. Suchocki, "The Anatman and the Consequent Nature," in Center for Process Studies, *Papers of the Buddhism-Conference of the CPS* (Claremont: CPS-files, 1978), 2-5.

25. Cf. Suchocki, *End*, 110.

26. Cf. Suchocki, *God*, 205.

27. Suchocki, "Anatman," 5.

her understanding of God as *primordial superject*, which includes a new concept of God's "primordial satisfaction" and brings forth a new understanding of God's "creative effectiveness" in the world.[28] The condition to conceptualize God as primordial superject is to understand God's process as everlasting satisfaction. Other than any world-occasion, God's "actuality" is satisfied in originating from an infinite mental pole that is the measure of every intensity whatsoever, but unmeasured by any measure.[29] God's infinite intensity does not need (and not even allow for) any subjective aim to be reached by God's process in order to gain satisfaction. On the contrary, since God's infinite intensity reaches beyond any possible process to be fulfilled, aim to be reached, and satisfaction to be gained, God's satisfaction is primordial.[30] Hence, God's subjective aim is "perfected" and — in reversal of the poles that follows from this infinity of the mental pole — directed towards the world: *its* intensity, *its* well-being, *its* satisfaction.[31] Moreover, God's physical pole, while being in constant "movement" by the integration of the world's satisfied processes, is an everlasting transformation *within* God's infinite satisfaction rather than a transformation *into* God's satisfaction. In its directedness towards the world, God's superjectivity "effects" the world's creative process with all-encompassing wisdom and concrete understanding, without being "perfected" (unmovable) and "perfect" (lost in the past). In God's everlasting presence, satisfaction neither needs final determination of the process that is God nor demands objectivity as loss of subjective immediacy so as to be effective for the becoming of the world's occasions.[32]

2. Eschatological Realms

With these five features of Suchocki's eschatological God, the "end of evil" truly marks *the* Eschaton: the "end" of any world as we know it as conditioned by evil; the "end" as just reconciliation of the evil deci-

---

28. Suchocki, *End*, 138-143.
29. Whitehead, *Process*, 47.
30. Cf. Suchocki, "Ground," 241.
31. Suchocki, *End*, 144f.
32. Suchocki, "Ground," 244ff.

sions and effects in the world-process; the "end" of the series of cosmic epochs as the realm of time, inheritance, and decision. However, we may ask: What does it all *mean?* What is the world all about when its "aim" is its "end"? What sense does a process make that needs to be redeemed beyond itself to gain its final identity? Especially within Whitehead's process framework, the question must arise: Is the Eschaton, the "final end" of evil (the end of the conditions of its rise and the reconciliation of its destructions), what Whitehead wants us to think about the meaning of his analysis of process? While being theologically satisfying, the Eschaton seems to be contradictory in relation to Whitehead's world-centeredness: Does his assessment, philosophy being concerned with "*the* Universe," not imply that "the *Process*" is the final aim of his cosmology rather than all process's end in a final Eschaton?[33] What the "end of evil" in Suchocki's theology ends is, indeed, in Whitehead's eyes, the *condition* for the process to appear — although it might, at the same time, allow for evil to arise.[34] All three characteristics of the world-process — time, causation, and decision — mark the potentialities of evil to arise, but, at the same time, the process perpetually to proliferate. The end of evil is the end of the process: But why, then, has it begun in the first place?

Time is the most basic condition for the process: it is becoming and perishing; and becoming and perishing belong to the most basic features of the world-process as "process of processes."[35] Actualities, in their immediacy, arise in time, although in non-physical time, and perish, thereby producing quanta of physical time.[36] A universe without time is no universe, or at least: no universe as process.[37] However, time is also the most basic feature of the rise of evil; even more, its most basic manifestation: perpetual perishing, the loss of immediacy and subjectivity, the vanishing of the past.[38]

---

33. Cf. A. N. Whitehead, *Adventures of Ideas* (New York: Free Press, 1967), 150.

34. Cf. Whitehead, *Process*, 340; cf. *Adventures*, 259.

35. Whitehead, *Process*, 22. From Whitehead's early *Concept of Nature* (repr. Cambridge: Cambridge UP, 1993) on, time has become the most decisive feature for the specific structures of process. Cf. *Adventures*, 295: "process" is the "temporal advance" of the world.

36. Cf. Whitehead, *Process*, 283ff.

37. Cf. Whitehead, *Adventures*, 295.

38. Cf. Cobb and Griffin, *Process Theology*, 121.

Causation is *the* elementary relation in the temporal world.[39] Over against the philosophical tradition of Descartes, Hume, and Kant, Whitehead was most eager to demonstrate that all relations within the universe ground in *real* interconnectedness rather than projection.[40] His revolutionary concept of prehension cuts through every subjectivist philosophy's dualistic abyss between experience and reality. Every actuality is an "occasion of experience," of the generation of immediacy out of an objective world that causally produces subjectivity, novelty, and continuity. Causation as repetition of satisfied occasions in new occasions lays the ground for structure, complexity, and organic evolution in the universe by demanding routes of inheritance to crystallize,[41] thereby leading to continuous reproductions of the past in an ever-becoming and permanently extending universe.[42] Nevertheless, causation is a basic condition for the rise of evil since it produces a "power of the past" to grow over against new impulses; it hinders unrealized possibilities to get a grip on the process so as to lead to new directions of the process. Evil may be interpreted as inheritance of a past that insists on and fortifies a certain order over against novelty, creativity, and the imaginations of freedom; it may bind us to repetition of bad decisions; it may deceive us to the chains of past patterns that oppose our advance into novelty, freedom, intensity, and satisfaction.[43]

Decision belongs to the heart of the concept of the "process of processes."[44] Every occasion is a decision among potentialities, a determination of itself within a past world that appears as its real potentiality and within a range of unrealized possibilities that allow for alternative ways of determination.[45] Neither does causation (real po-

---

39. For the analysis of the temporal/causal process cf. M. Hampe, *Die Wahrnehmungen der Organismen: Über die Voraussetzung einer naturalistischen Theorie der Erfahrung in der Metaphysik Whiteheads* (Göttingen, 1990), 116-167.

40. Cf. Whitehead, *Process*, xiii.

41. Cf. B. Kasprzik, "Whiteheads metaphysische Option," *Allgemeine Zeitschrift für Philosophie* 13 (1988): 19-36.

42. Cf. R. Wiehl, "Aktualität und Extensivität in Whiteheads Kosmo-Psychologie," in M. Hampe and H. Maassen, eds., *Die Gifford-Lectures. Materialien zu Whiteheads 'Prozess und Realität'*, vol. 2 (Frankfurt: Suhrkamp, 1991), 313-368.

43. Cf. Suchocki, *God*, 14-27.

44. Cf. R. Rorty, "Matter and Event," in L. Ford and G. Kline, eds., *Explorations in Whitehead's Philosophy* (New York: Fordham UP, 1983), 68-103.

45. Cf. Whitehead, *Process*, 22f.

tentiality) determine the process completely, nor can forms (pure possibilities) actualize the occasion. The "essence" of the occasion's actuality is solely its decision.[46] Because of the decision of the occasion about its own becoming, satisfaction, past, and causation manifest the universe as *history* rather than as a machine. In being decision, process is profoundly creative and, in its end (although relative to its position within the history of the universe), free.[47] Nevertheless, we must see freedom of decision as the most important condition for the constitution of the most deadly form of evil: the conscious decision to commit evil acts.[48] Again, the very condition of the process to be process is, at the same time, the most problematic basis for the process fundamentally to be shaped by evil.

It is central to Suchocki's *The End of Evil* to recognize Whitehead's consciousness of this nexus between process and evil.[49] Especially in *Adventures of Ideas*, Whitehead reflects on this nexus of process and evil.[50] Process as fusion of infinity with the finite, of becoming with perishing, of imaginative novelty with the pain of its imprisonment in historical conditions, not allowing for its realization, generates beauty and evil — one might be tempted to say — necessarily at once. Imperfection and discord belong to the process as such.[51] So, how can we wish to gain an "end of evil" without losing the most vital characteristics of the universe? To be a process of intensities and extensities, of which we think in categories of "aim," *per definitionem* means to chant its creativity rather than its end. "End" seems to be tantamount to the "end of process," the "end of creativity," the "end of the world" — the *disappearance* of the process as such.

However, Whitehead is cautious in drawing such precipitatous conclusions for he, in fact, develops a notion of *the* "end" (of creation, of evil) while entertaining conceptions of "eschatological realms" that, although they connote the end of evil, are *not* the end of the world's

---

46. Cf. G. Deleuze, *The Fold: Leibniz and the Baroque* (Minneapolis: University of Minnesota Press, 1993), 76-82.

47. Cf. L. Ford, "Afterword," in Ford and Kline, eds., *Explorations*, 305-345.

48. Suchocki, *God*, 25.

49. Suchocki, *End*, 61-80.

50. Whitehead, *Adventures*, 258f.

51. Ibid., 257.

process.[52] In *Process and Reality* this appears as paradox: although Whitehead refers to the end of evil as the "final end of creation,"[53] he knows of at least *three* "eschatological realms" that, while beyond the evil and temporal state of this cosmic epoch, still are "world."[54]

First, Whitehead imagines the realm of a coming *cosmic epoch* on which temporality, as we know it, does not impose its basic evil character of perpetual perishing anymore: "Why should there not be novelty without loss of this direct unison of immediacy among things [in the present]?"[55] For this "eschatological realm," Whitehead assumes a divine reconciliation of preserved immediacy and perpetual novelty without the loss of immediacy into the past (mere objective immortality). This "cosmic epoch" would be of significantly different character in relation to the temporal character of the series of cosmic epochs for which the "metaphysical characteristics" of time (becoming and perishing), causation, and decision apply.[56]

Second, Whitehead reaches beyond any *temporal* world into the "eschatological realm" of the consequent nature of God in its function to be *the* symbol of the end of evil — the *kingdom of God*.[57] Here, God revives the lost immediacy of the perished occasions in time. In God's consequent nature, Whitehead boldly states, there will be "no loss, no obstruction," but a "retention of mutual immediacy"[58] of all occasions. "In everlastingness, immediacy is reconciled with objective immortality."[59] In God's eschatological nature, God transmutes every "temporal actuality" into "a living, ever-present fact."[60] Clearly, while beyond any world of time, causation, and decision, the everlastingness in God's kingdom is the eschatological *life* of resurrected occasions in universal communication with all occasions of their personal societies (as their personal identity), all other occasions (in mutual self-

---

52. Cf. R. Faber, *Prozesstheologie: Zu ihrer Wuerdigung und kritischen Erneuerung* (Mainz: Gruenewald, 2000), 574-585.

53. Whitehead, *Process*, 349.

54. Cf. Faber, *Poet*, 242-244.

55. Whitehead, *Process*, 340.

56. Cf. ibid., 91f.

57. Cf. ibid., 350; cf. Cobb and Griffin, *Process Theology*, 118-124.

58. Whitehead, *Process*, 346.

59. Ibid., 351.

60. Ibid., 350.

transcendence and immanence) and God.[61] For this realm of the kingdom, a new notion of subjectivity/superjectivity must apply: that of an everlastingly *self-transcendent subjectivity* that is everlastingly *living superjectivity*.[62]

Third, Whitehead even thinks of a *final realm* that reconciles what the first two "eschatological realms" still divide. With the "eschatological epoch" and the "kingdom of God," a dichotomy of realms remains. Either we may think of them as "existing" together ("at the same time"), or we may understand the "kingdom of God" as being coextensive to all cosmic epochs.[63] Nevertheless, Whitehead must have felt the dichotomy of this conception when he recognized that the "eschatological reconciliation" must reach beyond the bifurcation of perished occasions and their Divine prehension in God. As reconciliation of their lost identity in the history of the temporal world (objective immortality) *and* their transcended identity as moment of God's experience (Divine prehension), Whitehead proposes that the past occasions *themselves* will experience salvation in God's prehension.[64] He boldly states that "the *temporal occasions* are completed by their *everlasting union* with *their transformed selves*" in the "final absolute 'wisdom'"[65] of God. Here, the eschatological unison really reaches even *beyond the difference* of the temporal world (and be it a world without perishing) and the kingdom of God.

3. The Conversion of Processes

All "eschatological realms" invoke a true life of "temporal occasions" *beyond* the conditions for evil, beyond time, causation, and decision in "everlasting identity" — beyond becoming, but as living fact; beyond

61. Cf. Suchocki, *God*, 202ff.

62. Cf. R. Faber, "Apocalypse in God: On the Power of God in Process Eschatology," *Process Studies* 31/2 (2002): 67-76.

63. The difference between the cosmic past of the occasions "themselves" and their prehension in God as moment of God's consequent nature remains; cf. W. Christian, *An Interpretation of Whitehead's Metaphysics*, 2nd ed. (New Haven: Yale UP, 1967), 368-370.

64. Cf. Faber, *Poet*, 244.

65. Whitehead, *Process*, 347; italics added.

causation, but in mutual transformation; beyond decision, but in satis-fied enjoyment. Still, the *difference* of temporality and everlastingness remains. The question is: How do time and everlastingness relate to one another? Especially the "third realm" detects the deficit: the (miss-ing) *unification* of time and everlastingness into "everlasting union."[66] This would be *the* Eschaton, the "final end of creation," where the di-chotomy vanishes and redemption is the expression of this final unifi-cation of the history of the world — or, for that matter, of all worlds (cosmic epochs) — and the history of the worlds in God. On the other hand, if the Eschaton really ends all worlds in the *unification of the differ-ence* of time and everlastingness: Why does the *difference* of time and everlastingness, God and world, primordial and consequent nature of God remain at all? In other words: Why creation, in the first place?

Whitehead answers with his dual eschatology:[67] that the *final Advent* of God, the Eschaton, is, at the same time, the *supreme Adven-ture* of God with the world, the *origin* of the creative process.[68] In *Pro-cess and Reality*, Whitehead connotes the "final end of creation" with the "complete adjustment of the immediacy of joy" and the end of suffering.[69] In this redemptive state, the "end is existence in the per-fect unity"[70] of immediacy and objective immortality in the "per-fected system"[71] of the Divine wisdom.[72] Nevertheless, even if the "final end" reaches beyond the duality of the temporal world and the kingdom of God, it never appears to be the "end of creation" *as such.* On the contrary, the "end of creation" as the end of suffering para-doxically *demands* the ongoing temporal advance of the creation — ac-cording to the "fourth phase" of the creative process at the end of *Pro-cess and Reality*: the "love of God for the world" flows back into the world whereby God is the "great companion" of the world.[73] In *Ad-ventures of Ideas*, Whitehead speaks of the "Final Fact"[74] and the "final

---

66. Ibid.
67. Cf. Faber, *Poet*, 237f.
68. Cf. Faber, "Apocalypse," 87-90.
69. Cf. Whitehead, *Process*, 349.
70. Ibid.
71. Ibid., 346.
72. Cf. ibid., 351.
73. Cf. ibid.
74. Whitehead, *Adventures*, 296.

Beauty"[75] of the world — clearly notions of the "end" of the temporal world beyond its evil and, for the same reason, temporal conditions. Nevertheless, he never embraced the view that the "Final Fact" really ends the world. On the contrary, the "final end"[76] appears to be the "initial Eros"[77] of the temporal world. Somehow, Whitehead seems to think that *the* Eschaton *initiates* creation as time, causation, and decision, rather than ends it.[78]

Obviously, this is the paradox. On the one hand, *the* Eschaton means the "Final Fact," "the final end of creation" "where suffering attains its end," the *final* "satisfaction" of the world-process. On the other hand, there is a presence of this end *within* the process both as its creative initiation (as Eros) and as the feeling of its everlasting reconciliation (as Peace).[79] Regarding a "balanced complexity,"[80] two main solutions to understand this paradox may fail. First, if we think of the Eschaton as an event in which the world ends and somehow disappears, we might gain understanding of the Eschaton as eschatological power affecting the ongoing process from the eschatological future, but this solution tends to annihilate the process when this Eschaton finally happens. The "Final Fact" would be the disappearance of the world (and God).[81] Second, if we think of *the* Eschaton as symbolizing the ongoing process[82] within a virtually infinite chain of cosmic epochs,[83] we might reinterpret God's eschatological power as creation of every occasion from its future (initial aim), but this solution tends to dissolve the Eschaton into an endless process that never gains final satisfaction.[84] The first solution resembles the eschatology of Pannenberg and Moltmann; the second solution seems to meet Lewis Ford's approach.[85] Both conceptions introduce God as *eschato-*

75. Ibid., 295.

76. Whitehead, *Process*, 349.

77. Whitehead, *Adventures*, 295.

78. Cf. Faber, *Poet*, 230-244.

79. Whitehead, ibid., 295f.

80. Whitehead, *Process*, 278.

81. Cf. T. J. J. Altizer, *The Gospel of Christian Atheism* (Philadelphia: The Westminster Press, 1966), 102-131.

82. Whitehead, *Process*, 350.

83. Ibid., 91f.

84. Cf. Cobb and Griffin, *Process Theology*, 118-124.

85. Cf. Faber, *Poet*, 230-244.

logical power that effects the world *from the future*, but they fail to accomplish a contrasted complexity: the *togetherness* of process and Eschaton, of "the Advance of the Temporal World" *and* the "Final Fact,"[86] of *advent* and *adventure*. Therefore, in a complex contrast, their togetherness must allow us to understand God's *eschatological* power to be *creative* of the world *from* its *final* future.[87]

In order to understand *the* Eschaton as the *creative* Eschaton, Suchocki's eschatological God may guide us. Her account rests on one of Whitehead's bold remarks on the nature of God and God's relation to the world, which — at the very end of *Process and Reality* — envisions God and world to be "in the grip of the . . . creative advance into novelty" by which either of them "is the instrument of novelty for each other."[88] In this creative interrelation, however, God and world "move conversely to each other."[89] Suchocki reads this passage as "reversal of the poles,"[90] that is, that God's process, unlike any world-process, *originates* not only from God's primordial nature but from its "primordial satisfaction," which grows in "everlasting concrescence."[91] As "everlasting concrescence," this God, indeed, is an *eschatological* reality that is beyond any creation but with infinite *receptivity* of the temporal creation; as "primordial satisfaction," however, God is the *origin* of the temporal creation. Because of the eschatological reality of God as "primordial superject," God originally self-transcends Godself to create the temporal world, and creation may not need to end in order to bring forth the kingdom of God.[92]

Nevertheless, this does not end the paradox. Although — through the *eschatological* nature of the superjectivity of God — God's kingdom is "present" within every cosmic epoch and in the creative process, without ending it,[93] the *duality* of temporal world and kingdom of God is maintained without ever reaching "the *final* end of cre-

86. Whitehead, *Adventures*, 295f.
87. Cf. R. Faber, "Zeitumkehr: Versuch über einen eschatologischen Schöpfungsbegriff," *Theologie und Philosophie* 75 (2000): 180-205.
88. Whitehead, *Process*, 349.
89. Ibid.
90. Cf. ibid., 348.
91. Cf. Suchocki, *End*, 141-146.
92. Cf. Suchocki, *God*, 198.
93. Cf. Whitehead, *Process*, 350f.

ation."[94] In order to understand *the* Eschaton not to be mere endless presence of initiation but to be *the* "end," we must aim beyond the *duality* of temporal world and kingdom of God — as the "third eschatological realm" has suggested.[95] We must even aim beyond the *difference* of primordial and consequent nature and their interaction that sustains the creative process as duality of time and everlastingness.[96]

For that reason, that is, to find a path to solve the paradox, I read Whitehead's phrase of the relation of the processes of God and the world, on which Suchocki built her "reversal of the poles," differently, namely as a proposition of a *radical inversion:* God and world, Whitehead says, "move *conversely* to each other *in every respect* to their process."[97] When God's process moves *conversely in every respect,* Whitehead's radical statement includes that God's concrescence and superjectivity not just happen *in reverse order,* but *in complete otherness* (although in intimate relation) to the world's process.[98] This is the thesis: the *complete inversion* of the processes *in every respect* may not appear prior to the recognition that they *coincide* in God.[99] This is the "conversion" of the processes: the radical inversion of God's process means the *non-difference* of what differs in creation — concrescence and transition, temporal world and kingdom of God. Now, in this radical form, God's primordial superjectivity reveals what we seek: the non-difference of time and everlastingness because of the *non-difference* of God's primordial and consequent nature — a non-difference that *originates* the process of *difference* in God and, based on the difference of God's natures, that of creation and salvation of the world.[100]

94. Ibid. 347; italics added. Cf. C. Keller, *Apocalypse Now and Then: A Feminist Guide to the End of the World* (Boston: Beacon Press, 1997).

95. Cf. Faber, *Poet,* 244.

96. Cf. R. Faber, "'Gottesmeer' — Versuch ueber die Ununterschiedenheit Gottes," in Th. Dienberg and M. Plattig, eds., *"Leben in Fuelle": Skizzen zur christlichen Spiritualitaet,* Theologie der Spiritualitaet, vol. 5 (Münster: Lit, 2001), 64-95.

97. Whitehead, *Process,* 349; italics added.

98. Cf. Faber, *Prozesstheologie,* 465-486. This "otherness" of God's process — although it appears beyond "process" — is still conceptualized within the same metaphysical notion of "process" that applies to the world.

99. Cf. R. Faber, "Trinity, Analogy and Coherence," in J. Bracken and M. Suchocki, eds., *Trinity in Process: A Relational Theology of God* (New York: Continuum, 1997), 147-171.

100. Cf. Faber, *Poet,* 136-143, 147.

Now, God's "superjective nature"[101] really *is* the "Final Fact" that, as "primordial superject of creativity,"[102] also is the *origin* of the creative process.[103] It is *final superjectivity* because it is *beyond* all differences of the processes; but as *creative primordiality*, it is the *origin* of all differences. In balanced complexity, the eschatological contrast states this: the "Final Fact" *creates* the world by *differentiating in creation what is non-different in God*. The Eschaton creates the process.

4. The Origin of Time

The eschatological thesis, now, is this: The Eschaton initiates the difference of "origin" and "end" because the superjective nature originates the difference between God's primordial and consequent nature. Hence, the Eschaton also initiates the difference between the temporal world (time, causation, and decision) and the everlasting perfection (livingness, transformation, and enjoyment). The question is this: When God is the non-difference of all differences in God (primordial and consequent nature), between God and world (time and everlastingness), and in the world (creativity and actuality), how can *the* Eschaton be *the* "origin of time" without becoming a new synonym for a *unilateral* creator of the world — a conception process theology strongly rejects?[104] How, if the superjective nature is beyond differences, can we avoid that God in God's absoluteness non-relationally sets the conditions for all communication whatsoever — even of Godself?[105]

Three insights in their combination will allow us avoiding this consequence. First, Whitehead's eschatological/creative notion of God as "primordial superject" in its radical understanding not only states the non-difference of subjectivity (self-causation) and objective

---

101. Whitehead, *Process*, 88.

102. Ibid., 32.

103. Cf. Faber, "Zeitumkehr," 195-201.

104. Cf. D. Griffin, *Reenchantment without Supernaturalism: A Process Philosophy of Religion*. Cornell Studies in the Philosophy of Religion (Ithaca: Cornell UP, 2001), 137-144.

105. Cf. C. Keller, *Face of the Deep: A Theology of Becoming* (London: Routledge, 2003), 3-24, 103-123.

immortality (other-causation), but produces a "converse process" that is the *inversion* of the relation of subjectivity and immortality as it is found in the world. While, in the world, satisfaction *ends* the subjective process, in God, it is the *origin* of its existence; and even more: it is the origin of all differences embracing God and world. While, in the world, superjectivity means self-transcendence *beyond* the subjective process, in God, it means the *origin* of all differences, which is self-transcendent precisely by *originating* subjectivity (self-causation) and immortality (other-causation).[106] Because of this inversion, by which the Divine superjectivity transcends itself *in* the difference of primordial and consequent nature, God opens an eschatological/creative space "between" God's primordial nature and consequent nature, which, by self-transcendently affecting the world-process,[107] originates time from the Eschaton.[108]

Second, we must not interpret the "superjective nature" of God as an absolute reality *beyond* God's "subjective natures"[109] (both primordial and consequent), but (by inverted superjectivity) as *total self-transcendence — into* the difference of God's natures, *into* the difference between God and world, and *into* all differences of the world.[110] The non-difference of God's primordial superjectivity is totally (that is, without reserve) *expressive* within the differences it originates. Hence, it is not a "third" reality "behind" the real differences, but is "real" by being the self-transcendent non-difference *of* the real differences.[111] It is neither identical with all that is in difference nor different from it, but as non-difference, it is the eschatological/creative space of its existence.

Third, Whitehead has a notion for this kind of non-different, self-transcendent space for all existence: the *chora* (Locus), the

106. Cf. Faber, *Poet*, 137-143.
107. Cf. Whitehead, *Process*, 32.
108. Cf. Faber, *Poet*, 161-170.
109. Cf. Whitehead, *Process*, 88.
110. Cf. R. Faber, " 'The Infinite Movement of Evanescence' — The Pythagorean Puzzle in Plato, Deleuze, and Whitehead," *American Journal of Theology and Philosophy* 21 (2000): 171-199.
111. Cf. R. Faber, "De-Ontologizing God: Levinas, Deleuze, and Whitehead," in C. Keller and A. Daniell, eds., *Process and Difference. Between Cosmological and Poststructuralist Postmodernism* (Albany: SUNY, 2002), 209-234.

hypodoche (Receptacle), the "Wherein" — based on a notion of Plato's *Timaios*.[112] The *chora* is Whitehead's notion of the *unity* of the universe — being "invisible, formless, and all-receptive."[113] It is formless emptiness, the all-relational space of communication, the "medium of intercommunication," and the "matrix of all things."[114] It is another name for "mutual immanence."[115] The *chora* is non-different from/ with/to all: it is neither identical with anything that exists within it nor different from anything of which it is the space of existence. In being formless emptiness, it does not impose itself or, for that matter, anything on the process of communication, although it is the origin of its existence. In being all-receptive, its unity does not force any particular togetherness, although nothing is "outside" its wholeness.[116]

The nexus of all three insights explicates the "end of evil" *as* "origin of time" without re-enthroning God, *the* Eschaton, as monological imperator.[117] The eschatological thesis is this: God's non-different superjectivity is self-transcendent, all-expressive, and empty; thereby, it is the condition of relationality without imposition.[118] In being *self-transcendent*, God's superjectivity is the eschatological/creative origin of all differences by providing a space of existence within the difference of God's primordial and consequent nature. In being *all-expressive*, this space is not referring to an absolute reality beyond all differences, but to an all-relational reality within the differences it originates, thereby providing communication. In being *empty*, this space of existence, which conditions communication, neither imposes the conditions of communication to be obeyed nor forces the directions of the decisions to be taken. In being *non-different* (self-transcendent, all-expressive, and empty), God's superjectivity, although it is the eschatological origin of difference, process, relationality, and, hence, of time, is neither absolute

---

112. Cf. Whitehead, *Adventures*, 187. Cf. Ch. Kann, *Fussnoten zu Platon: Philosophiegeschichte bei A. N. Whitehead*, Paradeigmata, vol. 23 (Hamburg: Meiner, 2001), 126-128.

113. Whitehead, *Adventures*, 187.

114. Ibid., 134. Cf. J. Bracken, *The Divine Matrix: Creativity as a Link between East and West* (New York: Orbis, 1995), 52-69.

115. Whitehead, *Adventures*, 201; cf. Faber, *Prozesstheologie*, 264-296.

116. Cf. Faber, *Poet*, 161-170, 244-251.

117. Cf. Whitehead, *Adventures*, 169.

118. Cf. Faber, *Poet*, 131-143, 191-204.

nor imposing, but all-relational and all-receptive — the "fostermother of all becoming."[119] God's eschatological/creative non-difference is the mother *chora*.

The creativeness of *the* Eschaton, reflected by the mother *chora*, resembles the *tsimtsum* in Isaak Luria's Kabbalah: In order to create, God *contracts* Godself, thereby originating a primordial space *within* God.[120] Somehow, this space, which is and, at the same time, is not God, can be identified neither with a "creation out of nothing" as in classical Christian theology[121] nor with a "creation out of chaos" as in the Platonic tradition.[122] In being the primordial non-difference of God as empty space of existence, it is somehow rather the "creation *of* nothingness."[123] The self-transcendent non-difference characterizes the Divine differences as *eschatological differences* and the space of existence as *eschatological space*. The mother *chora* is the *eschatological origin* of all communication, relationality, and process — and, hence, of the temporal world.[124]

However, a final question remains: How is *the* Eschaton precisely as *end of evil* the origin of time — so that it is not, at the same time, the origin of evil? I shall answer this question in three stages: reading the origin of time against its non-beginning; reading the end of evil as condition for the origin of time; and reading the theodicy as question directed to the *chora* as "nothingness of existence." All three steps refer to my departure from Suchocki's eschatology: the "conversion of processes,"[125] though — as I think — following her intention radically.[126]

First, while God's superjectivity is the non-difference of God's natures, in the *chora* — "in between" the difference of God's natures

---

119. Ibid., 134.

120. Cf. J. Moltmann, *God in Creation: A New Theology of Creation and the Spirit of God* (Minneapolis: Fortress, 1993), 87; cf. M. Hallamish, *An Introduction to the Kabbalah* (Albany: SUNY, 1999), 197-201.

121. Cf. Whitehead, *Adventures*, 236.

122. Cf. Whitehead, *Process*, 95.

123. Cf. Faber, *Poet*, 191-204.

124. Cf. ibid., 230-244.

125. Cf. Faber, "Trinity," 162; *Prozesstheologie*, 452-465; *Poet*, 137-143.

126. *In nuce*, the basic features of Suchocki's eschatology were already interpreted in her early article "The Metaphysical Ground of Whitehead's God" (1975).

and the world from God — the "con-version" happens as "processes in opposition" that constitute *two times*.[127] God's "eschatological time" comes from the future of creation and runs into the past of creation, whereas the world's "creative time" comes from the past and runs into the future. For the world, God's primordiality appears as its "future" (and in its future); for God, the world's satisfaction, which is the world's past (and in its past), is God's "future." The creative Eschaton crosses and touches the creation in every one of its accidents, but moves in the opposite direction.[128] Hence, in eschatological time, God's primordial nature initiates creative time *ex nihilo*, that is, out of absolute novelty,[129] and God's consequent nature redeems the past world. Because of this inversion, creative time has no absolute origin in its temporal past and no absolute end in its temporal future.[130] Whereas the world — on its way into the future — may await God as "absolute future" to be the end of time, in fact, God's primordial nature is the "absolute novelty" that, as future (and from the temporal future), *initiates* time indefinitely. And while the world may await redemption from/in the future as end of time, in fact, God's consequent nature is the redemptive Eschaton that happens to the *past* world (in the past of time).[131]

Second, while in God's superjectivity the "conversion of processes" is manifest as non-difference of God's natures, for the world, God's superjectivity happens *in the difference* of God's primordial and consequent nature, which originates the *chora* — the space of the nothingness of intercommunication *in* God *for* the world, and, hence, between God and world. The *chora* (in eschatological time) is the Divine origin and end of the temporal world, which in itself (in creative time) has no temporal beginning and end. Hence, the *chora* reveals a life-circle of God and the world in which God's *different* natures *mediate* the world through God's *non-different*, but self-transcendent superjectivity. Therefore, the origin of time is grounded in God's non-difference that, as self-transcendent relationality, is the empty space of *creative mediation* of the world between God's primordial and

---

127. Cf. Faber, "Zeitumkehr," 191-195.
128. Cf. Faber, *Poet*, 202.
129. Cf. Whitehead, *Adventures*, 236.
130. Cf. Faber, "Zeitumkehr," 203.
131. Cf. Faber, *Poet*, 234.

consequent nature, of the creation of the potentiality for existence and the integration for the actuality of existence. In this mediation, God's primordial nature (God's origination of time) always is conditioned by the consequent nature (God's receptiveness for actual time), as much as the consequent nature is conditioned by the primordial nature.[132] Hence, since the origin of time has the Divine life-circle as its *condition*, the origin of potential time is *mediated* by the redemption of actual time. Therefore we may say: the origin of time, indeed, is grounded in the end of evil, that is, in the primordiality of the redemptive love of God's self-transcendent superjectivity.[133]

Third, in the Divine difference between God's primordial and consequent nature, which opens the *chora*, God is the origin of communication that, in being the origin of time, is the condition for the *possibility* of evil. In process theology, a theodicy could follow from this "conversion" of processes, that is, the difference of the two times. Either it may excuse God for evil by introducing God's primordial nature as condition of creative freedom that allows for failure (a defense from creation out of nothing), or — as most process theologians assume — it may excuse God by appealing to God's relationality that has not created the world (a defense from creation out of chaos).[134] I do not accept either excuse, because, while the "conversion of processes" allows for both, it is neither: rather, the chora is the *creation of the nothingness of communication* in which "creation out of nothing" and "creation out of chaos" form a nexus of the counter-crossing inversion of creative and eschatological time. Since the *chora* as "medium of intercommunication"[135] does not impose any form of communication, that is, is empty (of form) and all-receptive,[136] God's relationality is not abolished by God's originality. When God's non-different self-transcendence originates the *chora*, it constitutes a "matrix of all things"[137] that is not God, but is in its relationality in "mutual immanence" with God.[138] Theodicy, then, speaks of God's "stature" to em-

132. Cf. Faber, *Prozesstheologie*, 234-243.
133. Whitehead, *Process*, 350f.
134. Cf. Griffin, ibid., 137f, 216-218.
135. Whitehead, *Adventures*, 134.
136. Cf. ibid., 187.
137. Ibid., 134.
138. Cf. ibid., 168.

brace the end of evil while allowing for its possibility as condition for the process.[139]

Theodicy speaks of the "Supreme Adventure."[140] That is, theodicy is the consequence of the paradox that God, *in being* the end of evil, *is* the origin of creation. God is the great "advent/ure:" in being the *advent*, the end of evil, God originates the *adventure* of time. In the Divine duality of the "advent/ure," evil, then, is the price for *existence*, and theodicy — instead of being an excuse for God's inability — is the *justification of existence*. "Existence" means that God's love longs for a "space of relationality" in which a world is *real* — in *real* relationality, *real* process, *real* temporality — rather than remains a mere dream within God's unfathomable potentiality.[141] In the great "advent/ure," existence is beyond God's dream of creation, and evil remains as price for God's insistence on the reality of a world beyond God's dream of its possible perfection.

---

139. This is the implication of Bernard Loomer's concept of God's "stature" or "size": cf. B. Loomer, "The Size of God," in W. Dean and L. Axel, eds., *The Size of God: The Theology of Bernard Loomer in Context* (Macon: Mercer UP, 1987); for its interpretation as theodicy cf. R. Faber, "Ambiguitaet und Groesse. Ueberlegungen zu einer skeptischen Theodizee," *Impulse* 56/4 (2000): 3-6.

140. Whitehead, *Adventures*, 295.

141. Cf. Faber, *Poet*, 286f.

An Alternative Theory
of Subjective Immortality

Lewis S. Ford 4, 10

Many theologians distinguish between two different understandings of the hereafter. Theories of the immortality of the soul hold that the natural potentialities of the soul are sufficient to guarantee the self a life to come. Plato's *Phaedo* inaugurated this line of thinking, which has been severely criticized in recent analytic thinking. Theories of the resurrection of the body hold that the individual cannot survive death unless it receives from God a resurrection body. This alternative at first sight appears less plausible, or at least less susceptible to philosophical examination, until it is realized that "body" may be quite different from the mortal body. "Body" essentially means that surrounding context or environment which can sustain the self after death. In contrast to notions of an immortal soul, this "body" is not an essential factor belonging to the soul but something specially received from God to sustain it in the hereafter.

Marjorie Suchocki proposes that God's complete prehension of each occasion's satisfaction, because it prehends the occasion completely, including its subjectivity, is the basis for that occasion's life after the death of the physical body. This gives a novel interpretation to the "resurrection body," for it is God's experience itself which sustains the self in the hereafter. Thus the "resurrection body" becomes truly a "spiritual body" constituted out of the divine life.

Taken on its own merits her theory is quite possible. Whether it is true depends on rational and empirical considerations, and we lack the experience which can only come from first-hand acquaintance with that which lies beyond death. Nor can we dispense with empirical criteria, as would be the case with metaphysical necessities, since life beyond death is a contingent matter. There might or might not be any life to come. On the other hand, if life after death is possible and desirable from a divine perspective, we might confidently expect that God would institute it. One indication that it could be divinely desirable is the whole history of evolution. If God has directed the course of evolution towards the increased presence of freedom, subjectivity and consciousness, would God not seek to preserve this precious and still relatively rare achievement from the destruction effected by the loss of the physical body?

I

My present contribution is essentially technical, based on the rational considerations of consistency and coherence. I propose an alternative, because her theory conflicts with what I take to be essential tenets of Whitehead's philosophy. But my alternative retains salient features of her account. I am convinced that complete prehension of the satisfaction will not yield subjective immortality, but the complete prehension of its subjective form might. Both approaches, moreover, see divine experience as functioning as the "resurrection body" sustaining the self in life after death.

The difficulty lies in her interpretation of Whitehead's notion of satisfaction, the culmination of the process of concrescence or actualization. The occasion as satisfied has an objective role for superseding occasions. As objective it can be prehended or appropriated into the life of these occasions. Suchocki acknowledges this objective role for finite occasions, but God is treated as an exception. She distinguishes between partial prehension, which is objective, and a complete, divine prehension, which includes the occasion's subjectivity. This presupposes, moreover, that the satisfaction has a measure of subjectivity and that subjectivity can be prehended.

The nature of subjectivity is deeply rooted in Whitehead's philosophy, and we should consider some of its antecedents. He rejected the "simple location" of scientific materialism whereby each particle was what it was independently of all others. His contrasting endeavor sought to show how each actuality could be constituted out of its relations (prehensions) to all other actualities. Yet if an event (occasion) is made up of these many relations, how is it that they come to be a single actuality? To explain this Whitehead devised a theory of concrescence, the growing together of many prehensions into one final concrete actuality. This is a process of determination, whereby the many indeterminacies as to how the initial prehensions were to be integrated are reduced to one actuality.

The actuality first comes into being with its determinateness. This means that the concrescence of determination lacks the final unity of being. Yet without concrescence there would be no being. The two aspects of actuality, becoming (coming to be) and being, require each other. Or in Whitehead's terms, the actuality is both subject and superject. The occasion is the subject of its own becoming, which becomes the superjective being for superseding occasions. (I take Whitehead to have preferred 'superject' to 'object' because it abstracts from any necessary relation to later occasions. But the 'superject' is the 'object' when considered with respect to some prehending occasion.)[1]

A being is an object inasmuch as it can be prehended, thus causally influencing one another. This suggests that the corresponding term, subject, can be identified with becoming. This proves apt, because then we can talk about the subject as the subject of its prehensions, that which is affected by that which it prehends. Just as the occasion is an instance of decision,[2] so the subject is the agent of that deciding by the way it unifies its many prehensions. Subjectivity at root means the way an occasion is dynamically affected and unifies its internal relations. Since every being requires such subjective becoming, subjectivity is a necessary feature of every actuality. Subjectivity in this sense is far more basic than mentality (which involves novelty) or consciousness, and is not to be understood simply as an attenuation of human subjectivity.

In becoming a being, a being no longer has a becoming. Also

---

1. Suchocki interprets superject otherwise: "Whitehead affirms this in referring to an entity as a subject-superject, for this term embraces creativity in its concrescent and transitional forms" (*End of Evil* [Albany: SUNY Press, 1988], 86). [Hereafter, EE.] This interpretation presupposes the notion of transitional creativity, which we shall consider anon.

2. *Process and Reality* (New York: Free Press, 1978), 43. Hereafter, PR.

were the becoming simply to continue becoming, no being would arise. This same consideration applies to subject and object. Whitehead thus analyzes the transition from subject to object in terms of perishing. The subjective immediacy of the process of unifying perishes in the attainment of final unity, which is objectively immortal. 'Perishing' emphasizes the radical (and temporal) nature of this transformation, but it has had the unfortunate consequence if applied to the whole occasion rather than only an aspect thereof.

By satisfaction he intended the final phase of concrescence in which the many feelings were all integrated into one. Originally this satisfaction was treated as a subjective feeling, but under the influence of the contrast between being and becoming, Whitehead determined that the satisfaction, as the final unity of the process, really lay outside of the process itself. Thus he writes:

> The process of concrescence terminates with the attainment of a fully *determinate* 'satisfaction'; and the creativity thereby passes over into the 'given' primary phase for the concrescence of other actual entities. . . . Completion is the perishing of immediacy. . . .[3]

Only that which is determinate can be prehended, and what is determinate lacks subjectivity. It follows that subjectivity cannot be prehended, which squares with our experience that we cannot perceive the subjectivity of another, or that contemporaries cannot causally interact. We should realize the metaphorical character of determination/indetermination here. The indeterminate is not simply that which can be perceived only with difficulty, such as a very foggy landscape. The indeterminate means that which (as yet) has no being (determinate unity) at all, and hence cannot be prehended at all. The passage from indetermination to determinateness is the passage into being.

Ordinarily 'being' is used in an inclusive sense to refer to anything having reality. Whitehead uses it primarily in a contrastive sense with 'becoming' which excludes subjectivity from being. This seems quite paradoxical in that we are quite certain of the being of our own subjectivity. In order to fit these two usages together, let us stipulate that 'becoming' refers to that which has being for oneself, while 'be-

3. PR, 85.

ing' means that which has being for others. On process principles, then, that which has being for oneself has no being for others, and that which has no being for others may have being for oneself. In other words, becoming has no being, and being has no becoming, or what is subject is not (yet) superject, and what is superject is (no longer) subject.

Were we to adopt a substance orientation, that which is subject might also be object. This would enable the subject to have being. The value of this orientation is preserved by the process principle that it takes time to be fully actual. In substance thought the underlying conditions or essence of an actuality is the same throughout the life of the substance. The corresponding conditions of a process actuality unfold. Thus while the becoming is essential to the actuality of the being, it must perish for the being to come into being. Thus subject and superject require each other, but appear sequentially, not all at once. Thus while subject in and of itself (in its own time) has being only for itself, it is essential for the actuality of the whole.

II

From this analysis of subjectivity in terms of being and becoming it follows that subjectivity cannot be prehended. It lacks the concrete unity of a being; it lacks its determinateness. It is not because our standpoint is limited or defective that we cannot prehend it, but rather that there is nothing (objectively) there to be prehended. God cannot prehend it anymore than God can prehend the future.

The satisfaction, as we have seen, is purely objective. It is only because the process of concrescence has been drained of its subjective activity that the satisfaction may appear. The unity of its being is the result (and termination) of the activity of unification. In virtue of its unity it can be prehended by others.

In order to bring about subjective immortality, so that the individual can enjoy subjectivity within the life of God, Suchocki requires that God's prehension of the satisfaction include the individual's subjectivity. This, however, is impossible, if we understand subjectivity in terms of becoming. Then satisfaction is devoid of subjectivity. Moreover, were it to have any subjectivity, it could not be prehended.

Subjectivity may be understood as the individualization of creativity, Thus, on Suchocki's supposition, but not in terms of my interpretation of Whitehead, the satisfaction's creativity can be passed along. "The occasion creates itself in concrescence, and forces the emergence of a future beyond itself in transition."[4] This brings about what has been called 'transitional creativity,' creativity invested in the superject whereby it acts upon supervening occasions. Because the satisfaction is held to enjoy creativity, some of the creativity of the concrescence can now be passed along in continuous succession to the superject.[5]

Alternatively, if both concrescence and superject were to be invested with creativity, the satisfaction could be regarded as also having creativity. Otherwise it could not serve as the link between these two. Thus satisfaction is "a mode of creativity, intermediate between the concrescent and transitional phases."[6] This departs from Whitehead's own practice of restricting creativity to the subjective activity of concrescence, as the previous quotation from *Process and Reality* indicates.[7]

There is a serious problem with transitional creativity. It is not with the notion of transition. Thus we can accept David Griffin's helpful suggestion that we

> replace the language of *perpetual perishing* with that of the *perpetual oscillation* between the two kinds of process, concrescence and transition. The creative advance of the world, therefore, involves a perpetual oscillation between efficient and final causation.[8]

The problem arises when, in explaining how transition works, we invest the superject with creativity. Then the superject acts upon later occasions in just the same way as efficient causes are thought to act in other philosophies. For Whitehead, however, efficient causation is to

---

4. *EE*, 86, immediately after previous quotation.

5. It is not clear how such continuous flow of creativity can be squared with the discontinuity of indivisible acts of becoming. Satisfaction as the termination of an occasion's creativity introduces the necessary discontinuity.

6. *EE*, 87.

7. PR, 85.

8. David Ray Griffin, *Reenchantment without Supernaturalism* (Ithaca: Cornell University Press, 2001), 115.

be understood in terms of physical prehension.[9] The locus of the activity expressing creativity is then reversed. For ordinary theory, the cause actively imposes itself on the effect, whereas for Whitehead what is to become the effect actively appropriates its causes. Creativity passes from one concrescence to another because only the concrescences are instances of creativity. Neither the intervening satisfaction nor the superject exercises any creativity. There may be an oscillation between concrescence and transition, but this does not depend on investing the transition as such with any creativity of its own.

Transitional creativity functions in Suchocki's theory to invest the satisfaction intervening between the creativity of the concrescence and the creativity of the transition with its own creativity. Since subjectivity is the individualization of creativity, the satisfaction now has its own subjectivity, were this possible. Also, since the satisfaction can be prehended, it is possible for its subjectivity to be prehended. (This step is not really possible, because the satisfaction, to close up the activity of unification, and to be a datum for prehension, must be purely objective.) It is but a short step to argue that while all finite prehension is objective, God's complete prehension can embrace the subjectivity of the occasion as well.

Suchocki recognizes, in a long bibliographical note listing various process accounts of immortality, that her position is closest to that of Charles Hartshorne.[10] This is striking. Although Hartshorne was one of the foremost champions of objective immortality, the doctrine that all of our deeds and actions are cherished in God's memory forever, he has not claimed that we might enjoy an enduring life within God. This is found to be a selfish desire for continued persistence. In his eyes, any sort of subjective immortality is rendered unnecessary by objective immortality. The true meaning of immortality lies in the persistence of value. If all our deeds and actions are merely transitory, they lack enduring worth. God's remembering them objec-

9. PR, 236.
10. EE, 166: "Of the above, the position of Charles Hartshorne is closest to this present work. He argues, as do I, that immediacy is contained in the satisfaction, and therefore that God retains the immediacy of the satisfaction. In contrast to me, however, he does not understand the immediacy to undergo transformation; it is retained as the living memory of God." I assume this to be a transformation into a subjective life within God.

tively is sufficient to guarantee their permanence, and continued subjectivity by us is not needed.

On another level, however, when we consider the means rather than the end, both Suchocki and Hartshorne claim that God includes the subjectivity of the occasion. Hartshorne appeals to the perfection of divine inclusion. Inclusion, rather than prehension, is his paradigm category. This is why 'panentheism,' the doctrine that God both transcends and includes the world, most fittingly describes his position. William A. Christian many years ago argued that Whitehead is not a panentheist.[11] Inclusion includes subjectivity, whereas prehension, Whitehead's basic category, excludes it. Only that which is objective can be prehended. God does not fully include the world insofar as the world has subjectivity or contemporaneity.

(Earlier Hartshorne had argued that God experienced contemporaries, but gradually became convinced that this was not possible by reason of relativity physics.[12] Contemporaries, however, are still in concrescence and have not achieved the determinateness of being. Both the contemporary and the subjective have being for themselves but not [yet] being for others. They cannot be prehended.)

Whitehead describes God's experience as a "tenderness which loses nothing that can be saved."[13] What can be lost, some have claimed, is evil and strife. The goodness of God would forbid his experience of such radical negativity. Yet we are told that God is the fellow-sufferer who must therefore suffer evil. Evil is not lost, but is incorporated within God by "a wisdom which loses what in the temporal world is mere wreckage."[14] God's infinite conceptual imagination is able to transform it into the beauty of tragic evil.[15] If it is not evil, what is it that is lost? Note that Whitehead says that there is some-

---

11. William A. Christian, *An Interpretation of Whitehead's Metaphysics* (New Haven: Yale University Press, 1959), 404-409.

12. Frederic F. Fost, "Relativity Theory and Hartshorne's Dipolar Theism," pp. 89-99 in Lewis S. Ford, ed., *Two Process Philosophers*, AAR Studies in Religion 5 (Tallahassee: AAR, 1973).

13. PR, 346.

14. Ibid.

15. See my essay on "Divine Persuasion and the Triumph of Good," pp. 287-304 (particularly the final section) in Delwin Brown et al., eds., *Process Philosophy and Christian Thought* (Indianapolis: Bobbs-Merrill, 1971).

thing which is necessarily lost, which cannot be included in God's experience. I submit it must be subjectivity, which by its inherent nature is undetermined since still a process of determination; it is simply not there (objectively there) to be prehended, any more than the contingent future is determinately there.

Hartshorne assumes that subjectivity is something that can be included or prehended by another; Whitehead does not. The crucial difference is that Hartshorne does not accept Whitehead's contrast between concrescence and its subjective outcome:

> I never cared for his . . . analysis of the becoming of an actual entity (a concrete unit-happening) into 'early' and 'late' phases. I never could see in the 'perishing' of actual entities anything more than a misleading metaphor which, taken literally, contradicts the dictum, entities 'become but do not change.'[16]

Taken literally, i.e. as entities having (objective) being, shifts from one phase to another, and from subjective immediacy to determinate unity, would be instances of change. But this is not becoming, which is increasing determination. It involves the shift from the less to the more determinate, which does not acquire fully determinate unity until the satisfaction. This shift from the subject to the superject (object) can properly be appreciated as the 'perishing' of subjective indeterminacy. Because this indeterminacy is incorporated into the determinate being, it no longer exists to be prehended.

Hartshorne considers God, the Perfect Includer, to include the subjectivity of the occasion, but for Whitehead that subjectivity does not (objectively) exist to be included. This does not mean that subjectivity is not a real aspect of the occasion. The occasion could not have being without its becoming. As we have seen, many thinkers assume that if subjectivity has reality for an actuality, then this must be a necessary feature of its enduring essence. Whitehead assents to its necessary character, but conceives subject and object to be sequential, not concurrent.

This brief comparison of Hartshorne and Whitehead indicates that many of the same difficulties that we found in Suchocki's theory

---

16. Charles Hartshorne, *Whitehead's Philosophy: Selected Essays, 1935-1970* (Lincoln: University of Nebraska Press, 1972), 2.

are also in Hartshorne's, principally because both resort to the notion of the perfect inclusion of subjectivity. The similarities are great, yet a major disparity exists which must be accounted for. I think it possibly lies in the different uses to which they put their theories. 'Subjective immortality' primarily concerns the continuation of a living (human) person after death, and her approach promises to belong to this category. Hartshorne, on the other hand, is concerned with the perfect preservation of an occasion within God, without championing any further subjective life within the divine. More precisely, we may think of God as preserving the subjectivity of the immediately past occasion, without according it any new subjectivity thereafter.

III

If the subjectivity of becoming will not insure subjective immortality, will the employment of subjective form fare any better? The reason the process of determination fails is that it is too indeterminate (hence nonexistent in any objective sense) to be prehended, even by God. The subjective form (at least in its final form) is a fully definite form ordering all the initial prehensions of an occasion into a unified whole, and thus is quite prehensible. It can be experienced by God and taken up into the divine life.

Yet is the subjective form sufficiently subjective to be the vehicle of subjective immortality?

Although subjectivity basically pertains to the becoming of determination, Whitehead also applies it to concepts intimately associated with the subject, such as 'subjective aim' and 'subjective form.' The subject is the agency directing the process of determination, which requires an initial orientation supplied by the subjective aim.

Whitehead analyzes a prehension in terms of its datum prehended, its subject prehending the datum, and its subjective form, the way in which this datum is felt. Thus there is a contrast between the objective datum and the subjective reception, or more precisely, the form of the subjective reception. Subjective form may be initially illustrated in terms of emotional feelings, such as to experience something 'angrily' or 'serenely.' But the way some datum is felt can be expanded beyond these primitive examples. Whitehead shows the way by treating consciousness as the subjective form of a particular complex type.[17] Some things we feel 'consciously'. If subjective forms pertain to complex prehensions as well as simple ones, they can apply to the most complex form of all, the final satisfaction. The final subjective form is the way in which the final satisfaction is felt. Since it is felt as one prehension, it is the way in which all of its initial prehensions are ordered. What is so ordered, the initial prehensions, constitute the objective content of the occasion, in contrast to the ordering activities of the subject finalized in its subjective form.

The subjective form is the individualizing factor of an occasion. The near identity of subjective forms from occasion to occasion within a personally ordered society provides for an enduring continuity of experience. If the forms are conscious, then there is an enduring continuity of consciousness. Thus the form can individuate the enduring individual in this life, and insure that its individuality may persist into the divine experience.

Besides the continuity which repeated instances of subjective form may provide, there is also the potential novelty furnished by the initial subjective aim. This possibility provided by God is also oriented to the way the final satisfaction is ordered. Now aim and form differ. Aim comes from God, form from prior occasions. Aim is conceived as a special kind of prehension, form is considered an aspect of all prehensions. As they emerge initially, they may contrast in their content. But in the complex negotiation of concrescence an identification occurs. For the final subjective aim unifies the multiplicity of initial prehensions together. That unity is the way the occasion feels its experience, and this way is its final subjective form.

Subjective form, when energized by creativity, constitutes an occasion's subjectivity, for the subjective activity of concrescence is the individualization of creativity. As we have seen, the reiterated instantiation of the same, or nearly the same, subjective form in a series of occasions establishes the enduring subjectivity we experience in ourselves. Now God, in prehending an occasion's subjective form, experiences the objective contents of its experience in the same way in which the occasion experienced its contents. The subjective form, while it is objectively definite to be prehended, becomes the subjec-

17. PR, 266f.

tive means of divine experience. The material basis in the physical world is abstracted from, and the form receives a new basis in terms of the divine experience itself. Its mortal body is replaced by a 'resurrection body' which is none other than divine experience.

Because consciousness is part of higher organisms, the subjective form of the risen self should also be conscious. This poses a difficulty. Unless a compelling reason can be given why God prehends only an enduring individual's final subjective form, the one immediately preceding the death of the body, God would prehend all of its subjective forms. If these have transformative power functioning consciously within the divine life, then there should now be a conscious life in God paralleling our own. If so, why aren't we aware of this parallel consciousness in this life?

Possibly we are, although very faintly. It may be that certain forms of meditation, disciplined to detach us from the ordinary concerns of life, attain some measure of access to such consciousness. But our embodied selves, which are primarily oriented towards perception and action, need consciousnesses directed towards the here and now. Another consciousness, disengaged from perception and action, would be conflicting and distracting. It would serve no purpose with respect to the immediate demands for action. It may be present, but only as receding into the background.

If our account is reasonably correct, one's consciousness in death is not lost. But it is transformed. It no longer possesses the means to act in the physical world, nor does it have the means of perception to guide such action. Ordinary consciousness fails it. But the consciousness it has in the divine experience now comes to the fore. In the absence of competition from ordinary consciousness it can now be as rich and vivid as waking experience. Consciousness in the divine resumes the life of the self (within the divine) with all of its memories, memories which now may be more vivid than they were when competing with perception and action.

IV

So far we have considered the possibility of the presence of self in the divine life. We need also to inquire into the persistence of the self in the divine life, for that poses difficulties of its own. Specifically, it concerns the nature of the creative activity in the region of the self. If divine, then how is it individuated in itself? If creaturely, how can it participate in the divine experience? It cannot be neither, for then it has no activity, no experience, no being. It cannot be both in the sense that both exercise full creativity. That leads to intolerable conflict and chaos.

Let us explore three alternatives:

A. Since the self regains its life within the divine experience, it is the creative activity of God which sustains it. God experiences the ongoing world in multiple ways, in terms of each finite subjective form. God's experience does not stop here, but includes the integration of cognate subjective forms, the integration of partial spatiotemporal regions, up to a final unified experience of the universe as a whole.

The self with the consciousness contained within its subjective form accompanies this process, being first integrated within similar consciousness, but eventually experiencing things with an appreciation which has almost lost its width. Yet in this process the self makes no decisions; all are made for it. It is conscious of the process, but in a passive way. It can merely observe.

The self was originally individuated in terms of its original subjective form, but it has no means of continuing its individuality. It cannot stamp its own uniqueness on things. It lacks the capacity for making decision.

B. The self can make its own determinations, yet it has its basis within the divine life. The conflict foreseen above can be resolved by considering this process successively. First there is divine creativity which determines certain very general features of creativity, mostly metaphysical, but also pertaining to the value and purpose of individual selves; then there would be the activity of the self as further determining the creativity.[18]

These selves, unlike those in the first alternative, possess genu-

18. I realize this requires considerable modification of Whitehead's own metaphysics. I have undertaken the justification of this modification in *Transforming Process Theism* (Albany: State University of New York Press, 2000), chapter 8.

ine freedom. It would seem, certainly from process considerations, that freedom is essential for each individual. On the other hand, what guarantee is there, even in heavenly places, that freedom will entail conflict and evil? The vices of the body may be absent, but the medievals were quite aware of the presence of purely spiritual vices such as pride, envy, jealousy or covetousness.

If we consider these selves to possess the widest possible freedom, it becomes difficult to distinguish the divine creativity which sustains them from the divine creativity sustaining the physical world. In both instances divine creativity is not just God's but the source of creativity for all occasions.[19] We may suppose that in our cosmic epoch God determined the metaphysical principles and the contingent physical constants needed for the eventual emergence of life, and with life, for mind and consciousness. This is the basis for freedom. Apart from these extremely general features there would be simply chaos.

This is a material world in contrast with the heavenly realm. Yet the same general structure is present: Divine creativity is so structured as to permit a maximum creaturely freedom. To be sure, freedom must evolve on earth, for actuality first manifests itself in elementary particles, and requires a long evolution to its present form. There is no reason to believe that maximum freedom has been achieved even yet.

C. Some further factor in the divine determination of the creativity which it provides to postmortem selves could distinguish between the material and the spiritual worlds. Then freedom would depend upon a spiritual rather than a material basis. This spiritual context would be partially created by God as determining its underlying principles, but as partially determined creativity it would be grounds for its freedom. In addition to freedom, hopefully those principles would also afford for consciousness, happiness, sociality, and a reduction, should elimination be impossible, of evil.

Whatever alternative is finally adopted, it seems unlikely that the self will retain its subjective identity forever. There can be a widening of

19. Ibid.

its subjective form such that it experiences more and more, not just in terms of objective content, but in terms of the way it experiences. This process may be gradual, first incorporating the standpoints of loved ones and family, and of acquaintances. There may be increasing identification with the goals of organizations, thereby adopting their standpoints: the voluntary associations one belongs to, but also one's nation, then humanity throughout the earth, even extending to animals and possibly to intelligent life elsewhere. This ever-widening increase in the scope and power of the subjective form would be achieved most efficiently if God constituted the activity of the self as in the first alternative. It would be least efficiently achieved in the second alternative, where human freedom could egoistically hinder and even prevent further increase. The third alternative promises to be somewhere between these others.

At any rate, the ultimate goal of the individual self is to attain an appreciation of reality which transcends the bounds of individual concern, to attain the Buddhist goal of compassion for all sentient beings.

Eschatology as Metaphysics
under the Guise of Hope

Philip Clayton

It is not typical to do constructive metaphysics under the guise of hope. In fact, I am not sure that it is possible. It may be that the only rational response to questions of immortality and eschatology is *hope without metaphysics*, that is, a subjective longing coupled with agnosticism or skepticism about all extant metaphysical proposals on the topic. For those not willing to engage in the suspension of belief, the concept of hope must serve, I suggest, as the lens through which all constructive metaphysical work on eschatology is focused.

This axiom gives rise to two theses, which serve as the (sometimes silent) background for the following exploration. First, in eschatology, more than perhaps any other field, the insight of Kant and German Idealists is correct. Knowledge claims cannot be advanced apart from a consideration of the *status* of those claims: are they known? how are they known? how well are they known? Where faith outruns knowledge, the mere having of the faith does not itself serve as a reason to think that the resulting beliefs are true. This principle holds in particular for resurrection claims both past and future: "If . . . historical study declares itself unable to establish what 'really' happened on Easter, then all the more, faith is not able to do so; for faith cannot ascertain anything certain about events of the past that would perhaps be inaccessible to the historian."[1]

---

1. Wolfhart Pannenberg, *Jesus — God and Man*, 2nd ed., trans. Lewis Wilkins and Duane Priebe (Philadelphia: Westminster Press, 1968), p. 109.

This position stems from the epistemological principle that conviction, no matter how passionate, is not sufficient for knowledge. The degree of probability of any prediction is only as high as the strength of the analogy between previous events and the one now being predicted. In the case of an idealized physical system (say, one functioning under ideal Newtonian conditions) the analogy between past cases and the present case is nearly perfect. Hence the probability of the same outcome in the future is very high — as empirical experiments in fact reveal. Unfortunately, the question about the end of this entire cosmic epoch lies at precisely the opposite end of the epistemic continuum. We have never experienced the end of a universe and have no analogies to guide us. The same holds true for the question, "What happens after my death?" Thus the epistemic strength of our predictions on these subjects is much lower than in most other areas — no matter how passionately one may believe in, or long for, one or another sort of post-mortem state. Of course, the uncertainty of our knowledge does not dampen the degree of our hope; indeed, the passion of hope may even be increased by unknowing! Thus statements about immortality and the eschaton belong more naturally under the heading of hope than under the heading of knowledge. (One might then ask, Under what conditions is hope justified?)

Second, I have just argued that eschatological statements cannot be *more than* statements of hope. It is equally true that they cannot be *less than* statements of hope — at least not if they are to be religiously significant. A scientist might study various possible outcomes of the physical cosmos and assess the likelihood of each possible outcome. The fact that she finds some of the outcomes more attractive and others less attractive is completely irrelevant to her assessment of them *qua* scientific hypotheses. But in matters of religion things are otherwise. Here it matters greatly that the religious narrative or worldview endorsed by the believer makes the universe meaningful for her. A religious tradition or belief that does not establish a context of meaning for believers has ceased to be religiously effective. What then are the conditions under which talk of the eschaton can still meet the condition of hope? A believer can hope for an (eschatological) outcome only to the extent that she can relate it to her own self-conception, the values that she holds, and the projects with which she is concerned.

This very concern has often been raised in the context of debates about process eschatology. One wants to know, Does Whitehead's doctrine of objective immortality meet the hope condition? The future state in which God remembers everything that you thought or felt allows you to become data in the divine consciousness. But it is not a future state that includes the subjective or agential part of you. Is it then a future state that you can hope for?[2] Certainly not in the sense of hoping for a continuation of who you are as a person; Whitehead's notion allows only for a continuation of who you *were* as a person (or better, perhaps, a person-moment). Agency is an essential condition for ongoing personhood: not just the content of your thoughts or actions, but your ability to think the thoughts or perform the actions, would have to be preserved. Indeed, the moment of agency is just as crucial in the creative synthesis of an actual occasion as it is in everyday understandings of personhood. Subjective immortality, it seems, but not objective immortality, meets this condition.

We first examine traditional eschatology before turning to Marjorie Suchocki's eschatology and defense of subjective immortality. I focus in particular on the work of Wolfhart Pannenberg and Jürgen Moltmann, since their "theologies of the future" are primarily responsible for the renaissance of eschatology in the second half of the 20th century.

Traditional Christian Eschatology

The Greek adjective *eschaton* means last or final. The noun *to eschaton* thus came to mean the end of this age, and hence of the entire history of the cosmos. As the divinely appointed end, *to eschaton* also conveyed the sense of completion or fulfillment, the telos of history. One cannot overemphasize the importance of this completion within Christian theology. As Wolfhart Pannenberg writes, "The future of

---

2. If a body that is not yours is subjected to torture, you imagine that that person is experiencing pain. But it is his pain rather than yours. The situation is not changed if the body looks like your body, or if it is a body that used to be yours but is no longer. If the subjective element is no longer present in the future — if one is present only as "data" — then you are yourself no longer present.

God's kingdom for whose coming Christians pray in the words of Jesus (Matt. 6:10) is the epitome of Christian hope. All else that is related to it, including the resurrection of the dead and the last judgment, is a consequence of God's own coming to consummate his rule over his creation."[3]

Many early theologians had limited the significance of the eschaton to the belief in the second coming of Christ and the establishment of the kingdom of God. This interpretation tended to place the focus on the final judgment, at which wrongdoing would be punished and good rewarded. The result was a heavy emphasis on the justice of God and God's role as judge.[4] But in 20th-century theology the doctrine of eschatology came to take on a more significant role than it had played in earlier periods of systematic theology. Jürgen Moltmann, arguing that Christianity understands history only "from the perspective of the future," risked the thesis early in his career that *theology just is eschatology*.[5] Moltmann's entire ethics and politics stemmed from this awareness: "If the Christians hope for this future of God, they not only wait for it, but also look for it, love it, and strive for it. The eschatological will lead to decisions that are live options in the present. The decision for the goal determines the means and ways that lead to the goal" (p. 46). Hence all of theology, and all of the Christian life, stem from one's belief in the eschaton. Without this culmination, all Christian belief and practice become futile: "If we who are in Christ have hope only in this life and that is all, then we are of all people most miserable and to be pitied" (1 Cor. 15:19).

It is true that traditional eschatology did not always express the subtlety and richness of this understanding of eschatology. As John Macquarrie writes, "Traditional eschatology seemed to understand the consummation as a kind of escape from the vicissitudes of time, from

---

3. See Wolfhart Pannenberg, *Systematic Theology*, vol. 3, trans. Geoffrey Bromiley (Grand Rapids: Eerdmans, 1998), p. 527. The following references in the text to Pannenberg are from the same volume.

4. One can't help but wonder how much this emphasis was motivated by the desire to see one's enemies brought down: "vengeance is Mine, saith the Lord; I will repay" (Rom. 12:19).

5. Jürgen Moltmann, *The Future of Hope: Theology as Eschatology* (New York: Herder and Herder, 1970), e.g., p. 22. More recently see his *The Coming of God: Christian Eschatology* (Minneapolis: Fortress Press, 1996).

the 'change and decay' that we see all around, into a realm where nothing would be subject to change any more."[6]

The tendency toward eschatological escapism based on dichotomizing time and eternity must be judged as a shortcoming. Yet such weaknesses in some traditional formulations are not sufficient grounds for discarding the notion of an eschaton altogether. Thus I cannot follow the recommendation of Catherine Keller that we understand the New Creation as "the renewal of *this* creation — not the deadly expectation of the end of this one. If we ruin this one, there is no Daddy to make us a new one. . . . The confluence of past energy and future possibility . . . is dis/closed only in and as 'the love of life.'"[7] The same applies to Rudolf Bultmann's famous attempt to eliminate all future dimensions of the Christian hope, translating them into a fully "realized eschatology." To struggle with the Christian tradition means to struggle with the dimension of futurity. Pannenberg provides a succinct summary of the challenge: "The relation between time and eternity is the crucial problem in eschatology, and its solution has implication for all parts of Christian doctrine" (p. 595).

The scientific picture is not encouraging of this cosmic hope. If eschatologists seek to ground their hope in science, they will be disappointed. John Polkinghorne summarizes the scientific position:

> Our knowledge is not sufficiently accurate to enable us to be sure which tendency will ultimately win, but either way the observable universe is condemned to eventual futility. If expansion [of the universe] predominates, the galaxies will continue to move apart forever, at the same time condensing and decaying within themselves into ever-cooling low-grade radiation. If contraction predominates, the universe will eventually collapse upon itself into the fiery melting pot of the big crunch. In neither way is an obvious evolutionary fulfillment to be found.[8]

6. John Macquarrie, "Eschatology and Time," in Moltmann, *The Future of Hope*, p. 111.

7. Catherine Keller, "Pneumatic Nudges: The Theology of Moltmann, Feminism, and the Future," in Miroslav Volf et al., *The Future of Theology: Essays in Honor of Jürgen Moltmann* (Grand Rapids: Eerdmans, 1996), p. 153.

8. John Polkinghorne, "Eschatology: Some Questions and Some Insights from Science," in Polkinghorne and Michael Welker, eds., *The End of the World and the Ends of*

These two possibilities have been summarized as the "freeze or fry" scenario. Neither outcome seems greatly to be desired.

True, the (relatively recent) realization that the world is finite in space and time is closer to the biblical view than is the notion of an infinite, unchanging universe that dominated the medieval world-picture. Nevertheless, as Pannenberg notes, "the cosmic eschatology of the Bible that expects an imminent end to the world, even though no time table is set, is not congruent with scientific extrapolations regarding a possible end to the universe that look to a remote future" (p. 589). Kathryn Tanner draws out the consequence of this discrepancy in no uncertain terms: "the best scientific description of the day leaves little doubt that death is the end toward which our solar system and the universe as a whole are moving."[9]

In the absence of scientific support for the Christian hope, certain conservative scholars and popular Christian writers have turned instead to a dark futurology, seeking to find confirmation for Christian eschatological claims in the evidence that the world is going to hell in a handbasket, as the prophets foretold. Many, for example, have looked for "signs of the Apocalypse," proofs that the dire predictions in Revelation are being fulfilled. Hal Lindsey's *The Late Great Planet Earth* both expressed and spawned a strange Christian *Schadenfreude* in the wars and environmental disasters of the late modern age.[10]

In marked rejection of this trend, mainline Christian theologians have argued that no such "negative apologetics" is necessary to substantiate eschatological language. The role of the future and the need for hope are well enough attested in human existential experience; their continuing role is assured through "the inner logic of the historicity of our sense of meaning" (Pannenberg, p. 590). Pannenberg's anthropology, for example, argues that the notion of "history as a whole" — which obviously includes the idea of the end of history — is

---

God: Science and Theology on Eschatology (Harrisburg, PA: Trinity Press International, 2000), p. 31.

9. Kathryn Tanner, "Eschatology Without a Future?" in Polkinghorne and Welker, *The End of the World and the Ends of God*, p. 222.

10. Hal Lindsey, *The Late Great Planet Earth* (New York: HarperPaperbacks, [1970], 1992); see also Lindsey, *The 1980's: Countdown to Armageddon* (King of Prussia, PA: Westgate Press, 1980), and Lindsey, *The Road to Holocaust* (New York: Bantam Books, 1989).

a fundamental feature of our being in the world.[11] Pannenberg and Rahner, among others, have appealed to Heidegger's powerful demonstration of the centrality of "the future" for present human existence in the world *(Dasein)*. Each individual's death, for example, is for her the locus of the possibility of her becoming whole *(Ganz-sein-können)*.[12]

At present, then, Christian theology finds itself drawn toward a hope that it cannot prove. The idea of a hope after death and an end that fulfills history as a whole is as intrinsic to the Christian tradition as it is foreign to the projects of science. Theologians can draw on numerous resources in anthropology and phenomenology in order to explain this hope and anchor it in the structures and longings of human existence. But to translate the Christian hope without remnant into human existential (or aesthetical or political) terms is to eliminate one of the most fundamental features of the tradition. We live in the tension between these competing forces. Pannenberg nicely expresses the balance which it is the theologian's goal to achieve:

> The themes of eschatology call for *anthropological* demonstration. True, anthropological argument can have only a limited function in eschatology because eschatological hope depends finally on God's reality and power, not ours. But what has to be demonstrated anthropologically is still essential if we are to be able to hear that which is maintained and proclaimed as truly a matter of promise, and if it is to be credible as the promise of God. Thus anthropology is the soil on which we can argue for the universality of the Christian eschatological hope even if in the process we cannot offer final proofs for the contents of this hope, the fulfilling of which is far beyond our human resources and depends on God alone. (p. 542)

Eschatology exists in the dialectical tension between an awaited and hoped-for act on God's part and an active process of evaluation and *con-*

---

11. Wolfhart Pannenberg, *Anthropology in Theological Perspective* (Philadelphia: Westminster Press, 1985).

12. See Heidegger, *Being and Time* (New York: Harper & Row, 1962), esp. sections 46-53. See also Karl Rahner, *On the Theology of Death* (New York: Seabury Press, 1973).

struction on the part of human beings. To what extent this tension can be resolved within any constructive metaphysics remains to be seen.

Process, Participation, and Panentheism

For those familiar with the process tradition, this quick account of traditional Christian eschatology may seem discouraging. Are not the themes of process thought far removed from these concepts and desiderata? There are however some connections, both metaphysical and existential, between the notion of an eschaton or telos and Whitehead's experiential philosophy. Exploring these connections will allow us to evaluate to what extent Marjorie Suchocki's proposal can be linked with the theological traditions just summarized.

Perhaps the most important link lies in the notion of participation. A passing comment in Pannenberg's systematic theology suggests a strategy:

> The problem of linking the thought of an end of time with that of life, including eternal life, disappears only when we consider that *God and not nothing is the end of time.* As the finite is bounded by the infinite, so are time and the temporal by eternity. The end of the temporal, of time and history in general, thus means transition to eternity. This can mean participation in God's own eternal life. (pp. 593f.)

Participation is uniquely suited to express both the subjective/transformative dimension of eschatology and its objective features (actual temporal futurity, the end of time, and the actions of God).

Mystics have explored the experiential dimension of participation in the divine, ethicists its implications for action. For her part, the metaphysician must ask about its formulation as a comprehensive systematic theory of reality. The Western tradition offers at least four major models for conceiving participation[13] (the Eastern philosophical traditions are equally rich but require a separate presenta-

13. See Clayton, *The Problem of God in Modern Thought* (Grand Rapids: Eerdmans, 2000), chap. 3.

tion and analysis of their own). Foundational for all of them is Plato's concept that all finite things exist only by participating in their respective forms. The next two both stem from (separate) syntheses of Platonic participation with Aristotle's metaphysics. Plotinus and the Neoplatonic thinkers who followed him held that all finite things emerge from the One in a process of emanation, yet continue to exist only through participation in it. Thomas Aquinas, by contrast, accepted the existence of a world outside of and distinct from God, each object a real combination of form and matter in Aristotle's sense. Yet his metaphysics of being was still built upon Platonic participation, as was his theory of the transcendentals (being, goodness, beauty, the One). Descartes argued that the existence of finite beings implies the existence of an infinite, which is logically prior and must serve as their source. Hegel then showed that it is contradictory to imagine the finite as lying outside of the infinite; the true infinite must encompass all finite things and include them within itself. Finally, Whitehead advanced a systematic metaphysics in which creative moments or actual occasions exist for themselves but come to be contained within the consequent nature of God after the completion of their creative activity.

Whitehead's exclusion of the creative moment — what modern metaphysicians have called subjectivity — from participation in the divine[14] represents a major setback for the theological appropriation of his work. For this reason, some of the process thinkers who followed him have attempted to reduce the distance using a concept not found explicitly in Whitehead's work, the concept of panentheism. *Panentheism* is the thesis that all finite occasions exist within the divine, although God is also more than the finite world taken as a whole. Charles Hartshorne's reformulation of Whiteheadian philosophy in panentheistic terms opened the doors to a deeper rapprochement of Whitehead and traditional theology; and later process thinkers, including Marjorie Suchocki and Joseph Bracken, have attempted to deepen the conceptual connections. Thus, Suchocki claims, "The occasion is linked into the concrescence of God, even while remaining

---

14. It would have been possible for Whitehead to develop a stronger notion of participation even here, had he appealed to the close ontological link between God and Creativity. But in fact he failed adequately to develop this connection.

itself. Thus the peculiarity obtains that the occasion is *both* itself *and* God: it is apotheosized" (p. 102). Any success that one may have in addressing the dilemmas of eschatology, I suggest, will depend on one's ability to formulate an adequate Christian-process panentheism.

Suchocki's Defense of Subjective Immortality

For those interested in the dialogue between process and traditional eschatology, the most important claim in Marjorie Suchocki's eschatological work, *The End of Evil,* is probably her affirmation of subjective immortality. Suchocki realizes that, in the dialogue between Christian theologians and Whitehead, the latter's apparent denial of the immortality of human subjectivity has been a major stumbling block. For Whitehead, past occasions are available to the present actual occasion only as data. Likewise, the present entity's own subjectivity exists only in the creative moment of unification, the moment at which it transforms the "many" of its input into the "one" of its unique perspective on the world (PR 21). The moment this unification is completed, it passes out of existence *qua* subjective; its unique perspective persists only as data for later actual occasions. Whitehead held (or: seems generally to have held) that the same limitation applies to God as an experiencer: even God can only prehend past occasions as (objective) data. Admittedly, God's prehension is unlimited, whereas ours is finite; nevertheless, since subjectivity is momentary, it cannot be preserved in God's ongoing awareness, even if all the *facts* about individuals can be. Thus Whitehead advocated objective immortality while denying subjective immortality.

In her book (pp. 90-96) Suchocki affirms the subjective immortality of each actual occasion within God. I shall not analyze in detail her arguments for the viability of this shift within an "orthodox" Whiteheadian framework; that task is attempted elsewhere in this volume. Here our concern is more with the *theological implications* of this shift. Suffice it to say that Suchocki supports her reinterpretation of Whitehead by appealing to the *perfection* and *unlimited nature* of God's prehension of past occasions: the absence of negative prehension, the perfect harmony of feeling, and the complete retention by God of all details concerning the past occasion's experience. Without arguing a position on whether this reinterpretation is compatible with the fundamental tenets of Whitehead's metaphysics (I tend to agree with Joseph Bracken that the resulting position is neo-Whiteheadian rather than orthodox Whiteheadian), I suggest we consider what is presupposed and entailed by Suchocki's attempted enhancement of Whitehead. As hinted above, participation and panentheism provide the *Leitmotiv* for this analysis.

In her approach to the question of immortality, Suchocki might be said to be raising the ultimate challenge to panentheists: How seriously, how completely, how radically do you understand the inclusion of all things and all persons within God? Under this interpretation, Suchocki is really pushing the logic of locating all things, and hence all subjective agency, within the divine. The result is a more radical account of what it means to locate finite agency within the divine subject than panentheists are usually willing to admit.[15] For the most natural response to her interpretation of subjective immortality is, "But there can't be real flesh-and-blood existence within God. Either a person exists in the world in the fashion with which we are familiar in everyday experience, or a person is remembered by God after she no longer exists. You can't have an existence within God which at the same time preserves what it is to exist in the world!" Although this is an intuitively compelling response, it is not one that is open to the panentheist. Recall that panentheism is the view that all things exist within God, although God is also more than all (finite) things. That means that, for the panentheist, the normal state of existence *is* that all things have real flesh-and-blood existence, *and* that they exist at

---

15. In particular, she has thought through the implications of a panentheistic eschatology more rigorously than most panentheists have. To be consistent, any theologian who accepts panentheism must offer a panentheistic eschatology. Note that a number of theologians who are not panentheists concerning the present do endorse panentheism as the final state of creation. That is, creation in its perfected state must be located within God and as a part of God. This position is most clear in John Polkinghorne, *The God of Hope and the End of the World* (New Haven: Yale Univ. Press, 2001). Elsewhere Polkinghorne has also attacked panentheistic theologies *of the present* and defended "eschatological panentheism" as the only viable option. For more detail on panentheism, see Clayton, *God and Contemporary Science* (Edinburgh: Edinburgh University Press, 1997) and *The Problem of God in Modern Thought* (Grand Rapids: Eerdmans, 2000), as well as Arthur Peacocke and Clayton, *In Whom We Live and Move and Have Our Being* (Grand Rapids: Eerdmans, 2004).

the same time within the divine. Being within God and having full earthly existence cannot, for the panentheist, be incompatible.

Of course, Suchocki construes inner-worldly temporal progression differently from the way classical Christian theology does. In traditional theology persons were understood to be substances or subjects that persisted over time, enjoying "normal" existence for their allotted three-score-and-ten. After that they either cease to exist, or exist in a state of disembodied existence, for some period of time; and then comes the resurrection and a final, eternal state. Thus for Thomas Aquinas the disembodied soul as it exists prior to the final resurrection of the body exists in only a partial, shadowy existence. On the last day, the tradition held, the soul is reunited with the body, allowing the resurrected person to enjoy a fullness of existence in the direct presence of God. By contrast, Suchocki, following Whitehead, treats as the fundamental unit the individual moment of experiencing rather than the person's life as a whole. The moment each one of these "occasions," or instants of experience, ceases to exist as a subjective reality, it is prehended by God in its full *objective and subjective* nature. On this view, the moment that "you" — the point-instant you — cease to exist in your earthly, finite form, you begin to exist panentheistically, that is, within God.

The strange sound of this proposal does not, I suggest, stem from its panentheistic commitment. There is nothing in and of itself strange about things existing within the divine presence; such a view merely intensifies the notion of divine immanence, which has played a role in Western theism since the Patristic period. The strangeness comes when one tries to picture the whole thing more realistically, that is, when one tries to imagine how the transition from "outside" of God to "inside" of God takes place. At one moment you exist as a flesh-and-blood being, surrounded and influenced by other solid things like sticks and snow and orange juice; and then suddenly you find yourself existing as a thought within the mind of God. Once there, you find that the feeling of "what it is like to be you" and all your particular thoughts are still intact, right down to the level of the particular pleasure you had when you swam laps in the pool this morning. At this point silly questions arise: Did God transfer the actual pool into this God-internal place? Or does God merely make it seem as though the pool is there? Are you now like the disembodied "brain in a vat" made famous by Hilary Putnam, with artificial inputs deceiving you into thinking that you are still enjoying a full existence?[16]

And then suddenly one realizes how Suchocki is able to make this move "into" God without, as it were, losing anything along the way: hers is an idealist ontology, just as radically as Whitehead's was. It's well known that Whitehead as a panexperientialist (or what, before David Griffin, we called a "panpsychist") defends an ontology that consists solely of moments of experience. As an idealist he can say that sticks and snow and scorpions exist, and that you have flesh-and-blood existence; what this claim has to mean for him in the end, however, is that *aggregates of innumerably many moments of experience exist,* and these aggregates have the character of sticks and scorpions and the rest. Aggregates are derivative. If you re-create each of the innumerable moments of experience out of which they are composed, including their subjective aspects, then you have re-created the world as we know it. Nothing is lost.[17]

Is this not what Suchocki's view of subjective immortality really amounts to? First an incredibly complex series of mental events takes place *outside* of God, although they are of course influenced by God. And then immediately afterwards (literally: at the next temporal instant) these same events are mirrored within God in so complete and accurate a form that *nothing* has been lost — so complete indeed, that we should speak of the mirrored state as the continued existence of those very subjective events who, a moment ago, existed outside of God. It is, apparently, a powerful thing to be remembered by God!

16. Hilary Putnam, *Reason, Truth, and History* (Cambridge: Harvard University Press, 1981), chap. 1.

17. Note how this view comes extremely close to the structure of supervenience as developed by non-reductive physicalists in the philosophy of mind in recent years. Physicalists move in exactly the opposite direction, however: complicated physical systems give rise to emergent mental properties. To say that these mental properties "supervene" on the physical systems that give rise to them is just to say that, if you re-created the physical system in identical fashion, the identical mental properties would be *ipso facto* re-created in exactly the same way. On Whitehead's view as reconstructed by Suchocki, if you re-created all the mental events within God, you would have the same physical-seeming world that we now inhabit. Nothing would be lost. For more on supervenience theory, see Jaegwon Kim, *Supervenience and Mind: Selected Philosophical Essays* (New York: Cambridge University Press, 1993), and Kim, *Supervenience* (Burlington, VT: Ashgate/Dartmouth, 2002).

In one sense, the subjective event as it occurs and the subjective event as it is remembered are identical. In another sense, however, they are not. In this difference lies the opening for a doctrine of redemption in Suchocki's work. Remember that persons are, for Whitehead, a series of actual occasions with a particularly close connection between the particular moments of which they are composed. In your pre-panentheistic state (if that's the right way to characterize Suchocki's position) you — or rather, each moment of "you" — is presented with an ordered set of initial aims, and each moment has the opportunity to respond to the divine lure in its own way. Let's assume that, as with most of us, your individual moments do not respond in perfect accordance with these initial aims. As each of your moments passes out of its creative phase and becomes data for future moments, it is re-created within God. Moment by moment you are being built up again, panentheistically, within the eternal divine memory. Yet in this memory in which you now "live and move and have your being," there is no perishing; each of your moments continues to exist eternally *in the robust subjective sense in which it existed during the process of its concrescence.* This fact means, presumably, that the opportunity exists for "you" — the sum total of the occasions that constitute you — to respond differently to the divine lure. In this eternal state you can understand more fully, respond more perfectly, and participate more completely in the eternal divine life in which "the many become one." Herein lies redemption. Thus Suchocki writes

> The occasion is twice-born: first through its own self-creation, and second through God's total prehension of this self-creation. Its temporal birth is as fleeting as the concrescence that generated it; its divine birth, grounded in God's own concrescence, is as everlasting as God. The occasion is therefore reborn to subjective immortality. (p. 96)

No Subjective Immortality
without a Theory of Subjectivity

The End of Evil attempts to develop an adequate theory of immortality and redemption — one sufficient to genuinely address the problem of evil — while remaining as true as possible to Whiteheadian thought. Whenever she diverges from Whitehead, Suchocki does so only to the extent necessary to achieve her goals; whenever possible, she justifies her modifications of Whitehead's system using his own concepts and the conceptual openings they provide. Suppose we accept this methodological commitment for the moment as a given. It will still be crucial to acknowledge to what extent the results actually diverge from Whitehead and how significant these divergences are. In a sense the relationship of this chapter to Suchocki's project is analogous to Suchocki's relationship to Whitehead: I find openings in *her* concepts, the implications of which drive us yet another step further from *Process and Reality*. In particular, Suchocki's notion of subjective immortality, and the modifications of process thought that it entails, introduce new concepts into the process debate. When we explore the resources that these concepts provide, we find ourselves treading on new territory.

First, I suggest that Bracken is right in noting that Suchocki has actually introduced a new level of intersubjectivity into the God-world relationship. He writes, "Whitehead conceived prehension, even divine prehension, along the lines of a subject-object relationship. What Suchocki has done is to convert divine prehension of creaturely actual occasions into a subject-subject or intersubjective relationship" (cf. above, p. 7). As Bracken realizes, Whiteheadian occasions in the course of their own concrescence directly perceive only *objects*, viz. past occasions. Whitehead does not provide us with adequate conceptual resources for conceiving direct subject-to-subject relationships. Partly for this reason, Bracken's own (neo-Whiteheadian) reconceptualization of relationship in terms of interpenetrating fields represents an important advance over Whitehead's conception.[18]

The field concept also mitigates the negative effects of Whitehead's idealism. Contemporary physics has not yet unified the theories of electromagnetic fields, gravitational fields, and quantum fields.

---

18. See especially Joseph Bracken, *Society and Spirit: A Trinitarian Cosmology* (London and Toronto: Associated University Presses, 1991); *The Triune Symbol: Persons, Process and Community* (Lanham, MD: University Press of America, 1985); *The Divine Matrix: Creativity as Link between East and West* (Maryknoll, NY: Orbis Books, 1995); and his articles "Process Philosophy and Trinitarian Theology," Parts I and II, *Process Studies* 8/4 (1978): 217-30, and 11/2 (1981): 83-96; and "Energy-Events and Fields," *Process Studies* 18/3 (1989): 153-65.

Nonetheless, each of these physical fields shares the property of inter-relating matter and energy so that the two are no longer understood as completely discrete (even if the differences in the way they do this are highly significant). Bracken has recognized that this blurring of the old dichotomy between solid matter and ethereal energy has the potential to reduce the tension between mental subjects and physical objects that has bedeviled modern philosophy at least since Descartes. We return to the problem of the physical world, and its role in eschatology, after looking first at the theory of subjectivity.

In one of the more intriguing sections of *The End of Evil* Suchocki, having made the case for subjective immortality, begins to explore avenues that would allow for an actual occasion to experience redemption. She first considers the possibility that "each prehended immediacy, by being united with the totality of God, [might] then become as a series in its continued experience of God. This would entail that every occasion . . . is ultimately destined for a continual seriality in everlastingness" (p. 102). But, she points out, expanding each actual occasion into what would then become an *infinite series* of occasions would not actually bring about redemption. One might conclude that *future* occasions were redeemed in such a view, but the actual occasion itself would be left in its initial state.

Suchocki then rightly turns to the two types of time that are implied in Whitehead's system. "Serial time marked by transition" is the dominant understanding of time in Whitehead; it is the series of moments of concrescence or creativity, each one ending and bequeathing the creative task to the next generation of occasions. But Whitehead's philosophy also implies a "genetic time of concrescence," since each of the "moments" itself includes a number of (at least conceptual) stages. Suchocki does not believe that the latter really deserves to be called time, since in processes of this sort there is no loss. Yet she does grant that it represents a unique form of process: "each datum is refined *and* modified as the concrescent process takes place, for the datum is contrasted in relation to other data, and integrated accordingly into the satisfaction" (p. 103).

By contrast, I follow McTaggert in holding that every actual process in fact implies some notion of time. Time is just the measure or conceptualization of any given process. Clearly, the nature of time in these two major types of process will be different, and they may even be conceptually incommensurable. Still, it is sufficient to note that the process of concrescence is characterized by its own unique time. Let's call the time of concrescence *subjective time*. It would be a grave weakness if Whiteheadian process philosophy were unable to incorporate this sort of temporal process. In fact, *other* process thinkers — notably Hegel and Bergson, and above all Augustine — have developed highly sophisticated process philosophies of subjective time.

It would also be deeply troubling to exclude subjective time because, I suggest, there is no answer to the challenge of eschatology without an adequate notion of subjective time. As we saw in the section on traditional Christian eschatology, we have access to the idea of the "genuinely future" through the experience of meaning, which one can grasp by analyzing the structures of human existence in the world (Heidegger). These analyses of subjective time are not *sufficient* for an eschatology, but they are necessary components of any adequate account.[19]

For these reasons, I suppose, subjective time plays a much larger role in Suchocki's system than in Whitehead's. Indeed, it turns out that her notion of subjective time is extensive enough to imply a nascent theory of subjectivity. For example, Suchocki's view entails that there is reflexivity or self-awareness in the actual occasion. Her actual occasions, being apotheosized, are, as we saw, both themselves and God at the same time. Put differently, "the entity enjoys its own satisfaction *and* God's consciousness of it in the unity of God's now extremely complex subjectivity" (p. 102). Suchocki must consequently postulate a "dual consciousness" within each actual occasion: "the retained consciousness of the satisfaction, and the moving consciousness of God" (p. 103). "In apotheosis the occasion experiences itself and more than itself" (ibid.).

This reflexivity or self-awareness was at the very least not anticipated by Whitehead, and it may well be that it is irreconcilable with his theory of actual occasions. By introducing it, Suchocki is able in

19. Recall the quotation from Pannenberg: "True, anthropological argument can have only a limited function in eschatology because eschatological hope depends finally on God's reality and power, not ours. But what has to be demonstrated anthropologically is still essential if we are to be able to hear that which is maintained and proclaimed as truly a matter of promise, and if it is to be credible as the promise of God" (p. 542).

principle to do greater justice to the richness of concrescence, thus addressing one of the more serious limitations of Whitehead's metaphysics. If she is successful in this task, she would be better able to describe the profound impact of God on the actual occasion. But one would be able to determine the extent to which she is successful only by providing a fuller theory of the notion of subjectivity that lies behind subjective immortality. That task has not yet been completed.

What kind of theory of subjectivity *would* be adequate for thinking these new developments? First, the ontology must include subjects who are extended over time (that is, of course, subjective time). During the process of their concrescence — and remember that, on Suchocki's view, this process may be everlasting! — these extended occasions, or subjects for short, experience a dual consciousness: they are aware of their own prehension of and evaluation of data, and they are aware of God's input.

Moreover, this dual awareness continues over long stretches of (subjective) time, since only in this way can Suchocki account for redemption. According to the dynamic she describes, the subject is partially redeemed by its awareness of God's reaction to it, reforms itself in that new understanding, presents that reformed understanding to God, and is further redeemed by God's further response. One might even say that the basic structure of this subject is *self-reflexivity in community*. In a process of fundamental sociality, the subject experiences God as Other, comprehends within itself God's response to it, and then internalizes this response into itself, thereby becoming more than it was before. Readers will note a significant parallel: this process, which seems to lie at the core of Suchocki's conception, is almost indistinguishable from the process that underlies Hegel's theory of subjectivity![20]

20. See, among many works on subjectivity in Hegel, Michael Theunissen, *The Other: Studies in the Social Ontology of Husserl, Heidegger, Sartre, and Buber* (Cambridge: MIT Press, 1984); and Charles Taylor, *Hegel* (New York: Cambridge University Press, 1975). This view is also reminiscent of the concept of the Other in Emmanuel Levinas, *Totality and Infinity* (Pittsburgh: Duquesne University Press, 1969).

Process and Traditional Eschatology

The proposal developed by Marjorie Suchocki seeks to make sense of the conceptual possibility of subjective immortality. Given that many metaphysical conceptions, including Whitehead's own, failed to do this, this would be no mean achievement.[21] I have argued that the task, though intriguing, is incomplete, and that completing it requires drawing on conceptual resources that are not to be found in Whitehead.

Consider the proposal in summary. This eschatology centers on an entity capable of continued subjective existence after the moment of its earthly existence. It is able not only to be influenced by God, but also to become aware of that ongoing (eschatological) influence. It is thus capable of redemption, a fundamental Christian notion. It is likewise capable of intersubjective awareness and experience, allowing for the notion of a redeemed community (ecclesiology). Nonetheless, the entity in its post-mortem state exists in continuity with its earlier state: it is capable of retaining memories, experiences and moral attributes from its earthy existence, and it is described using the same metaphysical structure. At the same time, there is apparently no need for some of the more ambitious speculations and claims about the afterlife that continue to compromise other works in Christian eschatology.[22] And all of this takes place within (and makes crucial appeal to) the framework of panentheism, which many theologians today argue is the most adequate description of the God-world relationship.

Were one to be able to establish an adequate metaphysics of subjective immortality, two crucial tasks would still remain, both of them comparative. The first involves comparing this metaphysical system with other systems that support subjective immortality, seeking to discern which is the most plausible. If another system did a clearly *better* job of making subjective immortality plausible, one's work would be for naught; the more rational thing to do would be to endorse the more coherent conception. Conversely, if a number of metaphysical systems produce equally plausible theories of subjective im-

---

21. I am more struck by the overwhelming difficulty of the problem of evil, and thus more reticent to say that major progress has been accomplished in this area.

22. See John Polkinghorne, *The God of Hope*, and my review in the *Harvard Divinity Bulletin* 30/4 (Spring 2002), pp. 33f.

mortality, a different problem arises: one begins to worry that a rational resolution among the proposals is impossible. In this case, one begins to worry that metaphysical speculation about eschatological matters is like tennis without a net: any series of shots turns out to be adequate — one just has to make a large enough number of them. Thus the comparative task is crucial for determining the epistemic status of the outcome: should we endorse the results as true, or should we suspend belief on this topic?

A number of metaphysics support only objective immortality (including Whitehead's), or no immortality at all (most forms of naturalism and physicalism). By contrast, all systems that understand humans to have an immortal soul (Thomism, of course, but also most doctrines of reincarnation) equally support subjective immortality. Indeed, one need not be a Thomist, for one also finds coherent defenses of this notion in the context of Platonic or Neoplatonic doctrines of participation and emanation, within substance theories of the person (as in the Patristic authors), within many forms of panentheism, and within the framework of modern, Cartesian dualism.

(In fact, for *anyone* who accepts that there is an eternal God whose power is unlimited, it is always possible — and conceptually coherent — to assert that this God preserves the subjective side of each person after her death, even if no metaphysical category is employed that would otherwise guarantee such immortality. Such views are less satisfying metaphysically, of course, but they are not for that reason alone incoherent. Anyone who holds to the omnipotence of God can reasonably assert the possibility of subjective immortality, whatever the rest of her metaphysics looks like; she simply appeals to the free choice of an Agent who is able to bring anything to pass.)

Conversely, one would have to say that the metaphysically "tightest" defenses of subjective immortality are those systems that advocate a metaphysical substance that endures over time and that is in its very nature eternal. Such systems, one might say, win the battle by presupposing victory from the start. After them, the next most credible alternatives for defending immortality are those positions that begin with the idea of a subject that exists over an extended period of time. Since these positions take personhood or subjectivity as basic metaphysical categories, it is easier for them to give an account of post-mortem existence.

To the extent that a position is Whiteheadian, it interprets subjectivity primarily in terms of momentary occasions of experience and creativity. Suchocki has shown that such positions *can* be adapted to support subjective immortality. One must acknowledge at the end of the day, however, that systems based on momentary units of experience will have more work to do to get to subjective immortality than the ones just listed. (Of course, other systems face even more difficulty than process thought in getting to subjective immortality. One thinks, for example, of the attempt by Nancey Murphy and others to combine thoroughgoing physicalism with theism. Certainly this is an even more difficult task than combining process idealism with theism!) Suchocki can be more successful than Whitehead was in establishing the possibility of subjective immortality because she expands the notion of the actual occasion into the idea of a subject that is extended over time, and because she allows for direct inter-subjective causation between subjects — in short, because she has brought her Whiteheadian eschatology much closer to the major modern theories of the subject.

The second comparative task facing the theologian is to evaluate the link between a particular metaphysic (in this case, a neo-Whiteheadian ontology) and the core concepts of the Christian tradition. How close to, or how distant from, the central ideas of traditional eschatology is the thought-world that we have been exploring? In Suchocki's conception, although there is subjective immortality, there is no concept of an actual future eschaton. History as such does not have a culmination. Instead, individual subjects undergo a process of progressive redemption; as a byproduct of that process, communities of redeemed individuals may in principle be formed.

On reflection, perhaps it is not surprising that Suchocki leaves no place for an objective eschaton as conceived in biblical eschatology: "Then I saw a new heaven and a new earth, for the first heaven and the first earth had passed away, and there was no longer any sea" (Rev. 21:1). On her view, what we call the physical world is already derivative. In one sense, on this view there *is* no ultimately existing physical world; there are only the regular patterns inherited from past data, which form the basis for physical prehensions. The part of the world that consists of data and patterns can be retained within the mind of God and thus enjoy objective immortality — which, Suchocki would presumably argue, is all the immortality it needs. No moment of transition from this world to the next is needed since, she believes, that transition takes place continually in the consequent nature of God. Predictably, then, the only culmination or redemption it makes sense to hope for on her view is the ongoing community with God and with other persons or occasions. I believe that there are resources in process thought for doing greater justice to the inherent value of the physical and biological worlds (as in the work of Charles Birch), but those resources are not developed here.

Finally, how should the present conception be judged against the two criteria spelled out in the opening paragraphs of this chapter? Does it recognize its own epistemic limitations, and does it provide reason for hope? Little if any attention is given in *The End of Evil* to the epistemic limitations inherent in eschatological thinking. Suchocki's statements and arguments are made in the assertorical mode; one finds no hint of self-limitation or the regulative use of language. (Of course, one finds relatively few instances of such language in most metaphysical writing, so Suchocki is in good company.) Whiteheadians do emphasize the openness of all metaphysical systems, and Suchocki has been particularly outspoken in insisting on this feature as well.[23] Still, the epistemic status of eschatological language begs for more attention. How, for example, would one compare the assertions made about eschatology with assertions made within science or, for that matter, history? Concerns about the knowledge claims being raised do not admit of easy resolution.

Suchocki's system, if successful, scores better on the second criterion. A process philosophy with subjective immortality does in fact provide grounds for hope. To the extent that one experiences existence as a subject — a locus of activity, decision and valuation, including self-valuation — one inherently wishes for a continuation not just of the *memories* of one's existence but also of the principle of activity itself, since this principle is basic to our self-understanding and self-evaluation in the present. Suchocki's conception is consistent with such a hope.

---

23. See Suchocki's paper for the March, 2003, conference on Whitehead and Schleiermacher at the Center for Process Studies at Claremont, under the title "System without Certainty."

Behind the Veil: Evolutionary Naturalism and the Question of Immortality

John F. Haught

v/.10

The philosophy of naturalism — by which I mean the modern belief that "nature is all there is" — insists that our consciousness will not survive our dying. Endorsed by the physicalist claim that there is no immaterial reality, and by the Darwinian suspicion that ideas such as "soul" and "spirit" are best understood as adaptive fictions, naturalism claims that at death our consciousness vanishes into the void forever. And because epochs from now our universe itself will fade away as a consequence of excessive heat or cold (probably the latter), the naturalist must add that any larger history of sentience and consciousness in the cosmos will also expire utterly. There will be nothing or nobody to remember any trace of it.

Duke University philosopher Owen Flanagan delivers a sustained defense of the naturalist's rejection of life beyond death in his recent book *The Problem of the Soul*. He admits that most people believe that the human soul or self will live on after death. But, he argues, such beliefs are irrational, since science can provide no evidence to support them. Not only are they irrational, they are also an annoying impediment to the spread of naturalism, the prospering of which Flanagan takes to be the primary mission of contemporary philosophy. One might respond to him that even if they turn out to be misguided, beliefs in immortality don't cause any trouble. But Flanagan's rebuttal is that indeed "they are causing trouble." He explains:

> Most philosophers and scientists in the twenty-first century see their job as making the world safe for a fully naturalistic view of

things. The beliefs in nonnatural properties of persons, indeed of any nonnatural things, including — yes — God, stand in the way of understanding our natures truthfully and locating what makes life meaningful in a nonillusory way. . . . .Furthermore, historical evidence abounds that sectarian religious beliefs not only lack rational [i.e. scientific] evidence or support, but they are at least partly at the root of terrible human practices — religious wars, terrorism, and torture. Yes, I know the answer; such calamities come at the hands of fanatics. Even if this is true, the fact is that fanatics are fanatics because they believe that what they believe is indubitably true.[1]

There are varieties of naturalism, but Flanagan's is unabashedly materialistic. Since as far back as the 17th Century the harder forms of naturalism have almost always been accompanied by what Alfred North Whitehead calls "scientific materialism," the belief that the lifeless and mindless abstractions of science are the ontological foundation of all that is real.[2] Their commitment to this belief system makes it impossible for adherents of naturalism such as Flanagan to accept any prospect of conscious life after death. And it also logically excludes the possibility that all the human centuries of effort and creativity can have any permanent significance. The great American psychologist and philosopher William James expressed in the frankest of terms just what materialist naturalism implies as far as the human quest for immortality is concerned:

> That is the sting of it, that in the vast driftings of the cosmic weather, though many a jewelled shore appears, and many an enchanted cloud-bank floats away, long lingering ere it be dissolved — even as our world now lingers for our joy — yet when these transient products are gone, nothing, absolutely *nothing* remains, to represent those particular qualities, those elements of preciousness which they may have enshrined. Dead and gone are they,

1. Owen Flanagan, *The Problem of the Soul: Two Visions of Mind and How to Reconcile Them* (New York: Basic Books, 2002), 167-68.

2. Alfred North Whitehead, *Science and the Modern World* (New York: The Free Press, 1967), 17. "Matter" here is really a name for the lifeless quantitative abstractions (especially what are called "primary qualities") of modern science.

gone utterly from the very sphere and room of being. Without an echo; without a memory; without an influence on aught that may come after, to make it care for similar ideals. This utter final wreck and tragedy is of the essence of scientific materialism as at present understood.[3]

Flanagan, by the logic of his own commitments, has to agree with this assessment. The majority of the world's people, on the other hand, would consider the final extinguishing of mind and spirit to be the greatest of evils. The possibility that consciousness — not to mention all of its historical expressions — could end up in the pit of absolute nothingness is unthinkable. This revulsion is not enough by itself to validate rationally the hope for immortality, of course. But since the large majority of people still believe in some form of survival after death — whether through bodily resurrection, the soul's immortality, or reincarnation culminating in a state of final liberation — we may be forgiven for continuing to wonder whether they are indulging in nothing more than wishful thinking. As sociologist Peter Berger has argued, our everyday gestures of laughing, playing and hoping all arise from a deeply lodged intuition that the empirical world, circumscribed as it is by death, is only a small part of a much wider metaphysical setting in which death may indeed prove, after all, not to be the final word. Even those who formally affirm the absolute finality of death still rebel, at least at some level of their being, against the notion that their own consciousness will ever come to an abrupt and definitive cessation. They continue to affirm in their hearts what their naturalism requires that they deny in their thoughts.[4]

But what about these thoughts? Is human rationality destined to remain completely estranged from our heart-felt hopes that consciousness can survive death? Sad as it may be, the naturalists reply, scientifically enlightened rationality now obliges us to abandon any such expectation. Science has shown, they maintain, that all anticipation of survival beyond death is completely illusory. And in contemporary science it is especially Darwinian insights that have decisively ex-

3. William James, *Pragmatism* (Cleveland: Meridian Books, 1964), 76.

4. Peter L. Berger, *A Rumor of Angels: Modern Society and the Rediscovery of the Supernatural* (Garden City, N.Y.: Doubleday, 1969).

posed the fanciful character of all human longing for conscious immortality.[5]

According to today's Darwinian naturalists, the *real* reason that Berger finds the denial of death's finality so deeply embedded in our nature has nothing at all to do with the actual existence of a transcendent dimension where the soul's survival could be sealed forever. There is a much simpler, purely natural explanation for such naive trust. The *ultimate* reason for belief in immortality is that this kind of belief, or at least the kind of cerebral apparatus that gives rise to dreams of endless existence, has proven to be adaptive in an evolutionary sense.[6] It has been adaptive, first of all, at the level of the individual human organism, and perhaps also at that of the religious group.[7] The hope for immortality has led persons and communities, for example, into the belief that they have an eternal worth, and such a conviction in turn has given them a reason to live well and bear children — in the face of all suspicions that life and the universe may in fact have no ultimate meaning.[8] Second, however, the sense of having a destiny beyond death is ultimately adaptive at the genetic level. Belief in immortality has allowed human genes to achieve their own kind of immortality. Indeed, the genes that long ago — probably during the Pleistocene — engineered brains that were able to entertain thoughts about immortality were the very genes that proved, on the average, to be the most reproductively successful. And these are the genes that took up residence in our own bodies and that still incline our brains to believe (falsely, of course) that we too are destined for immortal conscious existence.[9]

5. See, for example, Flanagan, 301-10; and Daniel C. Dennett, *Darwin's Dangerous Idea: Evolution and the Meaning of Life* (New York: Simon & Schuster, 1995).

6. Robert Hinde, *Why Gods Persist: A Scientific Approach to Religions* (New York: Routledge, 1999). Walter Burkert, *Creation of the Sacred: Tracks of Biology in Early Religions* (Cambridge, Mass.: Harvard University Press, 1996); Pascal Boyer, *Religion Explained: The Evolutionary Origins of Religious Thought* (New York: Basic Books, 2001).

7. Biologist David Sloan Wilson takes a "group-selection" approach to the explanation of religion in *Darwin's Cathedral: Evolution, Religion and the Nature of Society* (Chicago: University of Chicago Press, 2002).

8. The naturalist proposal that religion is adaptive fiction is clearly exemplifed by E. O. Wilson's book *Consilience: The Unity of Knowledge* (New York: Vintage Books, 1999).

9. This is why Pascal Boyer, in his immodestly titled book *Religion Explained*, refers to religious claims as "airy nothing." Some Darwinian naturalists are content to

Therefore, now that we can comprehend, by dint of Darwinism, the "genealogy" of our natural inclination to project the fiction of human "souls" into a deathless beyond, can't we finally dispense with all the bungling attempts by philosophy and theology to establish the *truth* of ideas of immortality? Since these ideas, or the kind of brains on which such ideas are parasitic, can now be explained quite economically in terms of adaptive functioning, do we need any further proof of their unreasonableness? If science finds that the sense of having an immortal soul or self has persisted so long because it is adaptive in an evolutionary sense, doesn't this make it all the less necessary for us to worry about whether such beliefs have an epistemically referential standing?[10]

At least this is how today's Darwinian naturalists typically deal with the notion of immortality, as well as with religious ideas more generally speaking. They do not doubt that we are born with brains that annoyingly still have a tendency to *believe* in gods. Likewise, they allow that the propensity to extend ourselves imaginatively toward endless life beyond the grave lies buried deeply and perhaps even permanently in the digital instructions that shape our brains. The kind of genetic trickery that gives rise to religious hope in humans is just one among countless ways by which strands of DNA work to get themselves passed on to the future. Consequently, since it now appears that the roots of religion lie more foundationally in biology than in culture, many of the Darwinian naturalists no longer expect historical or cultural change alone to eradicate our pious fantasizing.[11] Even during an age of scientific enlightenment, phantasms of deity and im-

---

say that religious ideas are themselves adaptive. Others, with a bit more restraint, argue that it is the kind of *brains* that give rise to religious fantasies, rather than necessarily the religious ideas themselves, that can be fully explained in Darwinian terms.

10. Some naturalists, such as Flanagan, apparently realize that the justification of beliefs is logically independent of where they came from. But their own belief that religion *must* be susceptible to an exclusively naturalist explanation compels them today to look to Darwin for ultimate, and if possible, adequate explanation. In general, however, most Darwinian critics of religion (see note 6) believe that by explaining religious ideas naturalistically they have also explained them away epistemologically. For a sustained critique of such rationalization, see Holmes Rolston III, *Genes, Genesis and God: Values and Their Origins in Natural and Human History* (New York: Cambridge University Press, 1999).

11. See, for example, Burkert, 2-8.

mortality will more than likely linger on, if for no other reason than that human genes continue to create brains inclined to entertain such "counterintuitive" conceits.

It is not surprising then that the new Darwinian interpreters of religion are not nearly so hostile or unsympathetic to religious believers as were earlier critics of religion. After all, the new generation of debunkers realize that they have the same genetic make-up as their religiously deluded conspecifics. A major exception to this restraint is the Oxford evolutionist Richard Dawkins, but most other Darwinian naturalists, although no less sure than Dawkins that Darwin has made religion completely implausible, are usually far more forgiving.[12] In general, the new devotees of "evolutionary psychology" are reluctant to criticize religious tendencies and habits too harshly or openly, in part because they must realize that without religion's adaptive effectiveness in their own ancestry they would not be here today. Even though they are convinced that the idea of immortality is entirely fictitious, some of them are willing to condone and even cultivate this illusion's flourishing among the scientifically naive.[13]

Former ages were generally able to respond much more positively to human anxiety about the finality of death than are many thoughtful people after Darwin. Yet even before Darwin's own ideas had become widely known, the English poet Alfred Lord Tennyson's grief-filled poem "In Memoriam" was already expressing an agonizing uncertainty about the implications of evolution.[14] The same protracted lament that recorded his vexation at "nature red in tooth and claw" also expressed his century's looming apprehensions about immortality:

12. See, for example, the books, cited above, by Boyer, Burkert, E. O. Wilson and David Sloan Wilson, all of whom are Darwinian materialists, but who do not express such scorn and overt hostility toward religion as does Dawkins in such books as *River Out of Eden* (New York: Basic Books, 1995) and *Climbing Mount Improbable* (New York: W. W. Norton & Co., 1996).

13. See, for example, Loyal Rue, *By the Grace of Guile: The Role of Deception in Natural History and Human Affairs* (New York: Oxford University Press, 1994), 82-127, 261-306. Rue calls religious ideas "lies," but he has no objection to our believing in them for the sake of evolutionary adaptation.

14. William E. Phipps, in an informative study of Darwin's own religious beliefs, notes that even before Darwin's *Origins* was published, Tennyson had already become familiar at least with the evolutionary ideas of Robert Chambers. *Darwin's Religious Odyssey* (Harrisburg, Pennsylvania: Trinity Press International, 2002), 95.

Behold we know not anything;
I can but trust that good shall fall
At last — far off — at last, to all,
And every winter change to spring.

So runs my dream: but what am I?
An infant crying in the night:
An infant crying for the light:
And with no language but a cry.

O life as futile, then, as frail!
O for thy voice to soothe and bless!
What hope of answer, or redress?
Behind the veil, behind the veil.[15]

Marjorie Suchocki's work is notable for its exceptional sensitivity to this sort of outcry. She is aware that all of us have experienced, or will experience, at least something of Tennyson's sense of loss. And this has led her to look deeply into Alfred North Whitehead's thoughts about what might last amidst all perishing. Digging beneath Whitehead's own hesitations about subjective immortality, she has reaffirmed the plausibility of what had been a much more widespread hope before the age of science.[16] In sympathy with her project, I offer the following reflections on perishing and immortality in a post-Darwinian world.

Beyond All Reach

Belief in immortality, of course, is inseparable from what we usually refer to as religion. But just what is religion? Religion, as Alfred North Whitehead has exquisitely put it,

15. Alfred Lord Tennyson, "In Memoriam." For a readable study of 19th Century British skepticism see A. N. Wilson, *God's Funeral* (New York: W. W. Norton, 1999).

16. Marjorie Hewitt Suchocki, *God, Christ, Church: A Practical Guide to Process Theology* (New York: Crossroad, 1982); *The End of Evil* (Albany: SUNY Press, 1988), 81-96; Lewis S. Ford and Marjorie Suchocki, "A Whiteheadian Reflection on Subjective Immortality," *Process Studies*, Vol. 7, No. 1, 1977, 1-13.

. . . is the vision of something which stands beyond, behind, and within, the passing flux of immediate things; something which is real, and yet waiting to be realized; something which is a remote possibility, and yet the greatest of present facts; something that gives meaning to all that passes, and yet eludes apprehension; something whose possession is the final good, and yet is beyond all reach; something which is the ultimate ideal, and the hopeless quest.[17]

Whitehead is not unwilling to name the "something" that stands beyond, behind, and within, the passing flux of immediate things "God." And he thinks of God as saving everlastingly all that appears to our limited vision to be mere transience.[18] Suchocki is right to argue that, if God is able to save all that perishes, and if we ourselves are not to perish absolutely, then that which "gives meaning to all that passes" must be able in some way to preserve everlastingly our own subjectivity. If immortality were only "objective," and our own subjectivity were to be snuffed out for good, it could hardly be maintained that God *saves* the world in anything but a trivial sense of the term. Still, one cannot help asking why that which allegedly delivers all beings from the stigma of impermanence has to be itself so unavailable to human experience now, so lacking in obviousness. Why does what Whitehead calls the final good and the greatest of present facts have to be beyond all reach? And, along with the reality of God, why does our own final destiny often appear to be so much in doubt?

An obvious, but too often overlooked, reason for all this uncertainty must be that the universe, in which our lives and our religious aspirations are now absorbed, is still in process. If the cosmos were a completed state of being, rather than still becoming, we might legitimately expect the veil to be drawn back so as to let complete clarity shine through all at once, as Tennyson's anguished "In Memoriam" implicitly requests. But if everything, including our own awareness

17. Whitehead, *Science and the Modern World*, 191-92.
18. Alfred North Whitehead, *Process and Reality*, corrected edition, edited by David Ray Griffin and Donald W. Sherburne (New York: The Free Press, 1968), 29, 60, 81-82, 86-104, 346-51; and Alfred North Whitehead, "Immortality," in Paul A. Schillpp, editor, *The Philosophy of Alfred North Whitehead* (Evanston and Chicago: Northwestern University Press, 1941), 682-700.

and knowledge, is not yet fully formed, there can — at least for now — be no crisp resolution in our frustrating attempts to determine whether our perishing is final or whether the creative process is indeed saved in God's everlasting compassion. The uncertainty within all religious hope is itself a function of the fact that humans, with all their aspirations, are part of an immense cosmos still in the making.[19] Since it is not yet fully actualized, it is not surprising that they can discern only dimly what this universe, and they within it, are really all about.

It is difficult, though, for humans to put up for long with the uncertainty of an unfinished cosmos. So they strain in various ways to make it complete. For example, as far apart as religious literalism and materialist naturalism are in most respects, at root they share an unseasonable demand for present certainty in an inevitably ambiguous — because still emerging — universe. The impetuosity of their common craving for foundational clarity does not really fit well into a world whose full flowering could never become manifest in any perishing present moment. But the craving is persistent — and often dangerous.

One of the constant temptations of religion, as theologian Charles Davis notes, is the obsession with certitude.[20] But one of Whitehead's most important achievements was to have shown that scientific materialism is also the direct consequence of an obsession with certitude. It stems from an enchantment with the apparent clarity of scientific abstractions that have lost contact with the actually confusing and complex cosmic process from which they were abstracted. The confounding of scientific clarity with what is truly fundamental about reality is, according to Whitehead, one of the modern mind's most problematic but persistent habits.[21] That it still underlies

19. This is a point made especially well by Pierre Teilhard de Chardin, *Christianity and Evolution*, trans. René Hague (New York: Harcourt Brace & Co., 1969), 81-84.

20. See Charles Davis, *Temptations of Religion* (New York: Harper & Row, 1974).

21. Whitehead, *Process and Reality*, 162, 173. For Whitehead ideas that are the clearest and most distinct are not necessarily the most in touch with the actual concrete world: "Those elements of our experience which stand out clearly and distinctly in our consciousness are not its basic facts" (162). And: "It must be remembered that clearness in consciousness is no evidence for primitiveness in the genetic process: the opposite doctrine is more nearly true" (173).

allegedly "scientific" attempts to wipe the ambiguities of religion off the map of contemporary intellectual culture is openly exemplified by Flanagan's *The Problem of the Soul*. This work — by one of America's most respected contemporary philosophers — argues with great fervor that in the interest of truth the "humanistic image" of ourselves as spiritual beings endowed with free will and religious tendencies must now be completely *replaced* by the more realistic "scientific image." The scientific image, for its part, entails that "we are animals that evolved according to the principles of natural selection." The humanistic and scientific images, Flanagan claims, are incompatible, so we must choose between them. "One image says humans are possessed of a spiritual part — an incorporeal mind or soul — and that one's life and eternal fate turn on the fate of this soul. The other image says that there is no such thing as the soul and thus that nothing — nothing at all — depends on its state." "When we die, we — or better, the particles that once composed us — return to nature's bosom, not to God's right hand."[22]

In the conclusion to his book, virtually every page of which chastises those of us with cloudier images of ourselves than his own, Flanagan asserts that people who choose the scientific image can look with unequalled clarity into the ultimate depths of themselves and nature. Indeed, beyond what naturalism is able to discern there lies absolutely nothing:

> . . . if you want more [than what naturalism allows], if you wish that your life had prospects for transcendent meaning, for more than the personal satisfaction and contentment you can achieve while you are alive, and more than what you will have contributed to the well-being of the world after you die, then you are still in the grip of illusions. Trust me, you can't get more. But what you can get, if you live well, is enough. Don't be greedy. Enough is enough.[23]

Perhaps if our universe were currently a completed and finalized state of being, and if clarity were the same as depth, Flanagan could

22. Flanagan, ix-x.
23. Flanagan, 319.

rightly demand such an end to all ambiguity. Transparency might then justifiably replace our presently befogged vision. But as long as the world remains in the process of coming into being, and we ourselves are fully participant in a still fragmentary creation, logically speaking we cannot realistically expect at any present moment to make out clearly what it is all about, let alone what lies beyond, behind or within the transient flux of events. It is inevitable therefore that what Whitehead calls "the greatest of present facts" will lie beyond all reach. And present uncertainty about our own destinies will be a correlate of this state of affairs. In making the world "safe for naturalism," on the other hand, Flanagan's ideal philosopher must strive to eliminate vagueness, uncertainty — and hence all forms of religious hope.

It is also true, of course, that in the context of an unfinished universe the reasons for despair may seem at times more persuasive than those that enkindle hope. The same century that produced Tennyson also gave birth to Algernon Charles Swinburne. Moved by a rising scientism and skepticism about the factual basis of Christian faith, this poet, no less than our philosopher Flanagan, was quite sure that all perishing is final:

> We thank with brief thanksgiving
> Whatever Gods may be
> That no life lives forever;
> That dead men rise up never;
> That even the weariest river
> Winds somewhere safe to sea.[24]

In the last century and a half the number of those who have migrated from Tennyson's anguished doubt to Swinburne's and Flanagan's clarity about the issue of immortality has gradually increased, in no small measure because of the appeal of Darwinian naturalism.[25]

---

24. Algernon Charles Swinburne, "The Garden of Persephone."

25. Again, Flanagan's naturalistic manifesto is a wonderfully clear recent illustration.

Perishing: Three Possible Perspectives

Flanagan's dream of a world in which the "humanistic image" will be completely replaced by the "scientific image" is not likely to be fulfilled, as even many Darwinian naturalists now reluctantly agree. It is much more probable that most humans will continue to trust, even if only tacitly, that death is not a definitive ending to awareness. For most humans, the prospect of an absolute perishing of consciousness would entail the final victory of evil over good.

Our own death is itself an instance of the fact of universal perishing, and it is the plain and simple fact of perishing, along with the inevitable fading of the past, as Alfred North Whitehead observes, that constitutes the core of the problem of evil for the religions of the world.[26] The flux of becoming and disintegration that caused Heraclitus to weep long ago is no less a reason for sadness today than it was for him. And the fact that exquisitely ordered living beings can eventually disintegrate into shapeless atomic stuff is especially to be lamented. The fact that the most precious entities, those endowed with life, mind, freedom and personality, are the most perishable of all is reason for unending meditation.

Human reflection on the fact of perishing has generally taken three distinct forms. Without getting too technical at this point, let us call these three options *naturalistic fatalism, otherworldly optimism* and *long-suffering hope.* (Henceforth I shall usually refer to these simply as *fatalism, optimism* and *hope.*) We may, of course, decide not to reflect seriously on the fact of impermanence at all. It is always possible to take refuge in the illusion that perishing is unreal and that we will somehow escape it ourselves. And so, *escapism* is a fourth, though not a serious, option.[27]

Fatalism views all loss as permanent and irredeemable. As the earlier quote from William James so clearly shows, it is resigned to

26. For Whitehead's discussion of "perishing" see especially *Process and Reality,* 340-41, 346-51.

27. Obviously the following typology does not capture all the nuance in the different understandings of human destiny. Moreover, I am using the terms fatalism, mysticism and hope in ways that a lengthier and more detailed historical study would considerably qualify. However, the point of a typology is to "seek simplicity." Afterwards one may distrust it.

the opinion that the stream of perishing events heads only toward complete nothingness, and that therefore the universe is ultimately "pointless." Fatalism also agrees that human life has no lasting purpose, although, unlike escapism, it sometimes allows for a tragic nobility in the courageous resignation to death and the final meaninglessness of the universe. Flanagan argues that the finally futile course of human lives can allow for moments of "flourishing," but he is absolutely sure that fatalism is the only interpretation of the cosmos that squares realistically with the flow of time, the remorseless laws of physics, Darwinian selection, and the far-off but inevitable demise of the universe.[28]

Otherworldly optimism, on the other hand, willingly acknowledges the fact of perishing but claims to experience, at least vaguely, an abiding and much more "real" world of permanence beneath or behind the transient flow of events. For the optimist the passage of time and the perpetual perishing of events in the visible cosmos is generally viewed as a kind of "veil" behind which lies the timeless splendor of the eternal. Time and history, in this reading, only lead us away from an absolute and unchanging Perfection. Accordingly, salvation must mean the retrieval of a fullness that exists in the mythical past or in an eternal present immune to the passage of time. And so, the meaning of our lives is to be found not in denying temporal loss, which would be escapism, but in overcoming time altogether in order to place ourselves in the atemporal presence of the divine. Since it is time that leads to loss, optimism must respond to loss by seeking the eternal beneath, behind or beyond time. Authentic life, it would follow, is a mighty struggle against the temporal flow, and religion's purpose is to teach us how to neutralize or vanquish the erosive passage of moments by stretching our souls even now toward the eternal.

Optimism is an appealing option, and it is one that many educated people still find attractive. Today those who embrace the otherworldly optimist's response to the world's perpetual perishing are often scientifically informed, but they generally consider modern science, including evolutionary ideas, to be religiously inconsequential. Since science is concerned only with the temporal world, its discoveries, including those of Darwin, can allegedly have little or no

28. Flanagan, 279-86, 315-17.

bearing on the religious sense of a timeless sacred world that underlies all appearances. Much contemporary theology is still attached to the optimist solution and, as a result, remains indifferent to science, evolution and cosmology. Ironically, it does so, as I shall argue later, at the risk of losing an appropriately robust understanding even of the individual person's destiny beyond death.

Our third option is long-suffering hope. Hope also acknowledges the fact of perpetual perishing, but it rejects as premature, untested and arbitrary the fatalist's judgment that perishing is ever final or that the cosmic process is "pointless." And, by way of distinguishing itself from what I am here calling otherworldly optimism, it trusts that the flow of time may lead the whole universe — and not just the individual soul — *forward*, toward an everlasting fulfillment that beckons, as it were, from the end of time. In this perspective the individual's concern about conscious survival after death is inseparable from the larger question of what eventually happens to the *entire* flow of perishing events that we call the universe. Whereas optimism (as I am understanding it typologically here) is acosmic, hope stays close to both human history and the physical course of events.[29] Hope does not try to neutralize, reverse or conquer time. Instead it pictures the vast temporal unfolding of the universe as being taken into the divine life and there saved from absolute loss.

Thus, in all the ambiguity of perishing, diminishment and creativity, hope views time as full of *promise*. Unlike otherworldly optimism, hope invites us to stay with time, not to negate it; for each moment of time is a seedling that sprouts toward an unprecedented future. What is permanent to the eyes of hope is not an eternal divine stillness lurking in the background, completely untouched by the flow of time. Rather what abides is a constant and faithful newness rising perpetually on the horizon of an always dawning future. This ever-faithful coming of a new future is the experiential basis for hope.

The permanence beyond perishing, in this third interpretation, is apprehended — obscurely, never clearly — by anticipation rather

---

29. Of course, there are instances of cosmic mysticism also, but most of these still deny or ignore the reality of time. A major exception is Teilhard de Chardin's "cosmic mysticism," which actually illustrates more approximately what I am calling "hope."

than by the immediate epiphany of a presently unchanging Plenitude. And the perpetual perishing that living beings all experience is not simply loss to which they must fatalistically resign themselves, but the effect of a constantly arriving future. As the future arrives afresh in each moment, the newness of being that it brings with it pushes the present into the past. But this past also abides in some way, entering causally into the shaping of the present and future. Hope, then, is a reverential and patient openness to the new, but also a posture that refuses to consign the past to complete oblivion. It looks toward a future redemption of all events that have faded into the past. It realistically allows the present to be pushed into the past, not in the spirit of tragic resignation, but in the expectancy that the redemptive future will in some way preserve and continually reconfigure the past by situating its "givenness" in an ever widening pattern of meaning. As events pass by they do not vanish into absolute nothingness. Otherwise, as Charles Hartshorne points out, we could not talk about them at all.[30] Instead the moments of time keep adding up and accumulating. They remain ingredients in each new present and lie open to being retained everlastingly by the future that lies "beyond all reach."

Fatalism, optimism and hope all have ancient pedigrees. Fatalism's remote exemplar is ancient Greek tragedy and stoicism. Optimism is foreshadowed by Platonic thought with its emphasis on an unchanging ideal world existing above time, untouched by perishing. And hope finds its classic expression in the prophetic or "eschatological" religious traditions that have understood time, in all of its transience, to be filled with the promise of a fulfillment beyond all reach. Abrahamic hope associates God with the *fulfillment* of time, history and creation rather than with an unchanging completeness existing serenely apart from the flow of perishable events.

I believe that in addressing the fact of loss in our own lives we are all obliged to choose from this three-fold set: fatalism, optimism and hope (or to opt out of choosing, by way of escapism). Of course, in actuality we often fabricate hybrid versions of the three options. Given the ambiguity of our actual lives, elements of fatalism, optimism and hope are usually intertwined with one another, and this

---

30. Charles Hartshorne, *The Logic of Perfection* (Lasalle, Illinois: Open Court Publishing Co., 1962), 250; 24-62.

tangle is itself commingled with some degree of escapism. In the history of religion, fatalism is often tinged with optimism, optimism laced with hope, and hope itself never completely cured of pessimism and impatience. Moreover, during the course of a single life one may oscillate back and forth along the range of options.

Nevertheless, where real life is tolerant of such ambiguity, theology is permitted to look for logical consistency. The three options cannot all be right. One of them — if indeed these are the only available options — must be more in tune with the nature of things, including what science has discovered, than are the others. Does science, and especially Darwinian science, match up better with fatalism, optimism or hope? Flanagan and other Darwinian naturalists are certain that Darwinism goes best with materialist fatalism, but is this necessarily so?

Let me set the stage for a response. We must all first choose, logically speaking, between fatalism on the one hand and optimism or hope on the other. This is a forced option since fatalism is incompatible with either of the other two. That is, we are logically compelled to decide between a view of things that discerns a saving permanence behind the veil of becoming and one that views all perishing as final.[31] One of these options is true and the other necessarily false. However, the alternative to fatalism forks off into both optimism and hope. Otherworldly optimism aspires to lift the shroud of impermanence abruptly in order to expose the permanence it conceals. Here the religious journey and the quest for immortality consist of making one's way back behind the veil of becoming and perishing to a fast and final union with unchanging Being. For Flanagan and his philosophical friends this acosmic optimism is the only alternative to their naturalistic fatalism.

But there is another religious option available. Long-suffering hope entails a different interpretation of the becoming and perishing that stand between human consciousness and the intuition of a permanence beyond. Here the stream of perishable events is *itself* the path to the eternal, not an obstacle on that path. The world of becom-

---

31. In actual life, of course, we may retire into an escapism that seeks to avoid choosing at all. But here we are looking at the options from the point of view of logic alone.

ing is a stream into whose current we willingly immerse ourselves now, for the eternal lies not so much "beneath" or "behind" the passing flux of immediate things as "up ahead," as the goal of the whole universe's temporal passage. Both optimism and hope, which Whitehead unfortunately tends to conflate, draw us toward the eternal. But optimism interprets the world's temporal flow as pulling us away from God. Time is a current that one must constantly struggle *against* in order to remain anchored to the really real that lies upstream.[32] Hope, on the other hand, is willing to suffer here and now the uncertainty of becoming and perishing, *wagering* (not seeing clearly) that somewhere — "far off, at last" — the river of events flows into that which abides without end. In the vision of hope, the stream of becoming is not something to climb out of in order to strand ourselves on an imagined embankment free from the natural flow. Rather, the flow of events is something that bears us along with it to the expansive sea in which the whole series of cosmic happenings, including our own life-stories, finds its ultimate fulfillment.

Fully aware of the risk of oversimplification here, let me nonetheless suggest again that each one of us born into this ambiguous, unfinished and perishing universe must, at least by the logic of default, choose between fatalism on the one hand and one of the other two ways of reading a transient universe on the other. Our first reading, the one most tempting to the scientific naturalist, may also be called cosmic pessimism. This approach reads things through tragedian eyes that see no lasting "point" to the universe since the world finally flows over a cliff into the pit of irretrievable impermanence. Here the transience of life and the final perishing of all things are taken as signals of the ultimate futility of the universe and the story of life within it. This interpretation seems most "realistic" to its many contemporary adherents because it professes not to go beyond the "facts" as these are made available by science.[33]

32. See the maps provided by the so-called "perennial philosophy," as, for example, in Sayyed Hossein Nasr, *Religion and the Order of Nature* (New York: Oxford University Press, 1996), 12.

33. *Cosmic* pessimism, as Flanagan's book illustrates, is not inconsistent with a certain kind of starry-eyed individual and social "optimism" that allows for a parochially human temporary "flourishing" (279-86; 15-17). I would propose, however, that the naturalist's inevitable *cosmic* pessimism is not at all the innocently disinterested

Optimism, as I am using the term here, is a kind of religious impatience. This option is an alluring one, for it speaks directly to our ineradicable longing for permanence. Interestingly, however, it often concurs with cosmic pessimism's conviction that the natural world itself perishes absolutely. It differs from naturalism in claiming that we, or at least our souls, do not really belong to nature, either now or eternally. The essential part of us stands permanently outside of nature, and the physical universe is ultimately insignificant except perhaps as a context for soul-making. Its great appeal is that it transports us abruptly into a Platonic beyond without letting us first taste fully of the fact of becoming and cosmic creativity. As Reinhold Niebuhr puts it, optimism (which he calls "mysticism") has a "tendency to flee the responsibilities of history and engage in premature adventures into eternity."[34] Unlike cosmic pessimism, optimism acknowledges the permanence "beyond, behind, and within, the passing flux of immediate things." But it tears itself away from this passing world, as though there were no inherent significance in participating long-sufferingly in the larger cosmic process of becoming. Virtually ignoring nonhuman life and evolution, it allows that there is only an instrumental value to the transient world and its evolution. The universe exists primarily as a school in which *humans* may prepare for an eternity outside of time. Consequently, optimism's religious impatience is unprepared to appreciate the narrative depth of the recently revealed fourteen billion years of cosmic time in which the human species has only lately appeared. The cosmic story re-

reading of nature that it professes to be. It is soaked in empirically unproven faith assumptions (such as scientism and materialism) that lead it toward a most arbitrary kind of selectivity in its choice of the particular slice of cosmological data that it takes as foundational. Whether in pursuit of Swinburne's Epicureanism, heroic absurdist stoicism, or a naturalist humanism, it leaves out many facets of nature that simply do not fit into the pessimistic paradigm (such as the perpetual replenishing of the future, and the fact of an indefinitely resourceful domain of "possibilities"). Although allegedly supported by Darwinism, cosmic pessimism can no longer claim the grounding in pure science that it has for the last century and a half. Reasons for this judgment are laid out in my two books *God After Darwin: A Theology of Evolution* (Boulder, Colo.: Westview Press, 2000) and especially *Deeper than Darwin: The Prospect for Religion in the Age of Evolution* (Boulder, Colo.: Westview Press, 2003).

34. Reinhold Niebuhr, "Introduction" to William James, *The Varieties of Religious Experience* (New York: Collier Books, 1961), 7.

mains essentially incidental to optimistic impetuosity. The other-worldly optimist opts cleanly out of this imperfect, perishing universe, refusing to watch it unfold at its own pace, along an indeterminate and richly creative trajectory.

Hope, on the other hand, is characterized by patient cosmic expectation. It shares with optimistic impatience an intuition of the permanence beyond all change. Yet it is borne toward the changeless not by a headlong hurdle out of the flux, but by staying patiently with the flow of events that carry an entire universe, and humans along with it, into the future. This patience, however, is not quietistic, but actively and enthusiastically participates in the ongoing creation of the universe. What remains permanent in this reading is not a primordial mythic *Urzeit* or a realm of static perfection untouched by time, but an ever fresh future that draws into itself the continual flow of time.

The name of this always faithful future — a future that no passage of time can ever erode, since the passage of time requires its constant arrival — is God. God, as Karl Rahner puts it, is the Absolute Future.[35] Beyond all relative futures, which will themselves eventually prove to be perishable, hope anticipates a Future that is beyond perishing. According to hope's reading of transience in the universe, impermanent things are not illusions to be discounted, but *promises* that already bear within themselves, always ambiguously, some aspect of the future that is always dawning. It is this reading that I would defend as more compatible with science than either optimistic impatience or naturalistic pessimism. Moreover, it is in terms of this hopeful response to perishing that we may find a congenial theological setting for Darwin's understanding of evolution. A "metaphysics of hope" is far more open to the actual discoveries of biology, genetics and geology than is the materialist fatalism that only feebly and fragmentarily contextualizes scientific information about life's evolution and the unfolding of the cosmos.

Unlike cosmic pessimism, a metaphysics of hope trusts that the entire universe may have a meaning or purposiveness which — because the world is still in the process of being created — is by necessity always somewhat hidden from view here and now. It may turn out

---

35. Karl Rahner, *Theological Investigations*, Vol. VI, trans. Karl and Boniface Kruger (Baltimore: Helicon, 1969), 59-68.

to be the case, then, that hope provides a much less selective and arbitrary reading of the data of current natural science than that given by the alleged "realism" of cosmic pessimism. Hope and promise, moreover, are notions logically compatible with the ambiguity and uncertainty of the present. It is not inconceivable that hope, rather than either cosmic pessimism or optimistic impatience, matches up most naturally with the picture of an unfinished universe that science is now laying out so lavishly.

Will I Survive?

However, here and now the pressing question, at least for many, is whether subjective consciousness will live on in some way after our deaths. Is such an expectation merely an illusion ultimately created by our genes in the interest of evolutionary adaptation, or is it (also) possibly a belief that — at least eventually — may turn out to be referentially true? In response, I shall make the following three points, even though here I cannot provide lengthy arguments for them.[36] First, the Darwinian naturalist's claim that human hope for immortality is purely fictitious because it, or the cerebral modules that underlie it, can be fully explained naturalistically in terms of Darwinian selection is a logical *non sequitur*. Second, this *non sequitur* itself is rooted not in science but in the materialist philosophical fatalism that still today, as in Whitehead's own lifetime, professes to be the only appropriate conceptual domicile for science. Third, and finally, I shall propose that henceforth theology should not take up the question of personal, subjective immortality except as a subordinate theme in the larger concern about the ultimate destiny of the entire universe. Let us consider each of these points in turn.

1. The Darwinian naturalist typically denies that there can be any real substance to religious hope in general, and the hope for immortality in particular, since these can be naturalistically explained as evolutionary adaptations. But such a judgment is rooted in a logical mistake. The *non sequitur* here is an instance of what has aptly been called

---

36. I have begun to do so more fully elsewhere, though much more remains to be done. See my *God After Darwin* and *Deeper than Darwin*.

the "if functional, therefore untrue" fallacy.[37] It simply does not follow that if belief in immortality is functionally adaptive in the biological sense, the content of that belief bears no relationship to reality. If the anticipation of immortality is pure illusion, then this would have to be established independently of whether or not such a belief promotes reproductive fitness.

Complex phenomena, moreover, require a plurality of levels of explanation, as even most scientists now agree. For example, the question of how life came about on earth can be answered at the levels of thermodynamics, organic chemistry, biology, biochemistry, biophysics and even astrophysics. Science is not reduced to accounting for life in terms of physics *rather than*, say, chemistry. Instead it is more likely to give an adequate account of life if it appeals to an explanatory pluralism. Likewise, theology is not necessarily interfering with science or diminishing all the scientific levels involved in the study of life's origin if it adds that life *also* (and ultimately) came about because of the generosity of God.

Flanagan, however, illustrates the naturalistic predilection for explanatory monism when he dogmatically proclaims, for example, that the features of life can be accounted for by Darwinian natural selection *rather than* by God. "Darwin's theory," he writes, "yields a credible and well-confirmed *alternative* to the Genesis story of creation."[38] It is this same kind of either/or thinking that lies behind his arbitrary assertion that people must choose between the humanistic and scientific images. Aside from revealing Flanagan's own implicit biblical literalism, such pronouncements also illustrate how easily scientific abstractions have been turned into bed-rock reality in the minds of contemporary naturalists. The mixing of an implicit biblical literalism with explanatory monism, however, is not at all rare among Darwinian naturalists.[39]

At their own respective levels of inquiry each way of accounting for life, including the Darwinian, can be pushed as far as possible

37. Rolston, *Genes, Genesis and God*, 347.

38. Flanagan, 204. Emphasis added.

39. For another clear example of this either/or approach (according to which the explanations of life must be *either* Providence *or* natural selection) see Gary Cziko, *Without Miracles: Universal Selection Theory and the Second Darwinian Revolution* (Cambridge, Mass.: MIT Press, 1995). I provide numerous other examples in *Deeper than Darwin*.

without needless fear that it is in competition with other scientific accounts, or for that matter with theological understanding. Good theology, after all, never interferes with science, but instead encourages the various natural sciences to carry out their respective inquiries to their methodological limits. What theology does not have to endorse, however, is the dogmatic claim that this or that science, or even the entirety of them, can ever give us an adequate understanding of life, or of anything else. Instead theology wagers that we are more likely to capture the full reality of things if we allow for an indefinitely deep hierarchy of explanations.

Thus, from the point of view of layered explanation or explanatory pluralism, there is no reason why the persistent human hope for immortality cannot be given *both* evolutionary *and* theological explanations simultaneously. Perhaps humans have clung to religious hope not only because it must in some sense be biologically adaptive, but also because it is aroused in us by the presence of a God who summons the whole cosmos, including conscious human subjects, toward a fulfilling future. Only an arbitrary explanatory monism — at which Darwinian naturalism is most accomplished — could logically rule out such a proposition. Scientific discovery itself cannot provide any sound basis for the Darwinian naturalist's judgment that immortality is *nothing but* an adaptive fiction.[40]

2. The Darwinian naturalist's habitual explanatory monism is itself more the consequence of an underlying materialist fatalism than of actual evidence. Quite predictably, however, those already inclined toward a materialist belief-system will see in Darwinian science the decisive confirmation of their pre-existing cosmic pessimism. For example, Stephen Jay Gould, by no means the severest critic of religion among recent Darwinians, openly claims that Darwin's science is inseparable from the "philosophical message" that the universe is purposeless and that "matter" is all there is.[41] Even physicist Steven Weinberg, famous for claiming that scientific clarity has only made the universe appear more and more pointless, discovers in Darwinism stronger reasons for his atheistic pessimism than he can find in phys-

---

40. This logical point is developed at much greater length in *Deeper Than Darwin*.

41. Stephen Jay Gould, *Ever Since Darwin* (New York: W. W. Norton, 1977), 12-13.

ics alone.[42] Increasingly over the last couple of decades Darwinian naturalism has become enshrined as the ultimate and adequate explanation of nearly all the manifestations of life, including ethics and religion. There is no good reason, though, for conflating good biology with scientific materialism. Such a confusion not only causes many religious believers unnecessarily to reject evolutionary science. As I have argued at length elsewhere, it also sabotages the worthy project of science education in cultures where the majority of people (quite rightly) see a contradiction between religious belief in God and immortality on the one hand, and materialist naturalism on the other.[43]

3. Nevertheless, what Darwinism, along with other natural sciences, can rightly claim is that we humans are indeed fully part of an evolving universe. And so, theology's preoccupation with our individual destinies can be separated only artificially from a deeper and wider concern about the cosmos as a whole and where it might end up. It is one of the felicitous consequences of evolutionary biology and cosmology that theology can no longer separate the issue of personal destiny from the larger topic of the universe's final outcome. Whether contemporary eschatology will begin to pay more attention to this linkage remains to be seen.

The doctrine of immortality, unfortunately, has flourished primarily in the context of an acosmic optimist impatience. Historically, belief in human survival beyond death seems to have fit most comfortably into a metaphysics that views the transient world of nature as itself essentially pointless — aside of course from its serving the purpose of being the backdrop for the human drama of salvation. As long as the physical universe itself was perceived as a setting only incidental or instrumental to the souls that temporarily inhabit it, our final resting place was generally pictured as a timeless spiritual realm existing altogether apart from the physical universe. To this day whenever the question of the plausibility of immortality arises, the usual assumption — as Flanagan's book illustrates — is that the only real alternative to fatalist materialism is an anticipation of the soul's final withdrawal from any contact with the cosmos at all.

---

42. Steven Weinberg, *Dreams of a Final Theory* (New York: Pantheon Books, 1992), 244-45.

43. See my books *God After Darwin* and *Deeper than Darwin*.

But there is a third possibility, that of a long-suffering hope concerned primarily with the destiny of the *whole* universe. This option ponders the question of human deliverance from death only within the ampler context of a concern for the entire universe.[44] Over the past half century science has provided indisputable evidence that the Big Bang universe is an unfinished story, a work-in-progress, and that our own emergence is continuous with that of other stages in natural history. Darwin had earlier shown that the journey of life is an immense experiment that has produced millions of species now extinct and that may still have other creative surprises in store. More recently astrophysics has extended the story of nature back into the past, into a cosmic preamble whose temporal magnitude had never been known before the twentieth century. Astrophysics now also foresees the prospect of the universe continuing on into an even more unfathomable depth of future time. Scientifically educated people realize, therefore, that humans are not situated above or beyond this ongoing cosmic story. The story is part of us, and we are an integral, though finite, part of it as it moves into an unknown future.

Humans exist within a cosmic evolution that has taken around fourteen billon years to get to where it is at present, and one that will last for many billions of years to come. Then, of course, it too will perish. And because we now understand how continuous the existence of conscious subjectivity is with the historical unfolding of an entire cosmos, we cannot help being concerned about the eventual perishing of the cosmos that is so constitutive of us. Where will all the moments of cosmic history — moments integral to our own personal stories — have gone when our universe itself fades away? Will they have simply disappeared into the void? If so, then a major portion of our own biographies will also have been lost forever.

In the face of the universe's own eventual "death" it is hard not to remain entranced by supernaturalist optimism since it proposes to satisfy cleanly and permanently the human longing to surmount the universe's perishability. However, attractive as it may appear in any moment of loss, otherworldly optimism remains unrealistically aloof from our new knowledge of the universe and our intimate confluence with it. Not only does its understanding of immortality leave much of

44. Or, perhaps, the "plurality" of universes.

us out of its partialized picture of fulfillment, it cannot answer any more satisfactorily than fatalism the question of cosmic destiny. Modern science has demonstrated that our own personal existence is tied both materially and historically into the fabric of the whole physical universe. We have no existence, even as conscious *subjects,* apart from the structure of the universe; and our own personal stories are intricately interwoven with the whole of cosmic history. Eschatology would do well to take this fact more deliberately into account than it has during all the epochs of otherworldly optimism.

The point is, if the universe as a whole were a futile drift toward absolute extinction, the significance of our own lives would be placed in question also.[45] For if humans are inseparable from the natural world, we simply cannot dualistically divorce our own search for significance from the question of what is going to happen to the entire universe. Perhaps we could have done so at a time when it seemed that our own existence and consciousness were only tenuously and accidentally connected to the physical world. But evolutionary biology, geology, neuroscience and astrophysics no longer allow us to think realistically even of human subjectivity as not belonging fully to the universe. Indeed, even our own longings for transcendence must also be those of an entire cosmic process if they are to be anything more than isolated, senseless gestures.

Our own personal existence does not terminate abruptly at the outer layer of our skin, but in subtle ways extends radially outwards into the whole of the natural environment, and temporally backwards to the first moment of cosmic origins. If this is so, then the questions of who we are, how we came to emerge from the cosmos, and whether we can expect to survive death, are inescapably linked to the issue of what the cosmos is and where it will end up. Consequently, any theological discussion of personal survival beyond death must bring along with it the question of whether in some sense the whole universe may be destined for redemption.

The thought that the *whole* of things can be saved in God may be easier to entertain if we learn to think, along with process thought,

---

45. Flanagan's ideal of temporary "flourishing" will have little appeal to those whose lives are not as comfortable and secure as that of the average twentieth-century academic.

that the universe is composed fundamentally of temporal events rather than spatialized parts. Material bits eventually dissolve and disappear forever, whereas events can add up or accumulate. Process thought will continue to be relevant to the question of human destiny, first, because it embeds us and our consciousness securely within the cosmos and, second, because it generously construes the cosmos in temporal rather than purely spatial terms. This conception allows that in God's compassionate feeling the *whole* series of cosmic occasions may escape the final wreckage that William James rightly took to be the logical consequence of materialism.

But, again, what about consciously subjective human destiny beyond death? The debate among Whiteheadians about whether immortality is only objective and not also subjective, will probably seem somewhat beside the point to the majority of religious believers. For them a merely objective immortality would differ very little from the fatalistic position sketched earlier. Thus, if process theology cannot make conceptual room for some form of subjective immortality it will not prosper among believers and theologians who "hope to enjoy forever" the vision of divine glory.

To make room for such belief it would seem that the main contribution of process thought would still lie in its defense of the idea of a God who is *absolutely related* to the universe and in whom the totality of cosmic events is internalized everlastingly.[46] *Theological* discussion of the reasonableness of hope for subjective immortality must base itself primarily on the trustworthiness of God and only secondarily on adjustments to Whitehead's metaphysics and cosmology. The theologian must ask whether God's relational power could be worthy of trust if God were thought of as presiding over the complete extinguishing of the conscious kind of subjectivity that allows humans to live in relation to God in the midst of the universe's perpetual perishing. Could we seriously contend that much of us would truly be saved everlastingly if our immortality were objective only? Objective immortality alone would differ too little from William James's portrait of the implications of materialism to provide any real religious consolation. To elicit worship and trust in the face of all loss, the divine power that

---

46. A doctrine made most explicit in Charles Hartshorne's book *The Divine Relativity* (New Haven: Yale University Press, 1948).

evokes and sustains conscious human subjectivity within the limits of a perishable, unfinished world must be able to do so also in a consummated one.

Cosmologically speaking, without God's preservation of the recently emergent *layer of consciousness* to which the universe is just now giving birth, the world *as a whole* would be largely lost. It would abide in God everlastingly only as a fragment of what it had eventually become. But if the world's Absolute Future is indeed also Absolute Relationality, then we would have a sufficient theological basis for our hopes, for the general awakening of consciousness that characterizes the latest chapter in *cosmic* emergence will never be stripped clean of its dimension of subjectivity without also diminishing God's own actuality. For this reason we can be grateful to Marjorie Suchocki for striving to show how subjective immortality may be consistent after all with the most important features of Whitehead's thought.[47]

47. See especially Suchocki's *The End of Evil*, 81-96.

Endings and Ends

4.10

Anna Case-Winters

Introduction

Traditional treatments of eschatology often deal with endings: the end of the world or the end of human life and the judgment and the consummation of all things. These are highly speculative areas of reflection, and there exists a wide theological spectrum on how these matters are best articulated and interpreted. This paper will problematize some of the prominent ways of thinking about "the end" and will propose reconsideration. The framework of process theology is exceedingly helpful for creative rethinking of Christian eschatology. Some of its best insights have been gleaned and presented very accessibly in the work of Marjorie Suchocki in her book *The End of Evil*[1] and also in her earlier work, *God-Christ-Church*.

Of Endings and Ends

Christian eschatology has been, it seems to me, most helpful when it shifts the discourse to talk less about *endings* and more about *ends* —

1. Marjorie Hewitt Suchocki, *The End of Evil: Process Eschatology in Historical Context* (Albany: State University of New York Press, 1988). Subsequent references to this book in the current chapter will be made immediately through page numbers in parentheses rather than with the aid of endnotes.

divine ends. It is the difference between centering on *end* in the sense of *terminus* or endpoint and *end* in the sense of *telos* or goal — not destination but destiny, not *endings* but *ends*. Inquiry into God's *purposes* frames the discourse on eschatology differently. Nevertheless, the question of endings does bear upon the matter of ends. For example, according to the scientific community, life on this planet will in fact have an ending when the sun has completed its life cycle. Proposals that there is such an endpoint may deepen our reflection upon the meaning and purpose of all things.[2]

A sense of meaning and purpose is a necessary ingredient in eschatological hope. Some visions engender hope and a "zest for life." The hope that is needed in our day is a hope that is greater than hope for a modest amelioration of our present circumstances. At the same time, there is need for a hope that is more tangible and immediate than Teilhard's "Omega Point." Process theology is uniquely able to compellingly articulate a hopeful vision in which divine ends are working persuasively and everlastingly in the process. This framework also engenders hope in its insistence that the future is genuinely open.

The Need for Reconsideration

Traditional understandings of Christian eschatology may benefit from reconsideration in several areas. Each of the following will be taken in turn, beginning with an effort to articulate where the difficulty lies and then showing how the resources of process thought, and Marjorie Suchocki's work in particular, resonate with the best insights of the tradition while providing a useful corrective to its distortions.

- Disconnection from scientific pictures of "endings" from a fear that they may pose a threat to meaning.
- Dual-destination thinking (heaven vs. hell) and a habit of

2. Kathryn Tanner has seen the connection clearly and poses the question whether there can be "Eschatology Without a Future?" See Tanner in *The End of the World and the Ends of God: Science and Theology on Eschatology*, ed. John Polkinghorne and Michael Welker (Harrisburg, Pa.: Trinity Press International, 2000), 222.

thought that separates judgment from redemption, assuming a destiny of judgment for some and redemption for others.

- A desiccated understanding of judgment that is easily laid aside altogether.
- An assumption of a guaranteed "triumph of the good" since God is "in control."
- A habit of collapsing into realized eschatology on the one hand or futurized eschatology on the other.

Illumination from the Field of Science

Why has Christian eschatology been so reluctant to consider scientific pictures of the world's end? While theology has affirmed the finitude of the creation, its state of being "not God," it has seemed to back away from scientific confirmations of creation's finitude. From the scientific community we learn that even if human beings do not themselves put an end to life on earth through environmental destruction or nuclear annihilation, there is still an endpoint in our future when the star which is our sun uses up its energy. Then, whether it all ends "with a bang or with a whimper," we face an ending to life as we know it. Perhaps the neglect of the scientific picture of this ending is a function of a supposed threat to meaning that this picture poses.

This may in part account for the neglect of conversation with science on this matter. However, even if it were granted that the scientific picture may pose a threat to meaning, theologians are not thereby excused from regarding it with utmost seriousness. Apart from honesty and realism, Christian hope may appear to be little more than "a consoling fantasy that somehow death is an illusion."[3] The threat must be faced in a realistic way and addressed as such.

Furthermore, theologically speaking, one may ask whether this threat is really qualitatively different from the threat to meaning which death, as such, already poses. Christian tradition has already

---

3. John Polkinghorne and Michael Welker, "Introduction: Science and Theology on the End of the World and the Ends of God," in *The End of the World and the Ends of God: Theology and Science on Eschatology*, ed. John Polkinghorne and Michael Welker, 12.

acknowledged the mortality of individual beings. Is the prospect of "the end of the world" *qualitatively* different from the threat that mortality poses to each life? Christian tradition has resisted the conclusion that human life is not meaningful because we are, as Heidegger observed, "beings toward death." The Christian claim is that, though death is real, it is not ultimate; only God is ultimate. There are ways of addressing these troubling questions theologically that have proven plausible and helpful.

Process thought is science-friendly and ready to converse about how the "end of the world" impacts theological eschatology. Without illumination from science, it is difficult to offer a "realistic" eschatology. Process theology has made a very fruitful proposal of the meaningfulness of existence in the face of the "perpetual perishing" that is our condition, and offered a way of thinking in which this reality is not the final word about our existence. When the divine "ends" are on center stage, "endings" become a relative thing. Process thought provides a ready bridge into conversation with science that may be of tremendous assistance in this endeavor.

If, as Ted Peters has suggested in his book *Science and Theology: The New Consonance*, the current conversations have evolved from a "methodological phase" through a "physics phase" and are now moving into a kind of "theological phase," the time is right for our entering a genuine conversation about the "endings" science pictures and their theological import. This encounter requires an enlarging of perspective from both fields. Theologians will be required to open their claims to more public forms of evaluation — rather than to seek to engage in special pleading and "immune them"[4] from the judgments of the sciences. "If the sciences are challenged by eschatological symbols to expand the scope of inquiry, theology, for its part, is made to confront in the most rigorous way possible the demand of publicly warranted truth claims."[5] Each field must acknowledge how it is caught up in a "hermeneutical circle" in which the "what" and the "how" of knowing are inextricably related. How things are known must accord with their nature, and that nature is revealed in what we know of them.[6] Both

---

4. Polkinghorne and Welker, 2.
5. Polkinghorne and Welker, 2.
6. Polkinghorne and Welker, 2.

theology and science share in common the quest for truth and more adequate ways of understanding and describing reality — seen and unseen. Both also have an interest in a realistic eschatology and the grounds for meaning and hope in the face of individual human and worldly finitude. There is a mutual illumination possible here that would prove highly advantageous in this connection.

Redemption and Judgment Reconsidered: God's Action in the Face of Evil

There is a prominent strand of thought within Christian tradition that separates judgment and redemption, assuming that some will be judged while others will be redeemed. There is a dual destination, a final divide between those who are saved and those who are condemned. The alternative approach articulated in process terms by Marjorie Suchocki is well grounded theologically and has much to commend it. She urges that there is a common destiny that all share, and it is one that includes judgment and redemption.[7] Further, it refers not so much to a final end point as to our ongoing history and our future with God.

The traditional concept of "heaven" as a place of perfection to be attained in the future is transformed into a present idea. It is what exists when the temporal world is perfected by its reception into the divine life. This has real effects in the real world, because God then offers this transformed state back to the world in the form of a vision and a lure. If there is a two-fold destiny it is held in common by all. It entails living deeply and richly in this life and participating everlastingly in the life of God. Redemption and judgment are a two-fold grace expressing God's creative-transformative love. Both happen here and now as well as at the "endpoints" of our lives.

There might be said to be a double aspect in God's redeeming judgment, but the differentiation has more to do with the *kind* of evil being addressed. In the face of evil as "perpetual perishing," grounded

7. This view is not altogether unlike perspectives found in more traditional theologians. Karl Barth for example assumes a joining of judgment and redemption. In fact, in his Christological treatments he speaks of both judgment and redemption as having already occurred for us in Christ. Christ as the "elect" of God has already experienced God's "yes" and God's "no."

in our finitude, God redeems. In the face of moral evil, grounded in our freedom, God judges.

In the Face of Evil as "Perpetual Perishing," God Redeems . . .

The deepest problem is temporality as such, with its "perpetual perishing." Whitehead puts it this way, "The ultimate evil in the temporal world is deeper than any specific evil. It lies in the fact that the past fades, that time is a 'perpetual perishing.'"[8] Joy, success, and the overcoming of evil, are all passing moments that do not last. Success does not finally succeed. As Jürgen Moltmann expresses this reality, "(E)very present passes, and what is past never returns. Expectations become experiences, and experiences turn into remembrances, and remembrances will in the end become the great forgetting that we call death. Yet something in us rises up in protest: 'Is that all this life has to offer?'"[9] There is, however, a conviction in Christian eschatology that this perpetual perishing is not the last word. "Death is the boundary of our lives, but not the boundary of God's relationship to us."[10]

This conviction is thoughtfully articulated in process theology. As Ground of Value,[11] God has a preserving, redeeming role. God as-

---

8. Alfred North Whitehead, *Process and Reality: An Essay in Cosmology*, Corrected Edition, ed. David Ray Griffin and Donald W. Sherburne (New York: The Free Press, 1978), 517.

9. Jürgen Moltmann, "Is There Life After Death?" in *The End of the World and the Ends of God: Theology and Science on Eschatology*, eds. John Polkinghorne and Michael Welker (Harrisburg, Pa.: Trinity Press International, 2000), 238.

10. Moltmann, 246.

11. Joseph Bracken, *Society and Spirit: A Trinitarian Cosmology* (London and Toronto: Associated University Presses, 1991), 159. Bracken proposes that a panentheism is the best way of understanding the God-World relation in Whitehead and that this understanding is enhanced by notions of society and spirit. In this view, God is immanent in the world and the world is immanent in God without loss of the independent status of either God or the world. "(A) genuinely panentheistic understanding of the God-world relationship will only be achieved if one thinks of God and the world as interpenetrating fields of activity with the field proper to creation contained within the even larger field of the divine intentional activity." Bracken's field-oriented approach avoids pantheism on the one hand and pancosmism on the other.

sures the everlasting value of each occasion by its preservation in the life of God. Each one gains an immortality in God and therefore in the temporal world. "The objective immortality of actual occasions requires the primordial permanence of God, whereby the creative advance ever re-establishes itself endowed with initial subjective aims derived from the relevance of God to the evolving world."[12]

> The problems of the fluency of God and of the everlastingness of passing experience are solved by the same factor in the universe. This factor is the temporal world perfected by its reception and its reformation, as a fulfillment of the primordial appetition that is the basis of all order. In this way God is completed by the individual, fluent satisfactions of finite fact, and the temporal occasions are completed by their everlasting union with their transformed selves, purged into conformation with the eternal order which is the final absolute 'wisdom.'[13]

"The many [are] absorbed everlastingly into the final unity."[14]

This approach is willing to acknowledge finitude and the passing of things and lodges their lasting significance in the internal life of God. In this way it resonates with theological reflections of both Karl Barth and Eberhard Jüngel. "Finitude means mortality," and "death in itself" is the "natural end of limited human existence."[15] It is *die Schattenseite* and not *das Nichtige*: the "shadowside" of creaturely existence and not "nothingness," evil in the stronger sense.[16] It is only the semblance of evil. "If through faith in God's grace people are freed from the fear resulting from sin and from the fear of death, they will also be freed for 'a natural death.' Their finite life is 'eternalized' in the memory of God: that is their redemption, not physical resurrection and the abolition of physical death."[17] Death places a "salutary limit to life."[18] It is not death

12. Whitehead, *Process and Reality*, 347.
13. Whitehead, *Process and Reality*, 346.
14. Whitehead, *Process and Reality*, 347.
15. Karl Barth, *Church Dogmatics*, trans. G. T. Thomson (Edinburgh: T&T Clark, 1960), III/2, 236-9.
16. Barth, CD III/3, 296ff.
17. Moltmann, 241.
18. Barth CD III/2, 629, 625.

that poses a problem for life, but rather life as we live it that "makes a radical problem of death." As Jüngel puts it, "the shadow cast by death (over human life) is no more than the haunting primordial shadow, now extended and magnified, which our life casts upon our ending."[19]

There is a sense in which the problem "perpetual perishing" receives a double response in process eschatology. One response is the phenomenon of *objective immortality*. Everything has lasting significance in the divine life; everything we do and are affects God everlastingly. Our enjoyment and our adding to the enjoyment of others contribute to God's own joy. Our pain and sorrow are nowhere more felt than in God's own being. Things do not simply "perish" as God acts with "tender care that nothing be lost."[20]

Another response to the problem is an affirmation of *subjective immortality* — a continuation of personal existence. This is proposed alongside objective immortality — the everlasting effects upon God and the world of our having lived. Subjective immortality would be a kind of continuation of our subjective selves though transformed. God prehends us in the fullness of our subjective experience. As our finite subjectivity is incorporated into the divine subjectivity we are transformed. "The mortal puts on immortality." "Transformation" is probably a more telling term than "immortality" for the latter might imply an everlasting continuation of what now is the case. Subjective immortality in God need not mean, for example, that, in the case of someone dying a painful death, that experience will have an everlasting continuation in the life of God. There is a transformed existence and a kind of continuing history with God that is opened up as one is taken into the life of God.

Both objective and subjective immortality address the problem of evil as "perpetual perishing." They provide a way of thinking that on the one hand acknowledges the reality of finitude and the passing of all things, but on the other hand affirms that God acts as One with a tender care that nothing of value be lost.

---

19. Eberhard Jüngel, *Death: The Riddle and the Mystery*, trans. Iain and Ute Nicol (Philadelphia: Westminster Press, 1974), 260.
20. Whitehead, *Process and Reality*, 535.

In the Face of Moral Evil, God Judges . . .

There is among many contemporary Christians a tendency to pass over the matter of judgment altogether. In common parlance today "judgmental" is a bad word, having only negative connotations. Theologically, the concept of judgment is desiccated when it is separated from redemption. Contemporary theologians, in their rejection of judgment, are perhaps reacting to some ways of thinking that do separate the two concepts. There are many accounts of judgment that we today find less compelling or even offensive. Puritan preachers, for example, were known to dwell on the imaginative elaboration of Hell's terrors in sermons designed to convert through vivid depictions of Hell. The Belgic Confession, written in a situation of persecution, promises that the elect "shall see the terrible vengeance which God shall execute on the wicked who most cruelly persecuted, oppressed and tormented them in this world." Part of the bliss of Heaven is taken to be the opportunity to witness the suffering of those who persecuted the faithful in this life. As Marjorie Suchocki notes, "Self-righteousness and revenge are odd entryways into a vision of the kingdom of God."[21]

While we may have inherited miscontruals of judgment from other times and places, better construals may be uncovered in Christian tradition. There have been many notable theologians through the centuries that have rejected theologically problematic readings. John Calvin, for example, interpreted biblical descriptions of the physical torment of Hell as metaphorical. They convey the sinner's experience of separation from God, which is a kind of self-imposed spiritual torment. Popular writer and theologian, C. S. Lewis, proposed that what happens after we die is that through eternity we become more and more who we are; for some this is Heaven for others, it is not! Others have urged a purgatorial view. Hendrikus Berkhof proposed that Hell be thought of as a kind of refining fire purging away the dross and purifying the precious metal. It is a judgment ordered toward redemption.

Perhaps we do well to lay aside notions of judgment that would separate judgment from redemption. But it will not do to simply cease

21. Marjorie Hewitt Suchocki, *God-Christ-Church: A Practical Guide to Process Theology* (New York: Crossroad, 1986), 178.

to speak in terms of divine judgment. If there is no judgment, there is no justice. If this life is all there is, and there is not something akin to resurrection and judgment, then at the end of it, evil will not have been seriously addressed. As Nietzsche insisted, "To redeem the past . . . that alone do I call redemption."[22] "No ultimate fulfillment is possible if the past remains unredeemed; an unredeemed past will keep every present (and future) unredeemed. The eschatological transition cannot therefore be only about being given a fresh beginning, but must also be about having all of one's failed beginnings, middles, and ends redeemed."[23] "Eschatological transition entails that that evil in human history be finally and unmistakably exposed and judged, and that the evil-doers themselves be transformed by God's grace, so that they can be freed from all evil, reconciled to one another and thus reach the state of new innocence." Polkinghorne and Welker also urge in the direction of an eschatological transition that will involve judgment.

> If it is intrinsic for human beings to be embodied in some form (so that resurrection, rather than spiritual survival, is the Christian hope), then it may be that they are intrinsically temporary beings. If that is so, the life of the new creation will have its own new time and its own new, salvific process. Judgment will then involve a coming to terms with the reality of ourselves, and a purgation of what we are in order to become what God wills us to be. Fulfillment will not happen in a timeless moment of illumination but through an everlasting exploration of the riches of the divine nature, an experience that may be characterized as our entering into "eschatological joy."[24]

In my opinion, what process offers is very fruitful speculation on the matter; it is a helpful correction to the problematic renderings — equally speculative ones — that were so focussed upon reward and punishment — dual-destiny thinking. Process perspectives represent

22. Friedrich Nietzsche, *Thus Spoke Zarathrustra: A Book for Everyone and No One,* trans. R. J. Hollingsdale (London: Penguin, 1969), 161.
23. Miroslav Volf, "Enter into Joy! Sin, Death, and the Life of the World to Come," in *The End of the World and the Ends of God: Theology and Science on Eschatology,* ed. John Polkinghorne and Michael Welker, 262.
24. Polkinghorne and Welker, 13.

a genuine advance in the effort to reconceive judgment and redemption as a common destiny for all. The proposal moves in ways consistent with essential insights of Christian tradition.

Suchocki illustrates her constructive proposal using the story of a woman burned as a witch as a kind of test case. The woman's experience of unjust condemnation and fire and agony and death is unredeemed and stands as a final mockery of God's justice if there are no resurrection and judgment in which this can be addressed. The function of resurrection and judgment is a setting right and a consummation of all things. It is not about eternal reward or punishment. Judgment is ordered toward redemption.

God's prehension of each occasion is at the same time a prehension of the initial aims with which it was provided. God sees both what we are and what we could have been. There is in this a moment-by-moment judgment, and as God moment by moment represents to us novel possibilities for good, there is the prospect of transformation, and out of each event God saves what is worth saving. At our end, in the resurrection when we are taken up into God's own being, we are co-present with God and experience ourselves as God experiences us. We "know as we are known." "Knowledge is judgment, a complete and utterly true sense of one's own contextual value" (109). We see what we were and what we could have been. To see ourselves in this way is to experience judgment. We know also, because we are co-present with God, what our effects have been in the world and upon other persons. Furthermore, we feel about those effects what God feels about them.

Following Suchocki's example of the judge who sentenced the woman to the flames, he will know her pain as God knows it, in all its intensity and agony. It is both an experience of her pain as she experienced it accompanied by the knowledge that this is his doing and a knowledge of what could have happened instead. These deeper levels of self-knowledge and knowledge of the world are what constitutes judgment. It is a self-knowledge that takes us outside ourselves.

Insofar as our actions were in conformity with the initial divine aim we will experience our inclusion in God as "Heaven"; insofar as they were not, we experience our inclusion in God as "Hell." Yet this is not an everlasting absolute experience of reward or punishment, for in our deepening self-knowledge and our deepening knowledge of the world we are opened up to that which is more than ourselves. For Hell to remain Hell, the individual ego would have to remain narrow. However, the boundary of the self-as-opposed-to-other breaks down; there is no longer an imprisonment in the ego. "The essence of an occasion's union with God is its final bursting of the bonds of selfhood even while affirming that selfhood" (110). The judge experiences the transformation of the woman burned for witchcraft, the woman experiences the judge's experience of her pain and his feelings of remorse. Each experiences the other's feelings as both are included in the life of God. Judgment moves into justice. Multiplicity moves deeper and deeper into divine unity; fragmentation is embraced in wholeness.

"Peace" is achieved when there is a "harmony of harmonies." This is not simply a monotony that comes from yielding to triviality. It is a complex and intense harmony. This is possible when "the restless egoism" of pursuing our own individual enjoyment broadens to take into account the enjoyment of others, the good of the whole. We get beyond preoccupation with personal satisfaction. Then our state of mind is much more like that of God who seeks the greatest good for all. As Suchocki puts it, "The essence of an occasion's union with God is its final bursting of the bonds of selfhood even while affirming that selfhood: the language is not paradoxical, for the reference is simply to a self, a value, which *is* in its givingness, its relatedness to a whole which by far transcends it" (110). She notes that Whitehead saw the dynamic union with God's primordial character in terms of this self-transcending Peace.

> Thus Peace carries with it a surpassing of personality. . . . Peace is the removal of inhibition and not its introduction. It results in a wider sweep of conscious interest. It enlarges the field of attention. Thus Peace is self control at its widest, — at the width where the 'self' has been lost, and interest has been transferred to coordinations wider than personality.[25]

Suchocki's process eschatology has deep resonances with the mystical tradition in which *theosis* is envisioned as the proper human

---

25. Alfred North Whitehead, *Adventures of Ideas* (New York: The Free Press, 1967), 288.

destiny. Like a drop of water returning to the sea, the self returns to God and finds its peace in this union or reunion. Suchocki's presentation has the advantage of presenting a continued consciousness and selfhood, an ongoing history in the life of God. There is not a mere continuation of what we are, but a transformed reality comes to be.

This view also resonates with understandings of judgment that assume a purgatorial purpose, a notion deeply rooted in the history of Christian tradition. The dogmatic starting point for the development of the idea of purgatory can be found in a declaration made in 1336 by Pope Benedict XII. He rejected the idea that those who die "sleep" until the resurrection at the Last Day. Rather they are immediately judged. In the presence of God, they are confronted with the truth about their lives and they judge themselves. Believers, then, experience the presence of God as light and fire, light that reveals the truth and fire that purifies until a true contemplation of God can occur in the beatific vision wherein "the pure in heart shall see God" (Matt. 5:8).[26] Or, following Calvin, we might think in terms of a great "watching and waking of the soul" after death, with which it "perceives" its healing and its completion and "experiences" its rebirth for the life of the world to come; its blessedness is "always in progress" before the judgment day.[27]

Suchocki's process approach to the matter of judgment has numerous advantages. It necessitates a giving up of notions of an absolute end to time and space and coming to think about the eschatological transition differently. It allows a continuing history with God, and it envisions this history to include both judgment and redemption for all. It foresees a setting right of all things in the life of God. The injustices done and suffered are addressed and not simply allowed to stand as a "final mockery" of divine goodness. It also pursues a social/relational pattern for judgment and redemption rather than an individualistic approach. Miroslav Volf has observed that "dealing adequately with sins suffered and committed can only be a social process. If those reconciled with God are not to remain unreconciled among themselves on account of their unreconciled pasts, and if history is there-

---

26. Moltmann, 247.

27. John Calvin, "Psychopannychia," in *Tracts and Treatises in Defense of the Reformed Faith,* trans. H. Beveridge (Grand Rapids: Eerdmans, 1958).

fore not to remain unredeemed, the final justification will have to be accompanied by the final social reconciliation. . . ."[28]

It should be recognized that this departs from the Augustinian vision in its universality. However, this would seem to be required, as Suchocki argues, because "finitude as well as freedom is implicated as the source of evil" (113). Another difference is that whereas the Augustinian view assumes a final judgment that is salvation or damnation, this proposal envisions judgment as a *transformation* "which moves from the experiential knowledge of one's effects to the inexorably required and purgative participation in God's own life" (113). The process view, however, shares with the Augustinian vision a conviction that there is judgment and that it entails everlasting consequence to the evils done and suffered. The world's salvation lies in the "Apotheosis of the World."[29]

Providing Hope Rather than Guaranteed Outcomes

There is a strong theme of hope available in the process reconstruction of Christian eschatology. God works persuasively and everlastingly for good. God never gives up. Evil has no finality. This stops well short of claiming that God controls the events of world process in such a way that God can guarantee particular outcomes. To take this position is to forgo a "guaranteed triumph of the good," a notion to which many cling. Cobb and Griffin[30] observe that a major reason why Christian faith has clung for so long to notions of God as controlling power is that it can hereby assure believers that God's will — despite all evidence to the contrary — is, or at the last will be, victorious. For the sake of this assurance, many Christians have been willing to risk seeing God as the author or the permitter of evil. Process theism lets go of notions of God as controlling and determining all things and therefore able to guarantee outcomes, but it thereby avoids God's indictability for evil. People assess this step very differently. For pro-

28. Volf, 263.
29. Whitehead, *Process and Reality*, 348.
30. John B. Cobb and David Ray Griffin, "Eschatology," in *Process Theology: An Introductory Exposition* (Philadelphia: Westminster Press, 1976).

cess thinkers the prospect that God is the author of evil is more theologically problematic than the assumption that God is not "in control." Nevertheless, even as the process approach lets go of affirmations that "God is in control" and "the guaranteed triumph of the good," it is able to maintain a motivating hope and it gains a plausible theodicy.

Process theology attributes the possibility of evil to finitude and freedom in the creation. For there to be any world that is "not-God" (the infinite One) there must be a world of finitude. It is finitude, though, that allows for perpetual perishing. For there to be any world — when being entails freedom/power — freedom is also a necessary ingredient of the creation. It is freedom, though, that is the condition of the possibility of moral evil. The possibility for good that relative freedom allows is in direct correspondence to possibility of evil. There are necessary risks that the divine creative love must take if freedom is to be real and if triviality is to be overcome. God, as Creator, may be held *responsible* for evil in this sense. Nevertheless, in the judgment of most it is better for the world *to be* than *not to be* and therefore God is not *indictable* for evil. God's "ends" are for good and not evil.

As for "outcomes" as such, process theology makes the more modest claim that no matter how great the evil in the world, God is acting persuasively upon the wreckage to bring from it whatever good is possible.

> God's role is not the combat of productive force with productive force, of destructive force with destructive force; it lies in the patient operation of the overpowering rationality of his conceptual harmonization. He does not create the world, he saves it; or more accurately he is the poet of the world, with tender patience leading it by his vision of truth, beauty, and goodness.[31]

Process theology further claims that this persuasive power with its infinite persistence is in fact the greatest of all powers. The power to open the future and to grant freedom to other actualities is a more worshipful[32] power than power of domination and absolute control.

---

31. Whitehead, *Process and Reality*, 346.

32. Hartshorne's derivation of divine perfections takes "worshipfulness" as a

This position even as it forgoes a guarantee of the triumph of the good, lays a firm foundation for hope. It may even provide a vision that is *more* motivating for human activity. Gordon Kaufman in *Theology for a Nuclear Age* pointed out that strong views of "God in control" are not generally motivating when it comes to such things as prevention of a nuclear holocaust. Those who believe God is in control, guaranteeing divinely willed outcomes, may either say, "God will not let it happen," or "If it happens, it is because God willed it as a judgment on the human race and there is nothing we could have done to prevent it." Hope is perhaps more motivating than a guarantee.

Balancing "Realized" and "Futurized" Eschatology

There is a tendency in reflection on eschatology to collapse into either a realized eschatology on the one hand or a futurized eschatology on the other. Painting with broad strokes, these are liberal and conservative tendencies respectively. Realized eschatology thinks of God's ends as having to do primarily with a new quality of life in the here and now. This is, in a sense, to "reduce the complexity of eschatological symbols to ciphers of inner self-consciousness." Futurized eschatology, by contrast, seems to divest itself of hopes for historical realization of a new reality and to anticipate instead a radically different reality beyond history. The former thinks in terms of continuity while the latter thinks in terms of discontinuity.

Would it not be more helpful to live within a dialectic of the futurized/realized options? In Scripture, talk of resurrection/judgment/consummation is in the context of a transformation of all things. The vision is not one of a simple continuation of the present order nor is the *eschaton* envisioned as a completely other and unrelated reality. The eschatological symbols of Christian tradition in fact generally present a kind of continuity-discontinuity, what Polkinghorne and Welker have called the "strange logic of eschatology."[33] The

---

central criterion. He asks whether a particular attribute may be attributed to a being who is worthy of worship and whether this attribute represents something worthy of human emulation. If it fails to meet these standards, it should not be ascribed to God.

33. Polkinghorne and Welker, 2.

use of terms like "new creation" or "a new heaven and new earth" seems to signal both continuity and discontinuity. Anticipation of *the resurrection of the body* as instanced in the stories of Jesus' resurrection has this quality as well. His "spiritual body" walks and talks and eats breakfast, yet it passes through locked doors and is not always recognizable even to his disciples.[34] There is a strong current of continuity in dialectical relation with discontinuity throughout the eschatological expectations.

Perhaps the contrast between continuity and discontinuity is not to be articulated in terms of present and future so much as in terms of being between realities (*both* present and future) that either reflect or do not reflect the divine ends. There is a sense in which God's purposes are already at work, inaugurated in the incarnation, and a sense that they are not now fully realized. This contrast of the *already* and the *not yet* has figured prominently in Christian eschatology. In this view, God's purposes are both present reality *and* future hope.

Future hope dimensions are expressed in the hope for God's coming reign which would entail the establishment of peace and justice, the renewal of nature, and the inclusion of the nations. These are envisioned as happening at some climax or consummation of history anticipated in the future. But there is the contrasting view as well. Jesus' teaching in the parables, for example, proclaimed the *basileia tou theou* (the realm of God) in ways that would have been destabilizing to those holding an exclusively futuristic orientation. He spoke of God's reign as, in a sense, *already present*. It is like the mustard seed (Luke 13:19), inconspicuous, growing quietly, even now in our midst, hiddenly. "The kingdom of God is among you!" (Luke 17:21). The discontinuity of this manifestation is seen in the dramatic reversals (transformations) that occur. There are personal reversals as lives are reevaluated and experience *metanoia* (turning around), repentance of the past and opening up to a new future so different that one may be said to be "born again." Religious values are re-evaluated as in the tale of the Pharisee and the Publican, where, remarkably, it is the publican

---

34. In the story of Mary Magdalene at the tomb, when Mary first sees Jesus she thinks he is the gardener. She recognizes him only when he speaks her name. In the story of the disciples on the road to Emmaus, they walk and talk with Jesus all day but do not recognize him until the breaking of the bread.

(the presumed sinner) and not the Pharisee (presumed righteous) who is justified.

Suchocki's proposal of how judgment works in a cumulative way in our subjective immortality expresses a futuristic dimension to eschatology. It is a matter that is personal/individual, but not only so. As one is incorporated into the divine life, there is an integration of the self, no longer a collection of serial occasions, and an integration of the self with other realities.[35] According to Suchocki, "One could envisage then a multiple transcendence of personality in God: first a transcendence of seriality into the fullness of the self; second, a transcendence of selfhood through the mutuality of feeling with all other selves and occasions, and third and most deeply, a transcendence of selves into the Selfhood of God" (108). This process, as illustrated earlier, does not simply incorporate, but in fact transforms. There is a "reconciliation of all things." This is a hope that has been central to Christian eschatology. Miroslav Volf expresses it this way, "(T)he eschatological transition can be understood neither as an apocalyptic discarding of the old world and creation of a new one *ex nihilo* nor as a holistic integration of 'everything' into a 'totality.' Rather, the eschatological transition must be ultimately understood as the final 'reconciliation of all things,' grounded in the work of Christ the reconciler and accomplished by the Spirit of communion, as the process by which the whole creation along with human beings will be freed from transience and sin to reach the state of eternal peace and joy in the communion with the Triune God."[36]

Elsewhere, Suchocki articulates another dimension of Christian hope very much located within history. This is not in contrast with the futurized eschatology described above, but stands in a dialectical relation to it and, as Suchocki claims, may even be grounded in it. As she says, "The togetherness of all things in the infinite satisfaction of God is the ultimacy of love, pervading and transforming each participant through the power of God's own subjectivity. The aims for the world that spring from this divine love are themselves aims toward a richness of community, which is *as much named by love in the finite world as in the di-*

---

35. According to Suchocki, "The wholeness of a person's life is present, and not simply the concluding moment" (108).

36. Volf, 278.

vine reality" (123, italics mine). "Redemption beyond history is a basis for hope within history, affecting what is possible within history" (82). Even now, in the context of history, event by event, realities are judged, transformed, and redeemed according to the divine ends.

Process perspectives are especially well suited to articulate a vision of the realm of God as involving God's judgment, transformation, and redemption as present and ongoing reality as well as a cumulative one. Here and now, in the internal life of God, there is judgment, transformation, and redemption. There is also a future hope, both for a better historical reality and for an everlasting Harmony of harmonies.[37]

Conclusion

Traditional understandings of Christian eschatology may benefit from reconsideration in several areas: its relation to scientific understandings of the end of the world, its conception of judgment and the connection between judgment and redemption, the way in which God's goodness and power are best articulated in relation to world process, and in balancing present and future dimensions of the realization of God's ends. In each of these areas problems have arisen which invite attention. This paper has sought to illustrate how the resources of process thought, and Marjorie Suchocki's work in particular, resonate with the best insights of the tradition and provide a useful corrective to its distortions.

A brief summation of central convictions might include the following. In relation to the world, God is the source, companion, and end of all things. Finitude and freedom necessarily accompany any creation that is both "not God" and actual. Finitude entails the prospect of mortality and perpetual perishing. Freedom makes possible the capacity for created realities to shape our own destinies to some

37. "At the heart of the nature of things, there are always the dream of youth and the harvest of tragedy. The Adventure of the Universe starts with the dream and reaps tragic Beauty. This is the secret of the union of Zest with Peace: — That the suffering attains its end in a Harmony of Harmonies. The immediate experience of this Final Fact, with its union of Youth and tragedy, is the sense of Peace. In this way the World receives its persuasion toward such perfections as are possible for its diverse individual occasions." Whitehead, *Adventures of Ideas*, 296.

extent. However we may misstep in doing so, we cannot step outside the divine purposes for good which are at work everywhere and always upon the wreckage we make. The evils that result from finitude and freedom never have the last word. God works everlastingly for good: judging, redeeming and transforming.

In the end, according to Whitehead,

> The revolts of destructive evil, purely self-regarding, are dismissed into their triviality of merely individual facts; and yet the good they did achieve in individual joy, in individual sorrow, in the introduction of needed contrast, is yet saved by its relation to the completed whole. The image — and it is but an image — the image under which this operative growth of God's nature is best conceived, is that of a tender care that nothing be lost. The consequent nature of God is his judgment on the world. He saves the world as it passes into the immediacy of his own life. It is the judgment of a tenderness which loses nothing that can be saved. It is also the judgment of a wisdom which uses what in the temporal world is mere wreckage.[38]

38. Whitehead, *Process and Reality*, 346.

"Afterwords"

Marjorie Hewitt Suchocki

Christian eschatology is a funny business. Occasioned by both despair and hope, it deals with the starkest realities of our finite existence, and with the sheerest speculation available to us.

With regard to despair and hope, the very yearning for some resolution to the seemingly infinitely varied problem of human evil stems from reckoning with the horror of evil. Evil entails such waste of human potential, such endurance of human pain — most horrifically, unnecessary human-inflicted pain, such as torture, wars, egregious punishments. Evil entails as well human recklessness toward the world around us, intentionally or unintentionally decimating the things that make for well-being among all earth's living creatures. It is as if there are a power and zest toward "uncreation" in the human breast, a destructiveness that tears down, wears down, bears down on weakness in the name of false strength. And many fall by the wayside. If "what you see is what you get," then contra Christian hope, there is no redemption, no redress, for much of earth and its inhabitants.

It is well that Jürgen Moltmann begins a volume dedicated to eschatology with his thoughtful essay exploring the many dimensions of evil. Without the problem of egregious evil, eschatology would devolve into little more than the desire for endless life in an idolatrous greed that surpasses the cynical lines from Proverbs, "three things there are that are never satisfied, four that will not say, 'Enough'" (30:15). The contemporary issue of eschatology is the issue of hope for redress of that which is named as evil. There is a strangely persistent hope that evil is not the last word; that God's justice is wide enough and deep enough to encompasses redress of the world's pains, finally wiping away every tear.

I will proceed in this concluding essay by sharing my responses to each of the eschatological essays that follow Joseph Bracken's summary of my *End of Evil,* and Moltmann's fine statement on the evils that must be addressed. Because any eschatology is necessarily an unfinished task, I take each writer as a conversation partner who aids me in my own continuing musings concerning unresolved issues in *The End of Evil.* The most challenging problems, as I see it, are these: How can an occasion in God be linked into the consciousness of God without violating the completeness of its finite satisfaction? Is it possible — as I argued — for an occasion to be "itself and more than itself" in God? And how can an immortality of *all* occasions of a person's experience be unified in such a way as to still make sense of the notion of "personal" immortality?

My responses will fall into three groups, although I hasten to add that given the overlap of issues within each essay, this grouping is arbitrary. For instance, in the first grouping both Robert Neville and Catherine Keller challenge the metaphysics as much as they do the viability of the eschatological quest. Nonetheless, as an organizational device, we deal first with responses related to the challenge of eschatology, then to the metaphysics, and finally to the hope of eschatology.

Group 1.
The Challenge of Eschatology:
Robert Neville, Catherine Keller

Robert Neville

Robert Neville suggests that to develop Christian eschatology around the basic requirement that it provide redress for history's evils is to depart from major New Testament eschatological themes and symbols, such as the eschatological role of Jesus, blood atonement, and the wrath of God. Furthermore, my eschatology interjects a central theme that is totally absent in the New Testament texts. Is this legitimate in a theology that names itself as Christian? Or must any eschatology, to be Christian, explicitly incorporate these themes?

As Neville notes, Christian eschatology has varied throughout the centuries in how it focuses upon evil. The resolutions of one age are not necessarily the resolutions of another. Hence, eschatology has dealt with various antinomies: immortality for mortality, forgiveness for guilt, meaning for meaninglessness, rewards for righteousness, punishment for sins. How one focuses on the issue of evil in large measure shapes the resulting eschatology, but throughout these historical developments, the biblical symbols have retained their shaping power. Redress for suffering within history's slaughterbench, Neville suggests, is a relatively recent way of focusing the eschatological problem, departing from the symbols in this regard.

Yet surely there are parallels in our old histories. For example John Dominic Crossan explains the notion of resurrection in relation to the Maccabees.[1] God, said the Judaism of its day, rewards the righteous with long full lives. Surely those Maccabees who were slaughtered during their defense of the temple were righteous, but they died. Has God failed; is God dumb to the plight of the righteous? An eschatological resurrection became the answer, providing a way to retain the conviction that God rewards the righteous despite their wrongful deaths. The contemporary call that *all* evil be redressed, and not simply evil that afflicts the righteous, is continuous with the innovation introduced during the Maccabean period, even while it goes beyond it. The "beyond" stems from our increased sensitivity to the interwoven complexities and ambiguities of what we name as "good" and "evil."

And in fact the history of Christian symbolism is a history of new wine constantly being poured into old wineskins. The living nature of a symbol is its adaptability to new conditions, new sensitivities. The constancy of the symbol is the way in which old meanings interfuse with the new in a mutual contextualization process, wherein past and present are reinterpreted in light of each other. In this process, the symbol continues to deepen and hence continues to influence the religious psyche. "Eschatology" as a symbol grows from old

---

1. John Dominic Crossan, *The Historical Jesus: The Life of a Mediterranean Jewish Peasant* (San Francisco: Harper San Francisco, 1991), 383-87.

needs, old perceptions, but is a living symbol precisely to the extent that it can adapt to new perceptions of dealing with human need.

Given all this, what of those ancient symbols — the eschatological role of Jesus, blood atonement, and divine wrath? Can I account for them? Or has *The End of Evil* left its Christian moorings for purely metaphysical speculation? The eschatological role of Jesus and divine wrath are the easiest to address, for the one is implicit and the other explicit in *The End of Evil*. Were it not for Jesus' preaching of a *basileia* where boundaries that divide us are wiped away, where there is healing of physical and spiritual sorrows, where there is a radical community sharing a common table and an all-too-uncommon love, how would one dare imagine everlasting dimensions to such a community? As for the wrath of God, I maintain that the judgment within God that brings about the transformation of the world in God is a valid application of the biblical symbol. Is wrath not the other side of violated love? Wrath is God's "no" to our violations of one another; it translates into divine judgment that is in fact necessary to our salvation. Without judgment, we would be left to our own consequences. With judgment comes the possibility of transformation.

Neville touches on blood atonement by suggesting that it indicates the awful cost to many — nonhuman and human — of our evolutionary history and our personal histories. Is there no reckoning of this cost? For him, reading Jesus' crucifixion as atonement provides the means to own our guilt as a species and as individuals. We exist through spilt blood; we are blood guilty: the crucifixion is witness. Except for naming the crucifixion "atonement," I resonate with his view. For me, the crucifixion is witness to our violence and our violations; it indicates that all the ills we do to others are felt by God as well. In a classic way, the crucifixion is the epitome of the devastations wrought by our bloodiness. But if by atonement Neville means that we are all vicariously punished in Jesus for our blood guilt, then I do not follow him — nor that part of our tradition — here.

Neville's whole discussion of symbol leads to some interesting possibilities relative to some of the issues I find in my own work. If a symbol is always itself and more than itself, can it provide an instructive parallel to one of my central questions? That is, can an occasion be itself and more than itself in God? A symbol retains its original meaning even as it accrues additional meanings. The very fact that

Neville can appeal to the biblical symbol of atonement is a case in point. Its original meaning is expiation for sins — but in its travels through the centuries, it takes on additional meanings (satisfaction, penal substitution) that are enfolded within the symbol without destroying its initial meaning. Can an occasion alive in God retain its original satisfaction, even while its incorporation into God's subjectivity continuously transforms its meaning? A similar process happens in history all the time: an event, completed, may have meant one thing, but as successor entities incorporate and interpret it, it becomes continuously completed in a novel way. For example, Victor Frankl experiences the horror of Auschwitz in a particular way, but without detracting from the original horror, in his ongoing experience he transforms the meaning of Auschwitz into *Man's Search for Meaning.* Countless persons, inspired by that book, have been encouraged to respond transformatively to their own tragedies. The single historical event of Frankl-in-Auschwitz, complete in itself and rife with evil, is nonetheless transformed through its continuous completion in Frankl's own life and in many others. In history, the original experience does not participate in these later transformations. To go back to the analogy of symbol, however, there is a sense in which the symbol *does* participate in its later history, even though the symbol is not alive in the sense that human beings are alive. My eschatology requires that a living occasion in God is itself and yet through participation in God becomes more than itself.

But these musings take me afield from Neville's fine essay. In sketching out his own eschatology he states that "the deep eschatological question is how our temporal lives add up eternally and how this relates to the dynamic eternity of God." In his understanding (which he opposes to a Whiteheadian view), God is eternal creator of a temporal world, so that creation itself is an eternal happening — not reduced to some past "big bang" moment of time, but from a temporal point of view, *always.* Because God is eternal creator, creation is always happening. A process way of putting it is to say that God is everlastingly creating; time itself results from the continuously given initial aims spurring a new present to emerge from the past toward its future. Eternity, Neville says, is "an infinitely more fulsome dynamic than can be laid out from the perspectives of any one point within temporal flow," and again, "the full ontological togetherness of our temporal lives is in eternity." But in *The End of Evil* I argued that who we are in God is precisely the full ontological togetherness of our temporal lives, necessarily so because God's prehension is not some unique "when you die" sort of thing, but continues throughout our lives in the way Neville suggests, from infancy through old age, all together, gathered in the Consequent Nature of God. This fullness is what leads to the problem that Lewis Ford will take up, the problem of "the million Marjories"! We are all of the selves we have ever been in God! The relation of time to eternity in my Whiteheadian view, then, is that God's everlastingly creating acts are the ground of time, even while being outside of our sequentially measured time. That which is created in time is subsequently prehended by God, so that God is both ground and terminus of time. Since God is an everlastingly concrescing entity, and since what we call time is the measurement of successive entities, God is everlasting rather than temporal. But I fail to see the substantive difference between Neville's notion of "eternity" and my notion of "everlastingness" relative to God. It seems to me that the same things are accomplished.

One more thing should be added to this conversation: Neville contrasts his notion of eternity with Whitehead's use of eternal objects in the primordial nature of God, whereas I am contrasting his notion with the consequent nature of God. But I argued as strongly as I could that the primordial nature cannot be static, since the unity of God requires that the consequent nature is everlastingly being enfolded within the primordial nature, and this enfolding is essential if relevant initial aims are to be provided to the world. The fullness of the Whiteheadian God is as dynamic as Neville's eternal God.

Catherine Keller

Keller's stunning work gives a sympathetic critique of the notion of sin in *The Fall to Violence* — she adamantly resists naming the suffering caused by the natural vulnerability of living creatures within the richness of earth's fecundity as "evil." This tends toward an all-too-familiar shifting of blame from ourselves to our circumstances, in a way reminiscent of Shakespeare's "The cause lies not in our stars, but in ourselves." Rather, we do better to focus the word "evil" on suffering intentionally caused on living creatures, traditionally named "sin." That word, she contends, has been so corrupted in common parlance as no longer to communicate. In its place, and in place of my own use of "needless violence," she proposes that we use the word "violation" when designating human-caused evil. I am in strong agreement with her argument and her conclusions.

She rightly recognizes the intentional ambiguity of my title — does the "end" of evil mean purpose, or finality? Both meanings are problematic. If I refer to some purpose that makes evil a means to an end, I risk justifying evil "while allowing it to deliver some eschatological fruit." If I mean that evil is finally left behind, I risk attempting the impossible task of extricating a duo that is inextricably intertwined in the ambiguity of existence. The termination of evil would be at the same time the termination of good.

But an eschatology based on a Whiteheadian notion of God requires the ambiguity of "the end" of evil without devolving into either the Scylla of "eschatological fruit" or the Charybdis of a false extrication of good from evil. Purpose, as Charles Birch is wont to tell us, is woven into the nature of things by virtue of God's initial aim, and also, if we read Whitehead's more theological passages, by virtue of God's insistence upon using that which is "wreckage." God and the world would be better off without our sorry brutalities, but God will use them nonetheless. I have argued that if God did not incorporate the evils of our world into the consequent nature, then God could not possibly know how to guide us in our next moments. We must deal with those evils; if God doesn't know them even more fully than we do, how could God's initial aims be at all helpful, let alone relevant to our situation? And if not even God can deal with evils creatively, transformatively, how on earth can we? But God can deal with evil creatively and transformatively only if God incorporates evil as well as good within the everlasting divine concrescence. My way of saying it has been that the edges of God are tragedy, but the depths of God are resurrection joy. If nothing is ever lost in God, then evil and good are indeed inextricably intertwined even as they both feed into God's ongoing purposes of increasing intensity, complexity, beauty — or what John Haught calls "deep relationality." Is this a satisfactory resolution to Keller's caution? I confess that I hope not, for an eschatology mindless of such cautions has forgotten its own necessary ambiguity.

Her major objections to eschatology as an end to evil within God are complex — and, indeed, compelling. First, the metaphysics I have used push me to state that in God, all freedom is God's own. Metaphysically, just as an actual entity is free in how it deals with what it has received, even so, God must be free to deal with what God receives. There is but God's freedom, dealing with the results of the freedoms of the universe. How God integrates those results depends upon God; therefore, if subjective immortality holds, then the subjectively immortal occasion participates in God's freedom rather than in an extension of its finite freedom. Alternatively, one could put it this way: the divine freedom now becomes an extension of the occasion's original freedom.

Keller argues almost intuitively against this alteration of freedom. But the only way finite freedom could be maintained in God in consonance with the metaphysics would be to introduce a double seriality of occasions: on the one hand, there would be the finite succession of entities within the universe — the freedom which we experience in our moment-by-moment living. But what if every occasion, prehended into God, generates yet another series, now within the context of the divine concrescence? The multiplicity entailed would be mind-boggling — but since when does infinite complexity within God require rejection of the concept? If there were continued seriality within God (and here Bracken's notion of divine intersubjectivity might come into play) wouldn't it be the case that the divine context would influence the continuing-freedom-within-God in a far more intense way than could be experienced in our continuing-freedom-within-history? If such a thought could be developed in a way that did not violate the fundamental metaphysical scheme, then the intuitive insistence that the freedom of God within the divine concrescence is compatible with innumerable instances of serialities might be suggested. The caveat is that when we utilize metaphysics to develop a "likely tale," in order to keep the "likeliness" of the tale, we are under the constraints of what the metaphysics allows.

But if such an eschatology could be developed, it would more adequately answer Keller's insight that God is no "divine sanitation department," and that God's "obliviousness to morals" indicates that the intensity of beauty within God draws from the contrasts with evil, rather than eliminating those contrasts. And it seems to me that her sensitivities are sound.

One final issue with Keller's critique should be raised before exploring the compatibilities with a freedom-retaining notion of eschatology within God with the intersubjective insights of Joseph Bracken. Keller opposes the notion so often used within process theology of the specificity of God's initial aim. The traditional notion of sin as "missing the mark" has been useful in exploiting the notion of a specific aim, suggesting that deviation from the aim is analogous to sin as missing some divinely appointed mark. But in *Fall to Violence* I argued that in most cases one must understand aims as far more general than specific, and far more open to "deviation" than a "missing-the-mark" definition of sin allows. I cited the case of deciding between options, both of which are good. Even though one might supposedly be the aim from God, in the nature of the case discernment is ambiguous, and God presumably works with whatever choice we make. Keller's movement even further away from ambiguous aims toward more amorphous aims seems appropriate to me. If God gives an aim for every single occasion that is peculiarly suited to that occasion, selecting from a vast multiplicity of eternal objects in order to find just this one perfect aim for the moment, and if God gives such aims to every occasion within the universe, and if there are billions of such occasions even within one human body, then arguing for specificity to the aims seems a bit ludicrous. In the past I have countered this by suggesting that "only a God" could provide such specificity to so vast a multitude of occasions. But I have also mused that perhaps God's aims are more like the rays of the sun — the same solar processes of fission, fusion, magnetic fields, and radiation produce an energy that swathes our earth in life-giving light. Each earthly element adapts the sun's light according to the specificities of its own becoming. Why wouldn't this be an apt image of God's aims for creation? Wouldn't the power of God's integration of the universe into the divine nature produce a radiance that bathes that universe in directional energy — but wouldn't that energy be adapted not so much by God for every occasion, but by the occasions themselves according to their varying contexts? It would still be an aim reflecting the divine good — what would be missing to popular piety is the sense of personalization that we hold so dear. But could it not be the case that the very radiance of God, reflecting a care that nothing be lost, could realistically be experienced as divine care, divine love, even though it embraces us from the vastly suprapersonal reality that such a divinity would be? Sin might be "missing the mark" as contradicting the divine radiance, but it would not be missing a very specific mark designed for just this occasion. It seems to me that initial aims in this more general sense do not defy the mind-boggling multiplicity required by specific aims for the quadrillion-plus occasions comprising the universe at every instant of its becoming.

Group II.
Whiteheadian Metaphysics:
Joseph Bracken, Roland Faber, Lewis Ford, Philip Clayton

Joseph Bracken

Joseph Bracken rightly points out that an important dictum of Whitehead's philosophy is that no occasion can be conscious of its own satisfaction, for such knowledge would be a component in the process and would thereby alter the satisfaction. In other words, consciousness of its own satisfaction would be contradictory, for it would add to the satisfaction, and therefore be a continuation of the concrescence. Self-reflexivity is not possible relative to an occasion. I strongly support this dictum, for I think it necessary to Whitehead's atomic structure. Contra Bracken, I do not hold that the "enjoyment" of the satisfaction is self-reflexive. Self-reflexivity is a mediated consciousness; it is the subject holding itself as an object. As such, it describes an occasion's prehension of its immediate past self, not the immediacy of its present satisfaction. "Enjoyment" is necessarily an unmediated consciousness. In any personal series of occasions, each successor occasion prehends the prior enjoyment reflexively. Thus what seems like self-reflexivity in human experience is actually reflection on an immediate past self. In a sense, then, self-consciousness is always one step behind itself; it is always "déjà-vu" — a making present of that which is actually past, as if it were indeed the present. With this adjustment, I can revise Bracken's summary statement to say that "satisfaction is the entity's *immediate* [better than active] enjoyment of *its fullness* [rather than 'what it has become'] and in that sense the ontological basis for its active . . . givingness to future actual occasions" (I have eliminated the phrase "self-presentation" because of its suggestion of reflexivity). Relative to the "givingness to the future," this occurs because the satisfaction includes appetition toward its successors. This appetition is in fact the transitional creativity that evokes the continuation of process and, in conscious occasions, what feels like self-reflexivity. These are admittedly fine points, but they make all the difference in maintaining Whitehead's atomic structure to reality. If satisfaction is a mediated, self-reflexive enjoyment, then it continues rather than concludes concrescence.

But given this, Bracken is nonetheless quite correct when he says I have introduced a subject-subject interaction between God and the world if in fact God prehends this unmediated enjoyment, this satisfaction, for the essence of the subject is indeed embodied in the satisfaction. The satisfaction is "process and outcome," as Whitehead notes, deeply presenting the subject to its successive prehenders — and in fact, evoking their prehensions through its own appetitions. God takes the entirety of this satisfaction — its enjoyment, its appetition — into the divine nature. Bracken then asks how the divinely prehended occasion can continue to exercise enjoyment within the divine life. My answer in *The End of Evil* is that the occasion exists not *with* God, as Bracken suggests, but *in* God, as a partaker of the divine nature. I argued that the continued existence of the subjectively immortal entity is possible not because of its own continued seriality of concrescence, but because of the divine concrescence, which is itself governed by the divine subjective aim. It is an eschatological apotheosis, not an eschatological perpetuation of self-contained existence. It requires, then, that God's consciousness, unlike the singularity of our own, be vastly multiple. It would be a many-splendored thing, grounded in God's continuous infolding of the world into the primordial vision, but experienced by God in and through multiple windows, prisms, perspectives, all of which are both themselves *and* God. It is because of this vision, guided by these metaphysics, that I have suggested in my earlier work (perhaps now to be revised in relation to Keller and now Bracken) that there is no freedom of the finite world in God — for how can an entity exercise freedom if it is no longer concrescing, but participating through its transitional feelings in the great concrescence of God? God's freedom governs God's concrescence, just as each entity's freedom governs each entity's concrescence. The form of divine community this requires, then, is both like and unlike finite forms of community, where individuality is constitutive of the form of unity attained. In God, the individualities of the world are cradled within the divine matrix, living through that divine matrix, governed by that divine matrix. Thus God is not a *member* of this community — rather, God *is* the community. The unity of God in the midst of the vast diversity of the consequent nature morphing into the primordial nature is established through the mutuality of subjective form, whereby each entity is related to all others, in and through the divine perspective.

But this vision undercuts both the retention of freedom so important to Keller and the fullness of intersubjectivity as argued by Bracken. If, as I suggested in response to Keller's work, the occasions in God are enabled by virtue of the divine concrescent activity to generate further seriality, and hence continued freedom, then Bracken's intersubjectivity holds, and a different kind of community would emerge within the divine nature.

Bracken argues that this different community is in fact Trinitarian — that the Christian intuitions of Trinity are connected to a deeply communal nature to God that is both threeness and oneness at the same time. While I can understand making this move in order to be consonant with the Christian symbol of the Trinity (and here Neville's work is relevant), it nonetheless seems to me that we should employ Occam's razor. The notion of God as an actual entity, concrescing through the reversal of the poles and therefore concrescing everlastingly, is sufficient to argue for the kind of communal eschatology I envision. There seem to be no internal grounds for introducing the kind of divine field composed of three that Bracken so ingeniously develops. However, having said this, if in fact one pushed the continued seriality of occasions in God, then intersubjectivity replaces the intrasubjectivity. Would Bracken's Trinitarian God allow the continued intersubjectivity that my total intrasubjectivity, multiple as it is, undercuts?

Roland Faber

Faber's recapitulation of my argument in *The End of Evil* is remarkably fine and true to my intentions in the text. Given this, I am intrigued by his suggestion that God's reconstitution of the world every moment within the divine life devalues the actual world. Does this make the world we experience simply a husk, with the kernel absorbed in God without remainder? If the world does not transcend God, if we have the kind of panentheism where the world is always entirely in God, then this would be a concern. But Whitehead's antinomies hold true. The world transcends God just as truly as God transcends the world. In its very successiveness, the world *qua* world is everlasting — actual entities may perish, but they are succeeded, and the world continues. The world is as everlasting in its multiplicity as God is in God's unity. God and the world presuppose one another. Thus an eschatology based on the mutual transcendence/immanence of God and the world cannot tolerate a devaluation of the world.

So long as there are a past and a God, there will be a world. The final identity of the world is what it successively does with itself; which is to say, its making of its own history constitutes its final worldly identity. God's absorption of each singular actual entity is the basis for relevance in the ongoing world's ever-immediate future; it is not the absorption of that future, sucking it into the vortex of God. God's redemption of the world within the divine nature is part of the total process, not the end of process. Since God's taking of the world into the divine self is the basis for the relevance of the successive initial aims (or radiance, if we follow the theme developed in regard to Keller?), the absorption into God is essential to the process of ongoingness. God is thus the ground of time, not the end of time. The end of evil is part of the process, not the end of the process.

In the latter part of his essay, Faber offers a most intriguing interpretation of what I have called the reversal of the polar structure in God. That is, for Whitehead God "originates" in the primordial vision, frequently described throughout *Process and Reality* in language virtually identical with his description of the finite occasion's satisfaction.[2] But this analogy to an occasion's mental pole is complemented by a physical pole, the consequent nature. The fullness of God is neither the primordial nature nor the consequent nature, but the dynamic and everlasting unification of the two. I then explored the implications of

---

2. I pointed this out long ago in "The Metaphysical Ground of the Whiteheadian God" (*Process Studies* 5/4, Winter, 1975).

this reversed concrescence in light of the internal dynamics of an actual entity — prehensions, subjective form, contrasts, propositions, subjective aim. This reversed concrescence in God provided the ground for the eschatology of *The End of Evil*. Faber suggests a different interpretation, with the intention of establishing (contra me) a final end to evil rather than the further consequences of evil within the divine concrescence.

Rather than reading the juxtaposition of primordial and consequent natures as a reversal of the polar structure, Faber reads it as a radical inversion. This, in turn, makes God completely other to the world. This otherness transcends all differences, so that in God all things coincide: primordial and consequent natures, concrescence and transition, time and everlastingness. The force of this coincidence of all opposites is a final superjectivity that is itself like a creative explosion that produces differentiation in time, e.g., a world of creatures. The togetherness of all things in God is an eternal "final fact," an eschaton. From this eschaton, comes time. This eschaton is itself eternal; it is the superjectivity of a God in whom all things are. Thus the eschaton precedes the world in every moment; but being eternal, it is never "past" to the world.

There are interesting possibilities for a conversation between Faber and Neville, checking to see commensuralities in their respective views. Perhaps it is the case that I am too wedded to the notion of the reversal of poles in Whitehead, and the strict application of the metaphysics of process to God, adapted only in light of the implications of the reversal. But I do not yet see how an eternal eschaton — before all worlds, with all worlds, beyond all worlds — differs from a Leibnizian best of all possible worlds that moves from its unity in the mind of God into the vast multiplicity of its unfolding. Clearly, further conversation with Faber — intensely complex metaphysical thinker that he is — is required.

Lewis S. Ford

Ah! Lewis Ford has been my conversation partner in matters eschatological for as long as I have known him! This consummate Whiteheadian metaphysician argues that subjectivity cannot be part of the satisfaction. Since, as he says, satisfaction is devoid of subjectivity, then satisfaction can have no form of creativity, neither what I rather inelegantly called "satisfactional creativity" or transitional creativity.

Ford's argument for subjectivity-less satisfaction stems from his clear distinction between becoming and being. He sees subjectivity as belonging solely to the former — subjectivity is concrescence, the sifting of prehensions, the resolving of indeterminacies in order to become one determinate being, the satisfaction. Determinate being is static being, for there is nothing left to resolve. Since everything is resolved, and since subjectivity can only be associated with dynamism, then there can be no subjectivity within the determinate satisfaction.

While I appreciate the clarity of his distinction between becoming and being, I am not convinced by his argument. Because of satisfaction, the subject is also superject (and Whitehead often hyphenates the terms), evoking occasions. But a static satisfaction cannot be superjective. Ford would heartily agree, and he resolves the ensuing problem of how new occasions can emerge by placing all initiating activity in God. The past is prehended by God who does not require superjectivity from the occasion, and the past is subsequently mediated to the nascent occasion by God through the initial aim — or so argues Ford. Ford often uses "counterintuitive" as an important device, and surely to say that our influences from the past come not from the past, but from God is counterintuitive. We experience a stubborn facticity, a givenness to the past that is temporal, not divine. We do so not only because of the "thereness" of the past, but because the past exercises superjectivity, an evocative power eliciting its successors.

Contra Ford, subjectivity belongs to the occasion as a whole — not restricted to its concrescence, but pervading its satisfaction as well. The subjectivity of an occasion is associated with its dynamism, which Ford restricts to its contrasting, sifting, comparing process of becoming, when indeterminacies are intricately interwoven toward a final determinacy. But this final determinacy must itself be dynamic, for it is a holding together in a decisive unity of that which the entity has become. Determinism is not a whittling away of one option after another until finally only one remains. Determinism is a coordinated facticity, a togetherness, a harmony, wherein the manyness of the beginning phases are now held into the unity of one satisfaction. This holding activity is the culmination of the occasion's subjectivity, not the demise of its subjectivity. Furthermore, it is Janus-faced. On the one hand, it is a holding that witnesses to its concrescent power, and on the other hand, it is a holding that generates its transitional power, so that it is a subject-superject. It is not first a subject and then a superject; it is the two together, a subject-superject. Its determinacy and its superjectivity (appetition, transitional creativity — all are synonyms) evoke a new becoming. But of course given the innumerable number of entities calling for a new future, the total effect for emerging occasions would be cacophonous were it not for the directionality derived from God's own superjectivity. Hence God and the past together evoke each new becoming.

As Ford knows from my earlier work, I hold that the reason why God can prehend the subjectivity of the occasion without violating metaphysical principles is that the subjectivity is not only determinate, it is there to be prehended. If a successor could prehend the entirety of the entity, it would prehend its subjectivity as well. But the finite successors are incapable of prehending the entirety of any other entity, since they must negate most of each preceding occasion. Therefore, finite prehensions yield objective rather than subjective immortality. God, from the fullness of the primordial nature, has no metaphysical need to negate any portion of prehended occasions — to the contrary, the relevance of aims depends on an absolute fullness of divine knowledge concerning each occasion's past. That is to say, present initial aims are relevant to the extent that God has based them on full knowledge of the past, integrated with God's wisdom concerning what might yet become. Such fullness of knowledge is gained through complete prehension of each occasion of experience. God prehends the entire occasion, and therefore its subjectivity.

In arguing that there is no transitional creativity, that all creativity is internal to concrescence, Ford overlooks the fact that in Whitehead God's initial aim is a form of transitional creativity. That is, even in Ford's system, the initial aim inaugurates the becoming of the occasion, but the initial aim is not internal to God's concrescence. Therefore, in principle there *is* transitional creativity; otherwise the aim is an anomaly in the system. And since God is not an exception to metaphysical principles, if God's satisfaction yields superjective creativity, then so does the finite satisfaction. Thus there is transitional creativity.

Curiously, Ford seems to give what he takes away when he moves to his discussion of subjective form as the vehicle for subjective immortality in God. He notes that every prehension is felt in a specific way, called subjective form. Further, the "mutuality of subjective forms," as I also argued in *The End of Evil*, becomes the vehicle whereby occasions within God feel other occasions within God. Consciousness, which Ford associates with satisfaction, is also a subjective form. "The final subjective form is the way the final satisfaction is felt," he says. But what is the difference between this and subjectivity? That is, if the satisfaction is *felt*, is it not subjectively experienced? And if it is subjectively experienced, is it not dynamic, an enjoyment, a holding together of the results of concrescence? Thus it seems to me that while Ford wants to limit subjectivity solely to concrescence, leaving satisfaction as a sort of husk-like being after the subjectivity has perished, he also re-introduces subjectivity into the satisfaction by means of subjective form. With this re-subjectifying of the satisfaction, my arguments for the dynamic form of creativity hold.

Philip Clayton

Clayton points out that Whitehead does not conform to the understanding of panentheism defined as all finite occasions existing within a God who nonetheless is more than this inclusion. But I hold that Whitehead's view of the mutual immanence and mutual transcendence of God and all finite reality is a far more viable form of panentheism than that which offers no separate reality to the world as such. The transcendence of the world is consonant with the strength of our own experience that we are ourselves, not God, existing in an equally finite world, not in God. And if this deep intuition is the case, then the world indeed transcends God, is truly other to God in and through being itself. What saves this view from a traditional mode of theism, whereby the world exists apart from but totally dependent upon a transcendent God, is the mutual immanence as well as mutual transcendence. God is immanent in the world through the world's continuous prehension of God's aims for the world. Insofar as these aims are integrated into the becoming occasion, to that degree God is immanent in the world. We live in a radically incarnational world, even

213

while being uniquely ourselves, finite, not-God. And likewise, insofar as God prehends the world, integrating that prehended world within the divine nature, then the world as resurrected is immanent in God. Mutual transcendence and immanence mark a Whiteheadian variation on the panentheistic theme. Participation in the nature of God then becomes the foundation for the adaptation of Whitehead's speculative philosophy toward a speculative eschatology.

Somewhat like Keller, Clayton assumes that subjective immortality in God implies agency on the part of the resurrected occasions. Previously, I argued that only God has agency within the divine nature. But Clayton, with Keller, would probably find resurrection into God meaningless apart from continued agency. But metaphysically, the only agency possible to a prehended subjectivity in God would be the appetition that reaches toward its completion in otherness, in this case, the "otherness" of God and the togetherness of all things in God — the community of God, if you will, as represented by the consequent nature. My argument was that this appetition becomes blended into God's subjective aim, and that the consciousness inherent in the appetition then experiences God's experience, albeit from the perspective of its own appetition. The resurrected occasion experiences God's agency in and through God's concrescence. This becomes the basis for judgment and transformation; it also yields the "always itself and more than itself" that I argued (thus at least partially answering Keller's insistence that evil not be "done away with" in God).

But I have never been entirely comfortable with my own argument. The problem, for me, was not any sense that continued subjective freedom and agency would be important for the occasion in God. To the contrary, it seemed to me that the experience of God's freedom would constitute the greatest freedom possible, and being conjoined with God's agency would likewise be the greatest agency possible: I envisioned an apotheosis of the world. But the problem as I saw it was the weakness of the argument itself. Metaphysically, the occasion is held in resurrected existence not through its own concrescence, but through God's. It is therefore a participant in God's concrescence — but can its finite appetition as integrated into God's subjectivity *experience* this transformation? Apart from such experience, then, there is no redress of evil.

If I heed the intuitions of Clayton as well as Keller, then the resurrected subject-superject evokes new becomings in God, just as its counterpart in the world evokes new becomings in the world. I once read that some physicists argue for multiple worlds on the basis that everything that could exist does exist. While this never seemed plausible to me, if the subject-superject generates new occasions in God, with God, then perhaps something like that multiple-worlds theory could be the case. The possibility resolves the problem of agency, and also introduces a type of freedom — although that freedom would be constricted not by the vicissitudes of finite existence, but by the overwhelming force of God's subjective aim. That is to say, while some problems are solved, other perhaps more intricate problems would be raised. But is not this the lure of doing eschatological metaphysics in any case?

Group III.
The Promise of Eschatology:
John Haught, Anna Case-Winters

John Haught

Haught argues persuasively that eschatologies must interact as faithfully as possible with the science of their day. Clearly, I agree with him heartily. While the traditional ground for asserting eschatological hope lies explicitly in an interpretation of selected biblical writings, an implicit or explicit ground is always speculative metaphysics. When theologians use metaphysics implicitly, then current philosophical assumptions about the nature of existence are woven into their theological constructions. To the extent that the assumptions are generally shared in the culture, the credence of the eschatology is reinforced. In times when such philosophical assumptions are in flux, then the philosophy must be argued rather than assumed. The twentieth century, with its vast advances in the sciences and its philosophical diversity, unsettled earlier assumptions about the nature of human existence. Thus any eschatology developed in the twentieth century and beyond must consider its metaphysics in light of what we can know through the sciences about the structure of this world.

This metaphysical task is essential. If eschatology refers to a particular way in which creatures continue to exist beyond their finite span of life, then the structures presumed to define existence must apply to the form of existence projected. Otherwise, there is little to separate eschatology from wishful thinking. Given the strong susceptibility of eschatology to such a charge, only insofar as eschatology employs a metaphysics consonant with our best understandings of what it means to exist can we follow the biblical injunction to "give a reason for the hope that lies within us."

I appreciate Haught's fundamentally supportive position with regard to the importance of subjective immortality. Given his long conversation with the sciences, Haught takes on the supposedly "scientific" position against eschatology in general, and immortality in particular. After discussing the naturalist position that all religious beliefs are reducible to the evolutionary importance of such beliefs in promoting the human species, he notes that the evolutionary nature of the world means that it is certainly unfinished, still in process, and therefore one cannot make final claims concerning where it can or cannot lead. There is a certain openness to an evolutionary world that renders provisional all definitive judgments about such large-scale things as purpose and immortality. Naturalists would do well to apply their skepticism about religious beliefs to their own pronouncements — which sound, to religious ears, very much like the religious dicta they decry.

In contrast, Haught opts for hope. Far from being totally dissociated from our experience, hope actually reflects our experience of a time — or, in Haught's poetic language, "each moment of time is a seedling that sprouts toward an unprecedented future." The future always comes to us with an element of newness, of that which goes beyond the grip of the past. In this case, the intuition of an ultimate newness that is in fact a transforming renewal is not divorced from our experience, but emerges from that experience. In rhetoric reminiscent of James' argument in "The Will to Believe," Haught argues for the viability of hope as an option toward the ambiguities and uncertainties of a cosmos deep in the throes of its continuous becoming.

What I find particularly instructive in his essay is his insistence that human subjective existence beyond death must not be separated from the fate of the cosmos as a whole. Humans are so deeply entwined in the relational network not only of earth, but of our universe, that to abstract our destiny from the fuller destiny of the cosmos is absurd. The abstracted fragment would be a poor witness not only to the emergent layer of consciousness in which it participates, but to the fullness of what is entailed in its very emergence. We must be headed toward an even deeper relationality, not to an abstracted relationality with all its roots dangling in a relationless void. Process philosophy, with its view that God prehends *every* occasion of the universe into the divine nature, and not simply those occasions belonging to human consciousness, offers a way to express hope in a cosmic destiny that depends upon the trustworthiness of God.

Anna Case Winters

This fine essay provides a fitting conclusion to my responses, for Case-Winters admirably summarizes the issues and hopes bound up in eschatology. Like Haught, she emphasizes the importance of developing eschatology in consonance with contemporary understandings of the world gained through the sciences. Her essential point is that eschatology must offer a two-fold source of hope: hope that speaks to more than the vagaries of history, and yet hope that inspires us to reach for deeper modes of community within history. We are an open-ended universe, an open-ended species. What shall be is affected but not determined by what has been. Therefore in thinking of ultimate and penultimate futures, we encounter mystery, as Catherine Keller notes. But the mystery is not enshrouded in clouds of ignorance. To switch the metaphor, the mystery trails "clouds of glory" that are intimated by our historical experiences as informed by the Christian gospel. To trust God is to trust that the mystery will yet work to our good. But if that were all that were accomplished, eschatology would have failed its most important task, which is to offer hope for history as well as everlastingness. Whitehead's metaphysics of deep relationality between God and the world indicates that what happens in God has an effect upon the world, offering transformative possibilities in the world that mirror to whatever extent possible the transformations accomplished within God. Everlasting eschatology does not refer to some future indeterminate historical time; it is coterminous with all time, receiving from all time, shaping all time. Because everlastingness is coterminous with our histories, its effect upon our histories is to offer hope that transformations toward good are possible in time, in history. Eschatology, then, is like a dance between everlastingness and temporality, each affecting the other. Were it not so — were everlastingness reduced to some nontemporal future — then eschatology would be, as Robert Neville points out, but a "pallid urgency." Eschatology necessarily offers possibilities for how we live here and now precisely because it exists in continuous interaction with the here and now. It is Whitehead's famous conclusion to *Process and Reality:* "In the fourth phase, the creative action completes itself. For the perfected actuality passes back into the temporal world, and qualifies this world so that each temporal actuality includes it as an immediate fact of relevant experience. For the kingdom of heaven is with us today."[3]

---

3. Alfred North Whitehead, *Process and Reality: An Essay in Cosmology,* corrected edition, ed. David Ray Griffin and Donald W. Sherburne (New York: Free Press, 1978), 351.

Contributors

Joseph A. Bracken, S.J.: Retired Professor of Theology at Xavier University, Cincinnati, Ohio. Author of *The One in the Many: A Contemporary Reconstruction of the God-World Relationship* (Grand Rapids: Eerdmans, 2001).

Anna Case-Winters: Professor of Theology, McCormick Theological Seminary, Chicago, Illinois. Author of *God's Power: Traditional Understandings and Contemporary Challenges* (Louisville: Westminster, 1990).

Philip Clayton: Ingraham Professor at the Claremont School of Theology and Professor of Philosophy and Religion at the Claremont Graduate University in Claremont, California. Author of *Mind and Emergence: From Quantum to Consciousness* (Oxford: Oxford University Press, 2004).

Roland Faber: Professor of Systematic Theology at the University of Vienna, Austria. Author of *God as Poet of the World* (Darmstadt, Germany: Wissenschaftliche Buchgesellschaft, 2004).

Lewis S. Ford: Professor of Philosophy and Religion Emeritus at Old Dominion University, Norfolk, Virginia. Author of *Transforming Process Theism* (Albany: State University of New York Press, 2000).

John F. Haught: Healey Distinguished Professor of Theology at Georgetown University, Washington, D.C. Author of *Deeper than Darwin* (Boulder, Colorado: Westview, 2003).

Catherine Keller: Professor of Constructive Theology, Theological School, Drew University, Madison, New Jersey. Author of *God and Power: A Counter-Apocalyptic Journey* (Minneapolis: Fortress, 2004).

Jürgen Moltmann: Retired Professor of Systematic Theology, Protestant Faculty of the University of Tübingen, Germany. Author of many books, including *The Coming of God: Christian Eschatology* (Minneapolis: Fortress, 1996).

Robert Cummings Neville: Professor of Philosophy, Religion, and Theology, Dean of Marsh Chapel, and University Chaplain at Boston University. Author of *Religion in Late Modernity* (Albany: State University of New York Press, 2003).

Marjorie Hewitt Suchocki: Professor Emerita, Claremont School of Theology, Claremont, California. Author of *Divinity and Diversity: A Christian Affirmation of Religious Pluralism* (Nashville: Abingdon, 2003).

Index

actual occasions, 1, 6-11, 60-62, 73-74, 78-90, 92-101, 113-24, 137-48, 175, 182-92, 198, 200-201, 204-15, 217
Advent/ure of God, 102-4, 112
Adventures of Ideas, 5, 79, 81, 99, 102, 195n37
agency (divine and created), 48-49, 60, 70, 115, 122 , 130, 138, 147, 149, 213-15
Agosin, M., 54n5
alienation, 3-4
Altizer, T., 28, 99n3, 103n81
ambiguity of good and evil, 46, 55, 65-69
anthropology, 134, 144n19
apocalyptic, viii, 13, 28, 30-31, 33-34, 46, 55, 57-59, 65-69, 133, 148, 178-79, 194
Aquinas, Thomas, 44n.19, 77, 84, 136, 139, 147
Aristotle, 77, 136
astrophysics, 174
atonement, theology of, 34-35, 43, 200-201
Augustine, 2, 26, 41, 54, 144, 190
Auschwitz, 201

Barth, K., 29, 61, 183
beauty, 65, 67, 99, 102-3, 203, 204
Becoming (vs. Being), 91-112, 115-17, 121-22, 157-58, 165-66
Berger, P., 152
Bergson, H., 144
Benedict XII, Pope, 189
Berkhof, H., 185
Between, the, 79, 82, 84, 107-9
Birch, C., 203
body (physical), 113, 124, 138-40
Böll, H., 22
bonding (vs. aggression), 53, 68
Boyer, P. 153nn6&9, 155n12
Bracken, J., 29, 61n3, 70n22, 72-90, 108n114, 136, 138, 142-43, 182n11, 198, 204, 205, 206-8
Brahman, 37
Brecht, B., 21
Buber, M., 64, 79
Buddhism, 29, 44nn19-20, 127
Bultmann, R., 132
Burkert, W., 153n6, 154n11, 155n12

Calvin, J., 185
Case-Winters, A., 177-96, 217-18
Causation, 97-98, 101, 103, 106, 118-19

certitude (vs. ambiguity), 158-60
chaos, 69-70, 126
chora, 109-11
Christian, W., 120
Clayton, P., 128-49, 213-15
Cobb, J., 91n2, 97n38, 100n57,
  103n84, 190
common element of form for a
  Whiteheadian society, 80-81, 88-
  90
community, 10, 43, 53, 62, 75, 84-87,
  146, 149, 181, 194, 199, 200, 207-8,
  214, 217
concrescence, 6-8, 10-11, 59-60, 114-
  24, 137, 139, 141, 143-45, 206-8,
  210-13, 214
consciousness (divine and human),
  114, 115, 122-27, 130, 144, 150-53,
  161, 164, 169, 175-76, 189, 206-8,
  213, 214, 217
contemporaneity, 116, 120
conversion of processes, 101-6, 109-
  12
cosmology, 57-59, 132-33, 142-43
creation, 57-59, 93, 99, 101-4, 109-12,
  160, 168-69, 172-74, 179, 195, 201-2
creation, end of, 196 (see also
  below, eschatology)
creation, new, 64
creation out of chaos, 109, 111
creation out of nothing, 42-45, 109,
  111, 194, 201
creative advance, 102, 104, 106, 110,
  118, 125-27, 183
creative Eschaton, 104, 106, 109-10
creative space, 108-12
creative time, 110-11
creativity (Whiteheadian), 5, 7, 8,
  40n17, 44-45, 69-70, 73, 76, 85,
  92, 98, 99, 106, 116, 118-19, 123,
  124-27, 136n14, 143, 183, 196, 203,
  207, 211-12
creativity, transitional, 118-19, 115n1,
  207, 211, 212

Crossan, J., 199
crucifixion of Jesus, 34, 36, 200
Czisko, G., 170n39

Darwin, C., 155, 162, 170, 173
Darwinism, 150, 152-55, 165, 169-72
Davis, C., 158
Dawkins, R., 155
death, 16, 34, 36-39, 43, 55-56,70,
  129, 133, 146, 150-54, 159-60, 161,
  169-75, 179-80, 183-84, 195
decision of an actual occasion, 5,
  59-62, 98-99, 101, 103, 106, 115,
  125-26, 149
Deleuze, G., 99n46
Demonic, 48, 54, 70
Dennett, D., 153n5
Derrida, J., 50n1, 64
Descartes, R., 44n20, 98, 136, 143,
  147
determinacy, 115-17, 120-22, 125, 210
difference, 102, 105-12
divine compassion/love, 57, 63, 66,
  69, 102, 112, 120, 157, 175, 200,
  205 (see also below, God)
divine concrescence, 59, 104-5, 202-
  4, 207-8, 210, 212, 214
divine consciousness, 198, 207
divine consequent nature, 6-11, 34,
  37, 40, 59-63, 65-69, 73-76, 83, 85-
  87, 93-95, 100-102, 105-12, 119-20,
  136, 141, 149, 196, 202, 203, 205,
  208, 209, 214
divine eschatological nature, 93-94,
  100, 105
divine initial aims, 5, 9-10, 33-34,
  62-64, 103, 141, 183, 187, 191, 201,
  203, 205-6, 209, 211-12, 213
divine intrasubjectivity, 208
divine judgment, 8, 30-31, 33, 34,
  36-38, 61, 65-66, 74, 131, 141, 179,
  181-82, 185-90, 196, 200, 214
divine life, 32, 34, 37, 40n17, 45, 59-
  61, 117, 122, 125-27, 135, 139, 141,

162-63, 175, 181-84, 194-95, 196, 207-8, 209
divine matrix, 78, 85-90, 108, 111, 208
divine persons, 26-27, 32, 36, 43, 83-87, 194
divine power, 50, 57, 60-61, 69, 104, 134, 147, 190-91
divine primordial nature, 6-11, 34, 40, 72, 75-76, 93-94, 102-11, 202, 208, 209, 212
divine wrath, 30-35, 38, 200
duality/dualism, 46-47, 52, 59, 98, 102-5, 112, 162, 165, 167, 172, 213

empathy, 51, 54, 71
End of Evil, viii-ix, 28n1, 29, 33, 47, 51, 58n8, 59n10, 60n11, 61n12, 63nn15-16, 64nn17-18, 66n20, 91, 92, 99, 115n1, 118nn4&6, 119n10, 137, 141, 143, 149, 177n1, 198, 200, 202, 207, 208, 213
End as goal or terminus, 47, 57-59, 65-69, 91-92, 96-97, 99-100, 101-6, 109, 130, 134, 135, 177-78, 179-80, 183, 185-90, 191, 195, 203, 209, 217-18
enjoyment (of actual occasion) 7-8, 73, 83, 87, 206-8, 213
epistemology, 128-29, 149, 154, 158
escapism, 161-63, 167-68
eschatological difference, 109-10
eschatological future, 92, 104
eschatological life, 100
eschatological origin, 109
eschatological realm, 91, 99-101, 104-5
eschatological space and time, 106-12
Eschatology, vii-ix, 1, 28-45, 47, 57-59, 65-69, 91-92, 102-4, 130-35, 148-49, 177-96, 197-218
Eschatology, realized, 31-34, 133-35, 179, 192-95

Eschaton as future event, 30-34, 40, 57, 66-67, 91, 102-9, 129, 131-33, 148-49, 179, 192-95, 210
eternal object, 202, 205
eternity, 41-44, 58-59, 66-67, 162-63, 164, 166-68
everlastingness (divine), 38-39, 58, 93-96, 100-101, 104, 201-2, 208-10
evil as God's responsibility, 190-91
evil as inhuman force, 48
evil as lying, 18-19
evil as perverse social structures, 21-23, 48-54
evil as privation, 17
evil as sickness, 16, 24-25
evil as sin, 16-17, 25-27, 47-54, 65-69, 200-201, 203, 205-6
evil as suffering, 46-47, 49-51, 68, 70, 102, 197, 203
evil as violation, 49-51
evil as violence, 47-57, 197, 200, 203
evil as waste, 197
evil, banality of, 12-16
evil, end of, 47, 57-59, 69-71, 72, 91-112, 204, 209-10
evil, fascination of, 12-16
evil, mitigated not terminated, 65-69
evil, moral, 1-11, 17, 99, 182, 185-90, 191
evil, origin of, 41n17, 47-51, 97, 111-12
evil, physical, 1-11, 16-17, 48, 52-53
evil, reversal of good, 19-23, 46, 55, 58, 63, 65-66, 70, 120, 126, 203
evil, systemic, 48-54
evolution, 153-55, 162, 167-69, 172-76, 200, 215-16
explanatory pluralism, 171

Faber, R., ix, 91-112, 208-10
Fall to Violence, 48, 51n2, 52n3, 53n4, 202, 205

fatalism, 161-62, 164-65, 166, 169, 171-72
feminism, 52, 54-57
Fergusson, D., 92n4
Ferraris, M., 50n1
Fiddes, P., 102n5
field theory, 142-43, 182n11, 208 (see also below, society as structured field of activity)
final end of creation, 96-97, 99-100, 102-3
Final Fact, 102-4, 210
finitude, 2-5, 133, 135-36, 179, 182, 183, 191, 195-96
Flanagan, O., 150-52, 153n.5, 154n10, 159-61, 165, 170, 172, 174n45
Ford, L., 42, 76, 92, 94n21, 99n47, 103, 113-27, 156m16, 210-13
Fost, F., 120n12
Foucault, M., 52
Frankl, V., 201
freedom, 23-26, 37, 41n17, 43, 59-62, 92, 98, 111, 114, 126, 182, 191, 195-96, 204-5, 207-8, 214-15
Freud, S., 26
Future, 42-43, 92-93, 104, 110, 131, 133-34, 163-64, 166, 168, 176, 202, 207, 209-10, 213-14, 218

Gebara, I., 46, 55-57
givingness of actual occasions, 206-7
God as Celestial City, 62-65
God as Creator, 42-44, 202
God as ground of meaning and value, 157, 168, 176, 182
God as Non-Difference, 106-12
God as Power of the Future, 92, 104
God as Primordial Superject, 96, 106-7, 109-112, 210, 212
God-Christ-Church, 29n5, 177, 185n21
God, eschatological nature of, 44-45, 157, 168, 176

God's experience, 113-14, 121, 122-24
God-world relationship, 6-11, 43-45, 101-12, 175-76, 200, 207, 209-10, 213-14, 218 (see also above, divine)
Good, guaranteed triumph of, 37-39, 44-45, 179, 190-92
Gould, S., 171
Griffin, D., 85n13, 91n2, 92n6, 97n38, 100n57, 103n84, 106n104, 111n134, 118n8, 140, 157n18, 182n8, 190
Gutiérrez, Gustavo, vii

Haag, H., 21
Hallamish, D., 109n120
harmony (divine), 2, 37-39, 44-45, 188, 195, 210
Hartshorne, C., 42, 84-85, 87, 119-22, 136, 164, 175n46, 191n.32
Haught, J., viii, 150-76, 215-17
heaven, 33-39, 59-62, 63-64, 130, 148, 178, 181, 185-90, 193
Hegel, G. W. F., 3-4, 136, 144-45
Heidegger, M., 134, 144, 180
hell, 30n8, 34, 36-39, 60-61, 178, 185-90
Heraclitus, 161
hermeneutical circle, 180
Hinde, R., 153n6
Hinduism 29, 37
hope (eschatological), 47, 51, 62-65, 70-71, 128-35, 149, 153, 161, 163-66, 168-69, 171, 173, 175-76, 178, 186, 190-92, 197, 215-18
Hume, D., 98

Idealism (German), 128
Idealism (Whiteheadian), 140
immanence of God in creation, 139, 209, 207-8, 213-14
immediacy, subjective, 59-61, 94-95, 100, 107, 119n10, 121
immortality, objective, 62, 73-74,

94, 96, 100, 116, 119-20, 122, 128-
30, 136, 147-49, 157, 175, 184, 196,
198, 207, 210-12
immortality, subjective, 1, 6-9, 37,
39-40, 59-62, 72-74, 77-78, 87-90,
94-95, 101-2, 113-27, 128-30, 137-49,
153-54, 169-76, 184, 194, 198, 204,
207, 210-12, 215-18
incarnation, 31-32, 43, 57, 64, 193
inclusion (divine), 120-22
indeterminacy, 69-71, 115-17, 119-22,
211, 216
individuation, 117, 119, 122-27
infinite, 93, 96, 104, 106, 133, 135-36
intersubjectivity, 7-9, 62-65, 72-75,
77-90, 110-11, 142, 146, 204, 205,
207-8
inversion, 105-6, 109-12, 210

James, W., 151-52, 161, 175, 216
Jesus the Christ, 30-32, 36-39, 43-45,
56-57, 67, 131, 181n7, 193, 194, 198-
200
Job, Book of, 14
Jones, J., 80n5
Judaism, 199
Jüngel, E., 183-84
justice, 33-35, 39-40, 49, 54-55, 68,
70-71, 197-201

Kabbalah, 109
Kann, C., 108n112
Kant, I., 3, 23, 42, 78, 98, 128
Kasprzik, B., 98n41
Kaufman, G., 192
Keller, C., viii, 12, 46-71, 105n94,
106n105, 132, 198, 202-6, 207-8,
214-15, 217
Kim, J., 140n17
Kingdom of God, 33, 38, 43, 59, 62-
65, 94-95, 100-101, 104-5, 131, 148,
193, 200, 218

Laszlo, E., 81-82

layered explanation, 171
Leibniz, G. W., 2, 44n19, 210
Levinas, E., 52, 145n20
Lewis, C. S., 185
life after death, 150-53, 161-76 (see
also above, immortality,
subjective)
Lindsay, H., 133
Loomers, B., 112n139
Luria, I., 109
Luther, M., 26, 36n11

Maccabees, Books of, 199
Macquarrie, J., 131, 132n6
Massen, H., 94n16
materialism (scientific), 114, 151,
155n12, 166n33, 171, 174
McGrath, A., 30n8
meaningfulness of life, 37-39, 41,
161-69, 172-76, 201, 203, 216-17
metaphysics, 35, 39, 41-45, 128-49,
198, 204, 207-8, 213-15
metaphysical necessity, 113, 126
Moltmann, J., vii, ix, 12-26, 92, 103,
109n120, 130-31, 182, 183n17,
189n26, 197-98
Murphy, N., 148

Nasai, S., 166n32
naturalism, 150-56, 159-60, 161, 171-
72
Neo-Platonism, 44n19, 136, 147
Neville, R., 28-45, 198-202, 210, 218
Niebuhr, R., 167
Nietzsche, F. W., 4, 186
non-difference, 106-12
Nothingness, 17, 20, 91, 109, 111-12,
151-52, 156, 161, 174, 184
novelty, 93, 98-99, 104, 110

optimism (otherworldly), 162-68
original sin, 51-54
oscillation, perpetual, 118

panentheism, 50, 118, 135-41, 146,
182n11, 202, 208, 209, 213, 214
panexperientialism, 140
Pannenberg, W., vii, 1n3, 92, 103,
128n1, 130-35, 144n19
participation, 135-37, 147, 202, 214
Past(ness), 41-42, 92-96, 100-101,
110, 202, 209-10, 212, 216
past, vanishing of, 97
Pauline epistles, 15, 30-32, 37, 84
peace, 60, 64, 95, 103, 188-89, 193-
94, 195n37
Peacocke, A., 138n15
permanence, 161-62, 165, 167, 169-76
perpetual perishing, 5, 87, 92, 97,
100-101, 116, 118, 121, 156-57, 160-
61, 161-69, 176, 182-84, 191, 195
personhood, 130, 147
Peters, T., 180
physicalism, 140n7, 147, 150
Plato, 17, 42-43, 108-9, 113, 136, 147,
164, 167
Plotinus, 136
pole (mental, physical), 93, 96
poles, reversal of, 93, 96, 105, 208,
209-10
Polkinghorne, J., 132, 138n15,
146n22, 178n2, 179n3, 180nn4-6,
182n9, 186
prehension (divine), 6-7, 11, 40n17,
73-74, 83, 87, 113-17, 121-24, 137,
139, 140-41, 187, 202, 204, 211-12,
214, 217
prehension (by actual occasion),
98, 113-17, 121-24, 206, 210-13, 214
primordiality, 93, 96, 106, 111
primordial superject(ivity), 92, 96,
106, 109-12, 210, 212 (see also
below, superjectivity)
promise, divine, 134, 163, 168-69
Process and Reality, 1n2, 8n4, 9n6, 76,
79-80, 90, 100, 102, 104, 115n2,
116n3, 118n7, 119n9, 120nn13&14,
123n17, 182n8, 209, 218

Purgatory, 60, 185, 189
Putnam, H., 139-40

Rahner, K., 134, 168
reconciliation, 34, 40
redemption, 6, 10-11, 26-27, 33-34,
57-62, 74, 87-90, 94, 102, 111, 141-
46, 179, 181-84, 187, 196
reincarnation, 37, 43-45, 147, 197,
204, 209, 210
relationality, 55-56, 62, 65-69, 95, 98,
100, 104, 105, 107, 111-12, 207-8,
211-12, 216-17
relations, subsistent, 84
relativism, 46-47, 55-56, 65-69
religion and science dialogue, 132,
149, 150-76, 178-81, 195, 215-16
resurrection of the body, 30n8, 88-
90, 100, 113-14, 124, 128, 131, 139,
183, 187, 189, 193, 199, 203, 214
Rolston, H., 154n10, 170n37
Rorty, R., 98n44
Rue, L., 155n13

salvation, 8-9, 34-35, 59-62, 94, 101,
106, 157, 175-76, 185-90, 192-96
Satan, 14-16, 19, 22, 48, 68
satisfaction (divine), 11, 96, 102,
107, 110, 196, 212
satisfaction (of actual occasion), 8,
11, 60, 73, 75, 99, 107, 110, 113-17,
118-19, 123, 144, 183, 198, 200,
206-8, 210-13
Scarry, E., 55
Schleiermacher, F., 3
Schwarz, H., vii
Schweitzer, A., vii
science and religion dialogue, 132,
149, 150-76, 178-81, 195, 215-16
self/selfhood, 51, 59-62, 101, 106,
113, 124-27, 184, 189, 194
self-transcendence, 51, 95, 101, 107,
109, 144-45, 149, 174

self-transcendent non-difference,
107, 109
self-transcendent superjectivity,
108-10
Sherburne, D., 157n18, 182n8
simple location, fallacy of, 114
sin (see above, evil as sin)
sin, collective, 49-50, 53-54
sociality, 126-27
society (Whiteheadian), 9-10, 13-15,
19-21, 77-90, 95, 110, 123, 140, 143,
145
society as structured field of activity, 77-90, 142-43
soul/body metaphor, 10, 85-90
soul/body relation, 10, 139, 150-55,
159, 163, 167
subjective aim (of actual occasion),
5, 8, 11, 183
subjective aim (of God), 8, 11, 17,
75, 86, 96
subjective form, 75, 88-90, 114, 122-
24, 208, 210, 213
subjective identity, 37, 42, 127, 139,
141, 145, 198
subjectivity (divine and created), 7,
34, 37, 59-62, 73-75, 83-84, 86-87,
93, 98-99, 100-101, 106-8, 113-27,
137-45, 147-48, 157, 175, 201, 206-8,
209-10, 210-13
subject-object relationship, 7, 73-74,
79, 82, 87, 116, 121, 142, 206-8,
210-13
substance, 79, 117, 136, 139, 147
Suchocki, M., viii-ix, 1-11, 28-45, 46-
71, 72-77, 83, 86-89, 91-112, 113-14,
115n1, 118-22, 130, 135-49, 156-57,
176, 177-78, 181, 185, 187-90, 194,
197-218
suffering, 35, 38, 40, 41, 43-45, 197,
199-201, 202-3 (see also above,
evil as suffering)
superject(ivity), 6, 73, 83, 92, 94,
96, 110-12, 115-18, 121, 210, 211-12,

214-15 (see also above, primordial
subjectivity)
Swinburne, A., 160
symbols, religious, 32, 36, 39-40,
44, 199-201
system, 81-82, 85

Tanner, K., 133, 178n2
Taylor, C., 145n20
Teilhard de Chardin, P., 158n19,
163n29, 178
Tennyson, A., 155-56, 160
theodicy, 109, 11-12, 181-90
theosis, 188-89
Theunissen, M., 145n20
Tillich, P., 29, 36n11, 38, 41
Time (vs. eternity), 41-44, 91-92,
94-95, 97, 100-101, 103-4, 106-12,
131-32, 135, 201-2, 209-10, 218
time, fulfillment of, 163-64, 172-76
time, ground of, 202, 209-10
time, origin of, 92, 102-3, 106-12,
173, 201-2
time, subjective, 144
transcendence 52, 70, 95, 101, 107,
112, 209, 213-14
transformation, 31-32, 57-59, 68, 74-
75, 88-90, 93, 95-96, 101, 116,
119n10, 125-27, 184, 187-90, 194,
196, 200-201, 203, 214, 217-18
transmutation, 80
Trinity (God as), 36, 83-84, 85-87,
194, 208
tsimtsum, 109

Ultimate Reality, 36-39, 44-45

violation (see sin as violation)
violence, needless, 49-51, 70-71
violence, propensity towards, 50
Volf, M., 186n23, 189, 190n28, 194

Weinberg, S., 171, 172n42
Weiss, J., vii

INDEX

Welker, M., 178n2, 179n3, 180nn4-6,
  182n9, 186, 192
Wesley, J., 61, 64
Whitehead, A. N., viii, 1-2, 4-11, 30,
  33, 34, 40, 44, 42, 44, 49, 53, 57,
  58-61, 66, 72-90, 93-112, 114-17,
  118-19, 120-22, 130, 135-49, 151, 156-
  58, 169, 175-76, 182, 183nn.12-14,
  184n20, 190n29, 191n31, 195n37,
  196, 201-2, 203, 206-7, 209-10,
  210-12, 213-14, 217-18
Wiehl, R., 98n42
Wildman, W., 45n21

Wilson, D., 153n7, 115n12
Wilson, E., 153n8, 155n12
women, oppression of, 50, 54-56
World as ongoing process, 33, 57-59,
  65-69, 95, 97, 99, 103-5, 107, 118,
  126, 157, 160, 163-69, 205, 208,
  210, 214-15, 216-17, 218
World, end of, 33, 57, 65, 91, 96-97,
  99-100, 103, 110, 129, 135, 148, 177-
  81, 195-96, 209
world process, goal of, 161-69, 173-
  76 (see also above, eschatology)